THE
NEW
VENTURE
HANDBOOK

THE
NEW
VENTURE
HANDBOOK

Everything You Need to Know to Start and Run Your Own Business

Ronald E. Merrill
and
Henry D. Sedgwick

amacom

American Management Association

This book is available at a special discount when ordered in bulk
quantities. For information, contact Special Sales Department,
AMACOM, a division of American Management Association,
135 West 50th Street, New York, NY 10020.

Library of Congress Cataloging-in-Publication Data

Merrill, Ronald E.
    The new venture handbook.

    Bibliography: p.
    Includes index.
    1. New business enterprises—Management. I. Sedgwick,
Henry D. II. Title.
    HD62.5.M46   1987   658.1'141   86-47818
    ISBN 0-8144-5895-5
    ISBN 0-8144-7680-5

Printing number

10 9 8 7 6 5 4 3 2 1

We hear much these days about mentors in big business. Well, entrepreneurs have mentors too, and we dedicate this book to Ron's:

Art Parthé
Stan Rich
Jerry Schaufeld

and to Harry's:

James Benno Rosenwald

Acknowledgments

We have benefited greatly from the experience and shrewd advice of our colleagues in the MIT Enterprise Forum in several cities. This is not to say that they should be held responsible for our views. We also wish to thank the many entrepreneurs we have worked with who have been immortalized—sometimes anonymously—in the examples and Cautionary Tales of this work. Finally, thanks are due to Nancy Brandwein, our editor at AMACOM, whose advice and suggestions materially strengthened this book.

Contents

Introduction

The capitalist, above all the entrepreneur, is not merely a dependent of capital, labor, and land; he defines and creates capital, lends value to land, and offers his own labor while giving effect to the otherwise amorphous labor of others. He is not chiefly a tool of markets but a maker of markets; not a scout of opportunities but a developer of opportunity; not an optimizer of resources but an inventor of them; not a reflexive respondent to existing demands but an innovator who evokes demand; not just a user of technology but a producer of it; not only a producer of garbage but a visionary who can transform it into wealth.

George Gilder
*The Spirit of Enterprise**

Yes.

Yes, you really should go ahead and start your own company. You're thinking about it, aren't you? Otherwise you wouldn't even have picked up this book. Of course, it's also possible that you have already started a company.

In either case, this book was written for you. Entrepreneurs are the lifeblood of the economy. It's they who create new industries and new jobs; who develop new technology and make it useful; who build new neighborhoods and revitalize old ones.

Of course, we may be a bit prejudiced on the subject. We're entrepreneurs ourselves.

*(New York: Simon & Schuster, 1984), pp. 16–17.

WHO CAN BENEFIT FROM THIS BOOK

This is a book for entrepreneurs by entrepreneurs. It was developed out of our years of experience as founders, CEOs, directors, investors, and advisors of a wide variety of small ventures. Our aim is to provide you with the management tools you need to plan and control your business.

The subject of entrepreneurship is so vast that nobody could possibly cover it completely in a single volume. We've chosen to focus primarily on the start-up process—planning the business and seeing it through its first few years of operation.

We haven't limited the book, however, to any particular type of business. Whether you're planning a new computer company or a neighborhood drug store, a pantyhose factory or a pushcart, basic business principles remain the same. Of course many of our specific tips apply only in certain types of business; we think you'll have no trouble deciding which advice is appropriate to your venture.

We've never encountered a truly "well-rounded" entrepreneur. There are many subjects you should master—sales, marketing, production, finance, R&D, and others. Every new CEO is strong in some areas, ignorant in others. So in each chapter we've tried to start pretty much at the beginning, then go on to a fairly advanced level. We've provided a bibliography for those who want to pursue some topics even further, and a glossary to help you with unfamiliar terms.

Finally, this book is not for CEOs only. An increasing proportion of new ventures are being built by complete management teams rather than being one-man shows. If you expect to fill a top slot, you can benefit by understanding the business as a whole, including the tasks and problems of your cofounders.

WHAT WE COVER

Here are a few of the important topics we'll be taking up in the following chapters:

  • How to analyze your personal needs and develop a venture that will fit them.

- The "Three M's" that are critical to building a successful venture (money isn't one of them).
- Why the bottom of a recession is the ideal time to start a new business.
- How to spot a dishonest employee before you hire.
- Why a market survey is *the* make-or-break factor in a new venture—and how to do a good one.
- How to understand your market and develop a coherent strategic plan.
- The "atomic bomb" of marketing—and why you should avoid using it.
- A critical step in the sales process that is often neglected even by experienced salespersons.
- A common mistake in production that can paralyze your start-up's output.
- Why fast growth and high profitability can lead to bankruptcy.
- Nine pitfalls that can cause immediate rejection of your business plan by investors.
- Money sources that most entrepreneurs ignore—and how to approach them effectively.

Our primary text focuses on how to analyze and *understand* the key aspects of a new venture. Then, to help you put these principles into practice, we provide a series of exercises to guide you in taking every step in the start-up process and in making critical decisions. In addition, each chapter contains checklists to give you a handle on the many important details that can affect your success.

The text is interspersed with many examples showing how real businesses handled specific problems. Some of these are taken from the business literature or news items; others from companies that we've worked with in the MIT Enterprise Forum; and many others from our personal experience as entrepreneurs.

Finally, to each chapter we've appended a "Cautionary Tale." Each of these is a short but complete account of a start-up in which one of us has been personally involved. These stories describe a variety of companies: a biotechnology start-up, a squid-fishing vessel, a new type of cosmetics company, a distributor of nuts and bolts, and others. Some were great successes, others total failures. Each one had something to teach us, and we think you'll also find them interesting and instructive. Each tale has some connection to the preceding chapter, but don't expect a tight correspondence; these are real-world companies, not textbook examples. They are included not to illustrate some particular point but to give you a feel for the dynamics of new ventures.

HAVE FUN

We love being entrepreneurs, and we love working with entrepreneurs. They are the world's most interesting, lively, and challenging companions. If you have not done so already— join us!

1
PREPARING YOURSELF

The market, like the Lord, helps those who help themselves. But, unlike the Lord, the market does not forgive those who know not what they do.

Warren Buffet*

In a way, starting a business is like taking a final exam. When you took an exam in school, your grade was determined mostly in advance—by how well you'd done your homework.

When you start a business, the same thing is true. The day you open your doors, the clock starts running. If you don't know what you're doing, it's too late to learn. If you haven't made the right preparations, it's too late to go back and do it properly. If you don't have a plan, it's too late to figure one out. Problems, decisions, hassles immediately start coming at you from all directions. There's never enough time to handle even the most urgent priorities, let alone go back and make up earlier omissions. And with every minute, your cash is ticking away.

Entrepreneurs are action-oriented people, eager to skip the preliminaries and get down to work. But the prestart-up, planning phase of your business is too precious to be wasted. The plans you make during this period will determine whether you succeed or fail. What's more, this is your last chance for a

*Quoted from the *1983 Annual Report* of Berkshire Hathaway.

calm, objective look at your business. To be able to think and plan at leisure, without having next month's cash flow to worry about, is a luxury you will come to appreciate when it's too late. Do your homework in advance—it pays.

You'll find this is a recurring theme in this chapter and throughout the book. The basic requirement for success as an entrepreneur is preparation. Study a subject *before* it comes up. Know the answer *before* the question is asked. Anticipate problems *before* they occur. You must become a fanatic about planning, precisely because you cannot plan everything. All too often, when the assembly line stops, when an employee makes a demand, when a customer has an objection, you'll be caught unprepared and you'll have to improvise. These unpleasant occasions can't be eliminated entirely, but the successful entrepreneur is the one who tries.

It's not only your success that's at stake but your happiness. At first, the image of the crisis manager may be attractive: solving problems on the spot, making snap decisions, beating deadlines by a hair. But for any but the most neurotic CEO, this sort of thing gets old quickly. Life is much more pleasant when things are going pretty much according to plan. Getting clobbered by an unexpected crisis can be stimulating as an occasional exception, but as a daily diet it's no fun at all.

So don't be in too much of a hurry to get started. Are you worried that a market opportunity will disappear if you don't move quickly? That's the kind of motive that has bought a lot of salted gold mines. In a hurry because you've lost your job? Watch out you don't lose your life savings also. Think you don't know enough to make a good plan? Going down in flames *is* very instructive, but it's a rather painful way to learn.

To start with, don't neglect the critical first step in starting your own business: preparing yourself, the entrepreneur. Being an entrepreneur has its advantages and its disadvantages, and it's well to be aware of them in advance.

THE PROS AND THE CONS

First, the bad news.

Starting a business is *risky*. The majority of new businesses fail. It's very unusual to start a business without putting up at least part of the money yourself. In fact, you may well have to invest all the money you have, or even more than you have— that is, go into debt. What's more, under certain circumstances you may be held personally responsible for offenses committed by your employees or agents. You could be wiped out if your business fails. That's not even the worst of it. If you raise money from friends or relatives—many of us do—then failure can become *really* unpleasant. Just imagine having to tell sweet old Aunt Mildred that her nest egg has gone west.

You risk not only money but your career. You may be giving up a good, secure job to follow your dream. It may not be easy to get another if you fail. The stigma of failure can hurt you professionally. In fact, even success can limit your options. Suppose your company does all right, but you find you don't enjoy small business. You may find it hard to go back to your old status—many large companies make it a point to avoid hiring people with small-business backgrounds, because they tend to be excessively independent.

As an entrepreneur you will face a lot of *hassles*. The larger and more successful your business becomes, the more time you'll have to spend on taxes, accounting, regulations, affirmative-action quotas, and a million similar annoyances.

As an entrepreneur you'll be under a lot of *stress*. The buck will stop with you. You have to make the hard decisions, deal with the unpleasant problems, take the responsibility and the risks. Running a business involves long hours of hard work, high risks, and high stakes, in an uncertain environment—a classic recipe for psychological and physiological stress.

Finally, entrepreneurs are *unpopular*. Don't be misled by all the media hype about the importance of small business. Small business is still business, and business remains the whipping boy of the Establishment. Government regards small business as a tax resource—to be consumed. Big business sees you as a threat—to be crushed. To labor, you are an exploiter of the working man—to be expropriated. Environmentalists regard you as a rapist of the environment—to be regulated.

Now the good news.

Running your own business gives you *freedom*—at least, as much freedom as it's possible to have this side of Tahiti. You decide when to arrive at work, when to go home, how to use your time, what projects to work on. All the little choices that were outside your control as an employee are now up to you. So are the larger choices that control your destiny. Whether you succeed or fail, it's your decisions, not somebody else's, that make the difference.

Being an entrepreneur is one of the few practical routes to *wealth*. Tax laws and other factors make it virtually impossible to create a fortune by saving out of a salary, no matter how well you are paid. If you can win a lottery, inherit millions from a rich uncle, or become a major movie star, fine. Otherwise, your best chance to get really filthy rich is to own your own company.

The entrepreneur has the opportunity for *achievement*. As an employee, especially of a big company, you have little opportunity to accomplish anything really substantial. It wouldn't fit in with company policy. It would interfere with existing projects. And if you were to do it and succeed, it would arouse envy and resentment among your less talented colleagues, upsetting the smooth operation of your department. If you are determined to reach a demanding goal, you may find the only route involves shaking free of the stifling corporate bureaucracy and working independently.

Ultimately, the most important advantage is *independence*. In becoming an entrepreneur, you select not just a different job but a different personality. You leave behind the limits that restricted your options. As an employee, you could not change your profession, because you were not "qualified" by the appropriate educational certificates. Now you can switch into any field that interests you. As a woman or a black, your career involved a constant struggle against prejudice. Now you can start at the top and succeed or fail entirely on your own merits. As the mother of young children or as a handicapped person, you were a nuisance to your employer. Now you can arrange your schedule, location, and working conditions to suit your needs.

THE STATISTICAL ENTREPRENEUR

But are you the "type" to succeed as an entrepreneur? There have been a number of studies of entrepreneurs that show that they have certain—statistically—common characteristics. It's therefore concluded that those lacking the "entrepreneurial personality" are unlikely to succeed. We disagree. To succeed as an entrepreneur, you need simply to make two commitments: first, that you are going to put in the necessary effort; second, that you will choose a business that fits your needs and talents.

Let's briefly consider the characteristics of the statistical entrepreneur.

- He is male. (However, women are now starting businesses in increasing numbers.)
- He is about 30 when he starts his business. Presumably it's difficult to start earlier because of the need to get education and experience and accumulate some seed money. On the other hand, if he waits too long, he may be tied down by family responsibilities.
- His father or some other close relative had his own business.
- He started making money in childhood—with a paper route, lemonade stand, lawn-mowing business, or the like.
- He takes moderate risks and sets goals just at the edge of his abilities.

If this profile fits you, you can take comfort in your resemblance to the typical entrepreneur. If not, don't worry too much. Small business is incredibly diverse. Successful entrepreneurs include Ph.D.s in mathematics, high-school dropouts, scions of rich families, penniless immigrants who couldn't speak English, whites, blacks, orientals, schoolboys, retirees, housewives, salesmen, scientists, soldiers, laid-back hippies, and men who wouldn't be caught dead without their three-piece suits. No average can truly characterize this array.

THE REAL ENTREPRENEUR

Perhaps too subtle for these statistical studies to measure are the character traits that are helpful to the successful entrepreneur. Here are some of the qualities that are typical of the real winners we've known.

Industrious. The employee is hardworking, usually, because his boss sees to it. The entrepreneur doesn't have a boss.

As you start your own business, there will be a tremendous amount of work to accomplish. In the early days you won't be able to hire much, if any, help. Many of the tasks you'll face will be unfamiliar, and you won't be very efficient in doing them. It's common for founders to work 60- or 80-hour weeks, especially in the early days. In fact, it's become a sort of macho display for entrepreneurs to brag about their long working hours, just as big-business executives boast about how many people they've fired. Although there comes a point where working to exhaustion is counterproductive, there's no question that starting a business involves a lot of very hard work. It helps if you're naturally industrious. Those of us who aren't need a lot of willpower.

Rugged. Working long hours without holiday or vacation under heavy stress will put a severe strain on your health. This is one reason businesses tend to be started by fairly young people. Before you begin, you should take steps to get into top shape, and make plans to stay in top shape. No matter how busy you get, be sure you take time to eat properly—regular meals, no junk food—and consider taking vitamin supplements. Another priority not to be neglected is exercise. Not only is it essential for your health, but a good, vigorous workout will help clear your mind, give you a refreshing break from constant worry, and improve your decisions. We've included several useful books on executive health in the Bibliography.

Stubborn. From the moment you get the first idea for your business, people are going to start trying to talk you out of it. Your family, your friends, your coworkers, your boss, your investors, your cofounders, your employees—any or all of these may try to persuade you to abandon or modify your project. The ability to resist such pressures seems to be an invariable characteristic of the true entrepreneur. If you listen to the pessimists, you'll never get started. If you quit when the going gets tough, you'll never succeed. Are you stubborn enough? Of course, there are disadvantages to being *too* stubborn—unless you have the good fortune to be right invariably.

Objective. A willingness to face facts—even unpleasant facts—is an invaluable asset. There may seem to be a contradiction here. How is it possible to be both stubborn and objective? Yet the successful entrepreneurs we've met seem to combine both traits. On the one hand, they are very resistant to the opinions of other people, even expert authorities. On the other hand, they have the utmost respect for reality and the self-discipline to change their own opinions when change is required by the facts.

Independent. An obvious qualification for the business founder is the ability to go it alone. Managers from a big-company background often have difficulty adjusting to the small-business environment. They miss the facilities, the staff, the resources that they have come to take for granted. They may also miss the camaraderie and support of their former working group. It is lonely at the top, even if it's the top of a very small organization.

Resilient. It's a very rare start-up that doesn't have at least one major crisis during its early growth. You're likely to experience some serious setbacks at one point or another. How do you respond to failure? Can you absorb a heavy blow—or several blows in succession—and bounce back?

Creative. Although starting a business doesn't take genius, it does seem to require a certain amount of creative spark or originality. A purely "me-too" or imitative business carries a heavy handicap in the market. Your business idea should have something new or innovative about it—a new product, an unusual marketing approach, a unique location. Once you've started, you'll have an ongoing need for original solutions to the many large and small problems that will come up.

Responsible. When small-business CEOs talk among themselves, they often use a put-down that reveals the naked essence of the entrepreneurial character. Be it an academic expert, an expensive management consultant, or a big-company executive, he may be dismissed with the phrase: "He's never had to meet a payroll." This really sums it up. The entrepreneur is responsible in an absolute sense, like the captain of a naval vessel or the commander of an army unit. To paraphrase the West Point ritual, the CEO is responsible for everything his company does or fails to do. In his hands lie the assets of his investors, the satisfaction of his customers, the livelihoods of his employees. The larger and more successful your company grows, the greater your responsibility. Do you enjoy responsibility?

A very important aspect of being an entrepreneur is the need to subordinate one's own ego to the enterprise itself. You've really got to be prepared to perform all manner of tasks, no matter how menial. When I got involved with Trig-A-Tape, with the exalted title of General Manager, I knew that we were short of capital. Although we had a secretary, there weren't a lot of hands to do what had to be done, so I found myself making out payrolls, cleaning the office, sometimes working on the production line to fill in for someone who was sick. I would do anything that freed other key people to perform their specialized tasks.

My job as head of a company is not only to be conductor of the symphony but to see that every part gets played. Everybody else in the company has a specific task to perform. The lead person is there to see that all elements go together effectively. If that means—as it has in my experience—that I go out and get the coffee because the secretary who normally does it is getting out an important letter, I just go out and get the coffee.

KNOW THYSELF

Few of us possess all of these valuable qualities to perfection. Fortunately, it's not necessary to be a paragon of entrepreneurial virtues to achieve success. Determination will make up many deficiencies. But most critical of all is fitting the nature of your business to your own needs, desires, and aptitudes. In order to start not just a business but the right business for you, you must thoroughly understand your own unique character and potentialities.

You'll probably find this self-analysis awkward; most of us haven't given such issues much thought since we were teenagers. Yet it's worth the trouble if it can prevent you from starting the wrong business. A surprising number of troubled start-ups have nothing wrong with them except mismatch. The founder is a good, skilled entrepreneur. The company is sound and well-positioned. But somehow it just isn't working out. When we analyze these cases, we invariably find that the entrepreneur has failed to think through his values and objectives. He has created a company that is not satisfying his personal needs.

A small design and consulting company developed a breakthrough that could revolutionize the multibillion-dollar integrated-circuit industry. Yet somehow this major innovation was not making progress. On analysis, it turned out that the founder simply didn't *want* to be the rich and famous CEO of a major growth company. He'd started his own company in order to have complete freedom to putter at the bench. That is what he enjoyed doing and what he wanted to go on doing. Very sensibly, he decided to pass up his great "opportunity" and stick to what he enjoyed doing.

After a series of vigorous disagreements with his superiors, the production manager left to start his own health-food company. In just a few years as CEO he had a successful concern—too successful. Its rapid growth demanded administrative work he hated. It also created a cash-flow dilemma—more equity was needed to finance the expansion, but investors were hesitant to put money into a one-man show. The CEO intensely disliked delegating authority, so he could not create a management team that would relieve him of administrative hassles and allow his company to grow. He had painted himself into a corner.

In the conventional wisdom, the entrepreneur is a sort of mild psychopath who has an unusual ability to start new ventures—but who needs to transform himself into a "manager" as his company matures. Somehow he must rid himself of the informal, intuitive, risk-taking style that served him in founding his company and become systematic, analytic, and conservative.

This classical model doesn't always apply in reality, though it has some validity. For one thing, "managers" and entrepreneurs are by no means such disjoint classes. One can be an entrepreneur and still possess the skills of systematic management—indeed, the purpose of this book is to help you do just that. A number of start-ups have reached the *Fortune* 500 with their original founders at the helm—Hewlett-Packard, Apple, and Compaq, to name three computer-industry examples. The ability to start a company is by no means incompatible with the ability to run an established company. This is fortunate, because the kind of massive transformation in personality so glibly prescribed is a rather tall order. Not many of us are capable of such a psychological metamorphosis, and not many of us desire it.

The fallacy in the traditional approach is its deification of the company. The company "demands" certain talents. The company "requires" a certain type of CEO. The company "needs" certain management systems. But you create the company; the company doesn't create you. As we'll see in the next chapter, companies come in all sizes, shapes, and colors. It's up to you to design and create a company that "demands," "requires," and "needs" what *you* can provide and want to provide.

We've constructed a series of exercises to help you define your goals. They aren't very elaborate; if you'd like to get into a deeper self-analysis, you may want to refer to some of the books listed in the Bibliography.

Most of us are reluctant to take goal-setting seriously because of past embarrassments—teenage vows, New Year's resolutions, and so on. Few of us reach the classical entrepreneurial age of 31 without unpleasant memories of promises made to ourselves and broken. But it is possible to set goals—even extremely ambitious goals—and meet them, if three simple principles are applied.

First, be guided by experience rather than speculation. The important questions for goal-setting are: What do I want? What am I good at? When these questions are answered on the basis of pure fantasy, the usual consequences are inappropriate goals and embarrassing failure. The very young must of necessity rely heavily on fantasy and guesswork; they have little experience to guide them. But successful adults choose the right goals by drawing on their memories of the past to suggest their plans for the future. What have I enjoyed? What have I done well at? These are the productive questions—with predictive answers.

Second, choose process goals rather than end-point goals. Any objective that is defined in momentary terms will yield only momentary satisfaction when achieved. The kind of goal beloved of inspirational authors—"be a millionaire by age 40" or "make Vice President next year"—is precisely the sort that gives only fleeting pleasure when accomplished. What's more, end-point goals have a nasty habit of becoming obsolete before you get there. Process goals, on the other hand, give continuing satisfaction and are less subject to the whims of fortune. Nor need process goals be vague: "spend 50 percent of my time at the bench" or "run a company with 50 to 100 employees" are process goals.

Third, build on strength. Far too often we choose goals intended to eliminate our weaknesses—for example, "get along better with the boss" or "learn cost accounting" or "become a better public speaker." Such objectives often turn out to be frightfully difficult to achieve; if attained, somehow they seem to bring disappointing results. Sometimes, of course, it's necessary to correct a serious deficiency. But when you are setting major goals, you should concentrate on identifying your strong points and making them even stronger. The "well-rounded" person is the mediocre person. There are no "well-rounded" geniuses.

In designing your business, you should begin by asking: Why do I want to start this business? What's in it for me? Using these questions as a starting point does not mean you should ignore the needs of your customers, your cofounders and employees, or your investors. It means instead that you should select customers, cofounders and employees, and investors whose needs complement your own. You can make sure your company satisfies their needs and yours also—provided you define your needs and design the company to suit them before start-up.

Our first exercise deals with the simple but by no means obvious question of day-to-day enjoyment of your work. What could be more ridiculous than quitting a secure, highly paid job because you're not enjoying your work; starting your own business with great effort, expense, and risk; and finding that you're still not having any fun? Unfortunately, this is the fate that befalls many entrepreneurs. There's no excuse for this error, because it can be avoided simply by designing your company, and your job within the company, to suit you. Do so in such a way as to maximize activities you enjoy and minimize activities you don't enjoy. This is not only for your sake but for the sake of the other people involved in the company. You, the founder, have got to be the spark plug of the company; if you're not totally excited and enthusiastic, success is unlikely. Furthermore, tasks you dislike are probably tasks you are not good at.

Exercise 1–1:
Part One: Your Needs and Strengths

A. Write down five activities that you do well, that you are really good at. They need not be strictly job-related; consider your hobbies and other pursuits also. However, list only items that you have experience in doing.

1. _____

2. _____

3. _____

4. _____

5. _____

B. List five activities that you truly enjoy. Again, these need not be strictly business-related, but confine yourself to pleasures that you have actually experienced in the past.

1. _____

2. _____

3. _____

4. _____

5. _____

C. Now go back over your whole life. Pick out the five happiest occasions of your life—your peak experiences—and list them.

1. _____

2. _____

3. _____

4. _____

5. _____

D. Finally, pick out the five greatest achievements of your life—the accomplishments of which you are most proud—and list them.

1. _____

2. _____

3. _____

4. _____

5. _____

Part Two: Your Perfect Day

This exercise is a controlled fantasy. Imagine that it is five years from today. You have started a company and it is successful. You are the CEO (or you hold whatever other position you would like). Now take a few sheets of paper and write down a complete account of a typical day in this fantasy, starting when you get up in the morning and ending when you go to bed. Describe all your activities in detail. What are your business appointments? What meetings (if any) do you attend? Who are your business associates and what are they like? What decisions do you make? How much of your time do you spend in the office, in the plant, in the lab, on the sales floor? What do you eat for your meals, and where? How much time do you spend with your family? What are your surroundings like—the building, the office, the furniture? What do you wear to work? Where are you located geographically?

As you work on this, refer back frequently to your answers in Part One of this exercise. Try to minimize speculative "I think I'd enjoy . . . " areas and maximize activities that you know from past experience you enjoy.

Part Three: The Entrepreneur Test—How You Score

There probably is no really good test of entrepreneurial capability, short of watching the subject start a company and seeing how she does. But the following test, based on a simple psychological principle, is likely to be as good as any.

Your Score: Refer to Part One, questions C and D. Compare your five most satisfying moments and your five greatest achievements and see how many items appear on both lists. In short, how much of your pleasure in life comes from achievement?

If all five items match, you sound too good to be true. Achievement is your whole life. If you set goals commensurate with your talents, you should succeed brilliantly and have a ball doing it. Before you start your company, call us so we can invest.

If three or four items match, you have good prospects as an entrepreneur, particularly if the matching items are business-related.

If less than three items match, do you flunk? Not at all. Chances are you're "competence-oriented" rather than "achievement-oriented"; that is, you are concerned more with developing your own abilities than with winning competitions. If this is the case, you should aim at developing a small "craft" business rather than a major growth company. Your best objective is probably to aim at a very small, personal operation designed to provide you with an interesting and enjoyable vocation rather than make piles of money.

SETTING YOUR PERSONAL GOALS

The next exercise concerns self-development. This has two aspects, the external and the internal.

External self-development involves your career progress. What qualifications do you want to acquire or improve? As an entrepreneur, you are free of the arbitrary restrictions that interfere with the development of new skills by employees. In the corporate climate, you may, for instance, be tagged as a scientist and automatically ruled out of consideration for management or any significant role outside the R&D department. You can bypass this obstruction by starting your own company and unilaterally redefining your career. If you later choose to return to the labor pool, you can usually make your new definition stick.

The internal aspect of self-development should also not be neglected. Becoming an entrepreneur gives you a chance to test your limits, to develop not only your skills but your character.

Next you should consider your financial objectives. Most entrepreneurs have a financial *motive*, but it's not as easy as it seems to set valid monetary *goals*. The key question is: what do you want the money *for*? Ayn Rand puts the principle eloquently:

> But money is only a tool. It will take you wherever you wish, but it will not replace you as the driver. It will give you the means for the satisfaction of your desires, but it will not provide you with desires.*

Once you know what use you have for money, you can decide how much money you need and how soon you need it. These decisions have critical implications for the objectives of your company.

Your company can also give you the means to satisfy your desires for status or other social rewards. As an entrepreneur, you may, if you choose, make a quantum jump in status—go in a day from "Assistant Supervisor" to "President and Chief Executive Officer." Of course, to make it stick, you've got to succeed! Still, the opportunity to skip the whole seniority ladder and award yourself whatever title, perks, and privileges you think appropriate can be invaluable if you use it shrewdly and cautiously.

There are other social goals you will want to consider. Does your current job keep you too isolated? Or, conversely, would you like to work in a less crowded environment? The atmosphere, the social environment, the company·culture—in founding your new company you can influence to a considerable extent how its people will interact. If you have your own ideas of what a workplace should be like, you can now implement them.

Atlas Shrugged (New York: Random House, 1957), p. 411.

Finally, you should set goals for achievement. It's been said, and truly, that the key to success is simply to aim at doing something extremely well. In founding and running Apple Computer, Jobs and Wozniak aimed not at entry to the *Fortune* 500 but at "bringing computers to the masses." By focusing on the latter achievement, they also accomplished the former. Perfecting a new technology, bringing a new product or service to market, putting out a product of superb quality, developing a company that really cares about its customers—it's goals of this type that make success stories. The winners are those who strive for excellence.

Exercise 1–2:
Your Personal Goals

A. Of the five strengths that you identified in Exercise 1-1, select three that you particularly want to improve even further during the next few years.

1. _____

2. _____

3. _____

B. Assume for the moment that your business is unsuccessful and you have to return to the job market. List three items you would like to be able to add to your résumé from your entrepreneurial experience.

1. _____

2. _____

3. _____

C. Decide (you may want to consult family members) which of the following economic levels you consider optimum.

Don't hesitate to define an intermediate step if none of the income levels listed is exactly what you want.

☐ Spectacularly wealthy—billions or at least hundreds of millions of dollars (another Getty or Hughes).

☐ Extremely rich—net worth in the tens of millions of dollars, able to lead a really luxurious life style.

☐ Very well off—net worth over $1 million, income over $100,000, able to lead the good life without worrying about the budget.

☐ Upper middle class—income over $50,000, able to live very comfortably and sock something away.

☐ Middle class—income $20,000–$50,000, living as other people do.

☐ Frugal—probably low income, money not an important factor to you, free lifestyle the real objective.

D. Assume you are able to earn as much money as you want. Which of the following items would you spend it on? Check as many as are appropriate.

☐ Highly luxurious lifestyle
☐ Big-ticket items—house, car, etc.
☐ Hobby or sports activities
☐ Family needs—children's education, etc.
☐ Charities
☐ Political activity—running for office or supporting favored candidates, etc.
☐ Building an estate
☐ Other (specify) _____

E. On the basis of your answers above, estimate your approximate financial needs over the coming years. Fill out the matrix on the next page with your estimates for income and net worth for the next two years, five years, ten years, and twenty years.

	Income	Net Worth
2 years from now		
5 years from now		
10 years from now		
20 years from now		

F. What social goals are important to you?

☐ High status—to be deferred to and treated with respect.
☐ Popularity—to be liked by colleagues and employees, have many friends, and so on.
☐ Independence—to be able to make your own decisions and live as you please without interference.
☐ Fame.
☐ Other (specify) _____

G. What do you want your company to *achieve?* To become a large organization? To revolutionize your industry? To be the perfect place for its employees to work? To solve a major social problem? To provide financial security for your family? To introduce a major technological innovation? Perhaps you want several things; but see if you can capture the essence briefly. Imagine that an investor asks you to define the purpose of your company in 25 words or less.

_____

_____

_____

_____

CHOOSING A COMPANY THAT FITS

Once you've defined your own goals and needs, you're in a position to decide on some of the characteristics of your company.

How big should it be? Do you want its growth to level off at some optimum size? If so, what size? And how will you maintain those limits?

> The owners of Zabar's, the famous New York delicatessen, have made a conscious decision to limit its size by the simple expedient of restricting it to one location—and requiring that a family member taste-test every item sold.

Perhaps you want your company to continue growing indefinitely. If so, will you stick with it and keep running it, no matter how large it becomes? Or will you step aside at some point and turn it over to new management? How fast do you want your company to grow? It's nice to get rich quickly, but very fast growth presents difficult management problems as well as high risks.

Where do you want to be within the company? No rule says you must be CEO, and you might be happier in a different slot.

> In planning Reaction Design, my original intent was to be the R&D Vice President. A friend was set as Marketing VP, and we sought a third cofounder to be CEO. After interviewing several candidates we gave up; it was hard to find the right person, and several of our investors felt I should be CEO since the project was my idea. It turned out that I was neither well-suited nor happy as CEO of a chemical company. I, the company, and the investors would have been better off if we'd stuck to the original plan.

What job will you take in the company, and what will your duties be?

What industry do you want to enter? Just because your training and experience lie in a certain area, you don't have to found your company in that industry. For instance, if you can't stand dealing with arbitrary government regulations, you'd better not start a chemical or pharmaceutical company—even if your background is in that industry.

How should you structure your company? What sort of operating style should it have? Where should it be located? These and many other questions can be rationally answered only on the basis of your personal goals.

COMMITMENT

Let's take stock. At this point, you should know what you want—your personal objectives—and what kind of company you need. Now comes the question of commitment. This is the subject of our final exercise.

You must make a realistic estimate of the amount of time you can devote to your new venture. The important word here is "realistic." Many entrepreneurs try to spend every waking minute on their companies; some even succeed in doing so. The companies seldom benefit. The prime responsibility of the CEO is to guide the company and give it a coherent strategy. This requires a lot of careful thought and an ability to see the whole company in context; neither is easy for a founder who is wrapped up in details 80 hours a week.

In the first flush of enthusiasm, you may feel ready to slay dragons and nonchalantly sign up for a workweek far longer than any you've experienced in the past. It can turn out to be more difficult than you expect to carry out such a commitment. This also applies, incidentally, to part-time businesses; you may not have as much "spare time" as you think you have. You should consider, too, that it is one thing to work a 90-hour week once, or even for a couple of months, and another thing to keep it up for years.

Related but not identical is the question of how much effort you can spare. You must consider your physical and mental stamina. Though you have 60 hours per week available for work, there may still be limits on how productive you can make that time. You cannot do push-ups for 60 hours, and neither can you do high-quality creative thinking. These limitations must be taken into account.

How much money can you commit? Again, be realistic. If you risk an amount that would devastate you if the company failed, you are not going to have a happy time—and will you make good business decisions under this kind of stress?

An important quality for the successful entrepreneur is the ability to live with a very low overhead. And I mean live with it—if not joyously, at least without being totally miserable. I have often seen people start businesses at a time when they were supporting a primary residence, a summer house, a boat, and other expensive toys that their salary from the new company couldn't possibly justify. There also may come a time when little or no salary can be taken. If you have a low fixed household overhead, whatever you want in variable expenses is fine; they can be cut back when necessary. But a heavy load of fixed commitments is very dangerous.

When I became involved with Trig-A-Tape, I think I had a salary of $8,000 a year (this was in 1957). I was then married and my wife worked, so we got along all right. But when the company got into difficulty and was about to fail, I stopped taking a salary. Happily, we had enough coming in from our meager investments and my wife's salary to ride out this period.

I frankly think that some of the financings that have been done by venture capitalists, allowing entrepreneurs to draw starting salaries in the $100,000 range, are ridiculous. There is something about personal financial control—a control of one's appetite, a willingness to defer satisfactions—that tends to spill over into the way one runs an enterprise. If you don't have money, you tend to save better than if you do.

This applies even when a business has become successful and is sold and the entrepreneur is deciding what to do next. In my case this has happened five times—so far. I still kept my overhead down because I didn't know what the future would hold. In my most recent experience, an investment of $2,500 in my baby-products company went to close to $2 million in a year and a half. After I sold out to Coca-Cola in 1981, I didn't rush out to buy a condo and a boat and a country house. I banked my gains, paid my children's college tuitions, and saved for what I knew could very well be a rainy day, until I started a new business and it became successful.

A question by no means minor is: Where does your family stand on this? If you're alone in the world, there's probably no problem. Otherwise you'd better be very careful.

To put it bluntly, the commitments you make to your company will come at the expense of your family. Time spent on your start-up will be unavailable for your family. Effort commitment is similar; you'll be using up energy that would otherwise be used for maintaining your marital relationship or playing with your children. The money you invest will be unavailable for buying a new car or filling other familial needs. Don't kid yourself on this issue, and don't try to kid your family.

You need to be sure that they understand what is involved, and that they are sincerely behind you. This is extremely difficult in most cases. Often a loyal wife, though scared to death of the financial risk, will pretend to favor her husband's ambitions. Or a husband, embarrassed to admit his old-fashioned notions, will conceal his disapproval of his wife's project. Children, afraid to anger their parents, may hide their resentment at being deprived of attention.

The best approach is negotiative. Tell them what you want to do and why. Be very frank about the consequences and how everybody will be affected. Ask for their support explicitly. Be ready to make some deals. Ask each member of the family what you can do to help them through the coming rough time and reassure them. Mother may want a commitment to maintain certain financial reserves, Junior a promise to attend his Little-League games. Make the necessary promises—and keep them. Too many businesspeople abuse their families. You wouldn't think of calling a business associate and saying, "Mr. Jones, I'm going to skip our appointment this afternoon because I want to meet with Mr. Smith—he's more important than you are." You keep your business commitments even if they're inconvenient—out of courtesy. Why not extend the same courtesy to your family?

A tip: if members of your family are willing to pitch in, even slightly, in working on your start-up, it will make them much more supportive. Give them a bit of a stake in your success. And when success comes, be sure to give them credit for supporting you.

I've been fortunate in having family support. In 1957 I was working at the Aluminum Company of Canada as a salesman. My then wife, whose experience with her father, her brother, and others she had known was that of men having their own businesses, couldn't really understand my working for a large company. I would come home depressed and frustrated, and when I finally decided to leave and start my first venture, she applauded— she'd wondered why it had taken me so long to come to that conclusion. When things began to get sticky at Trig-A-Tape, she was always supportive of my commitment to the company and never complained. It made a tremendous difference.

More recently, as I was developing my private investment banking activity, starting in 1982, I was fortunately involved with a woman who never allowed us to spend more than $25 between the two of us when we went out to dinner—and believe me, that is quite a trick in New York City. But she would study the alternatives very carefully and always come up with an excellent choice of restaurants, and we never did go over the budget.

Exercise 1–3:
Your Commitment

A. On a long-term basis, how much time can you spend on your business *without strain?* _____ hours/week.

B. During critical periods or emergencies, how much time could you spend for a few weeks flat out? _____ hours/week.

C. How much money can you spare for the expenses involved in the prestart-up phase of your business? $_____/ month.

D. How much money can you invest at start-up? $_____.

E. How long can you stand to go without any vacation? _____ years.

MAKING THE BREAK

Perhaps the touchiest operation in starting a company will be making the break with your current employer. If you're going into competition with your employer, or using technology you learned on the job, you may face some legal problems. Many technical types are dismayed to find that their ideas really are owned by the company that paid for them. See your lawyer at an early stage. If there's the slightest possibility that you'll be sued by your employer, have a contingency plan ready. Don't let yourself be taken by surprise.

If you're dissatisfied with your present job, you've probably been looking forward to the opportunity to tell off your boss. Don't do it. Just don't do it. You're going to have enough troubles, and you don't need any enemies. When you've become rich and powerful, you'll be in a position to tell the world how terrible your boss was and be listened to. By then you'll probably be above wasting your time on revenge. There's nothing like being highly successful to make you feel benevolent.

Checklist 1–1: Preparing Yourself

☐ Have you evaluated your capabilities as a prospective entrepreneur?

☐ If you were hiring someone else to be CEO of your business, would you hire someone with your résumé?

☐ Are you willing to do any task, however menial, to make your business a success?

☐ Do you know what you want from life?

☐ Do you know what tasks you are good at?

☐ Have you set goals based on your experience rather than fantasy?

☐ Are your goals process goals?

☐ Have you chosen as goals improving your strengths rather than eliminating weaknesses?

☐ Is your business aimed at some specific achievement rather than just making money "somehow"?

☐ Have you developed a new family budget, taking into account the financial commitments you are making to your company?

☐ Have you got the sincere backing of your family in entering this venture?

☐ Have you decided when and how to tell your boss you are leaving?

☐ Have you checked out all potential legal problems with your former employer and developed plans to deal with them?

☐ Have you asked your spouse or someone else who knows you well to confirm your concept of your personal character?

☐ Have you asked some objective source to evaluate the basis of your business and your qualifications to run it?

CAUTIONARY TALE: FOTO FINISHED

One of my early ventures was a company called FOTO COMP INC. The idea was to capitalize on phototypesetting technology by offering a "high-technology" typesetting service to magazine and book publishers in the New York area. For centuries, type had been set by hand and by machines called Linotypes, using metal matrixes or dyes and hot lead—a very primitive and cumbersome process even by the standards of the time. The phototypesetting technique had appeared in the early 1950s but somehow had not really taken off. There was a manufacturer of these devices which was very interested in getting some of its equipment out into a service-bureau environment so that publishers could become familiar with the machinery and its performance. I was approached by a friend of mine who had put together a business plan to found a company to operate service bureaus with this equipment.

I had just come off an overnight and very substantial success with my first venture. I was flushed with my ability to do things and eager to get going on another one. I had no particular idea how to find another deal, and this one came along and fell into my lap. My first mistake was to look upon it as my only opportunity, instead of exploring a number of alternatives. I didn't look for other deals but grabbed at this one and worked myself into a lather of enthusiasm, meeting constantly—and solely—with other people who were also enthusiastic. There was a great deal of optimism on the part of a technical group at Time, Inc., which had developed methods of using the equipment for setting type for the Time Book Division. Also enthusiastic, of course, was the firm that manufactured the photo-typesetting equipment. By that time, there were also a number of hangers-on who had joined the chorus.

I plunged ahead into the venture. I got financing from members of the board of directors of the manufacturer (acting as individuals) and some of their friends. Two of the technical people from Time came on as partners. We set up shop and got started. Almost immediately we ran into some problems that I simply had not examined in the initial plan.

First, were there enough trained people to operate this equipment—and if not, how long was it going to take to train neophytes in the use of it? We found that the answers were "no" and "much too long." This issue was completely overlooked in the business plan, and it turned out to be a major problem, because nobody in the typesetting community or indeed in any other existing labor force was familiar with the equipment. The time it took to train people was far, far greater than we had anticipated. I had made the mistake of relying on the technicians from Time, Inc., who had a way of answering specific questions with vague generalities.

A second problem also emerged early. The publishers whom I had interviewed prior to going into this venture—as to whether or not they would use this service—all said, "Yes, yes, yes, come to us when you're set up, and we'll give you work." What they were really saying—if I had been willing to listen carefully—was: "We are curious about this new technology. We might or might not at some point in time, one week or three years after you open, give you a small job to test your ability and the equipment's performance." But I read their answer to mean, "Of course we'll give you work, all you can possibly handle, and you will make a fortune on us."

Another truly major mistake was my choice of partners. These two technicians who had developed the system for Time, Inc., had done well for Time. The system worked very nicely for Time in the dedicated facility where Time produced type for its book series. What I neglected to explore was the cost of its operation. For Time and its editors, the important thing was to get these books produced as rapidly as possible. Time had an integrated operation: its people wrote the books, typeset the books, printed the books, and sold the books. This made it possible for Time to absorb a significantly higher cost for typesetting than a conventional publisher could. For Time, the purpose of this facility was to ease the work of its editors, not to reduce its typesetting costs. That little fact blew by me completely. It wasn't until we got heavily into our own operation and the majority of the capital had been spent in buying equipment and setting up shop and training people that I realized that there was a major question: Could we even compete on cost with the existing, though time-worn, technology?

Of course, by the time I realized all this it was too late. We were out of capital, we were butchering what jobs the publishers would give us, we were late, jobs were done badly, type was set incorrectly. You have no idea how upset magazine publishers get when you get typeset pages to them three days after the press was supposed to roll. Holding a press can cost them thousands of dollars a day.

The failure on my part to carefully scrutinize this venture before going into it cost me a great deal of money, time, embarrassment, and pain. I think if I had really *looked* at this project in the first place, I wouldn't have gone into it. There was just too much risk, and we, as a group, were simply too inexperienced in this particular activity.

Unfortunately, at that time I had not developed sufficient objectivity. I had to believe that this company was going to work. I was totally unable to accept any negative thoughts about it, so I didn't seek to find anybody who had another point of view—who would say that the market wasn't ready for this kind of service. I consulted only prejudiced parties—people like my partners from Time, Inc., and the directors of the manufacturer, who had a vested interest in being optimistic and pooh-poohing any caveats. I would pose all my questions in such a way as to elicit a positive response. In spite of all this, occasionally I would get a warning. I would be upset about it for a while and then I would just forget it.

If I'd known then what I know now, I would have proceeded very differently. Instead of jumping at the first opportunity that came along and hurrying into operation, I would sit down and think about my objectives. What, at that stage of my career, was I ready for? What was the logical next step? After thinking over these and some related questions, I could have examined a whole range of alternative ventures and picked one that would have had much better chances of success.

HDS

2

THE BUSINESS CONCEPT

In my opinion, no one can possibly achieve any real and lasting success or "get rich" in business by being a conformist. A businessman who wants to be successful cannot afford to imitate others. . . .

The successful businessman's nonconformity is most generally—and most obviously—evident in the manner and methods of his business operations and activities. These will be unorthodox in the sense that they are radically unlike those of his hidebound, less imaginative—and less successful—associates or competitors.

J. Paul Getty
*How To Be Rich**

Planning for your start-up must begin with a business concept. To develop a business concept, you need to go beyond your initial bright idea and answer three specific questions:

1. What are the *objectives* of the business?
2. What *kind* of business must you build in order to accomplish these objectives?
3. What will be *distinctive or unique* about your company?

*(New York: Playboy Press, 1965), p. 198.

THE TAXONOMY OF BUSINESS

In order to deal with these questions, we must first understand the taxonomy of business. There are millions of business entities in the United States. Many are quite young; in an average month there are over 45,000 new incorporations. On the other hand, some U.S. businesses date back to Colonial times. Businesses range in size from children's lemonade stands to multibillion-dollar behemoths like General Motors and Exxon. Though most businesses were started to make a profit for their founders, many have other purposes, such as providing jobs for their employees or even doing good works.

To start with, let's classify businesses by size. At the low end we find what might be called the *microbusiness*. This is a tiny creature, often run out of the home, a part-time or at most full-time activity for one person, though family members may pitch in. The lemonade stand falls in this category, as do the Amway distributor, the housewife who makes stuffed animals for sale, the carpenter who moonlights doing odd jobs, and the programmer who has a little software business on the side. The microbusiness is seldom incorporated, usually is managed very informally indeed, and has an amazingly low capitalization. Often it's part of the "underground economy."

The next step up is the *minibusiness*. This is big enough to have more than one person working full-time. Usually it has its own premises. A minibusiness may become fairly large, up to perhaps a thousand employees. The defining characteristic is that it is small enough to be managed by one person—not that it necessarily *is*, but that it can be. The most familiar minibusinesses are small retail outlets—grocery stores, barber shops, restaurants. However, minibusiness-size manufacturers and high-technology companies can be found swarming in industrial neighborhoods.

Now we come to the *mesobusiness*. This is an organization too large for one person to run, even with the assistance of aides. It requires a real top-management team: a group of people, each of whom has authority to make major decisions in some area of operation. Typically a mesobusiness will have from several hundred to several thousand employees. It may dominate a market in a geographical region, or it may be a minor player in a national market.

Finally, there is the *megabusiness*. It's possible for a meso-business to become so big and complex that its top-management team can no longer control it effectively. The company cannot just add more people to top management, because the group would become too large to operate as a team. It becomes necessary to split the company into divisions and provide each one with its own top-management team. Most of the "household name" companies would fall into the megabusiness category.

Now, "taxonomy" may not be the most precise word to describe the classification of businesses. A member of one biological species can never transform itself into a member of a different species. Business "species," however, are not such rigidly closed groups. Small businesses may grow larger. Big businesses may decline and shrink, or sometimes split up, thus forming smaller entities. And yet, there is surprisingly little movement between the four groups we have defined. A typical mesobusiness, for example, may grow somewhat larger or smaller from year to year. But it is very unlikely to make the transition to minibusiness structure, and even more unlikely to grow into a megabusiness.

This leads us to another criterion for business classification. Let us define a company that aspires to enter a higher "species" as "high-growth." On the other hand, we'll refer to a business that has no such ambition as "steady-state." A mega-business falls in the steady-state class by definition; it has no room for major growth. The vast majority of smaller businesses are also of the steady-state type. The transition from one business species to another is not only difficult but dangerous. Many a minibusiness has gone bankrupt during the attempted metamorphosis into a mesobusiness. There is a certain *cachet* to being a high-growth company; it's good for morale, not to mention the stock price. But management usually feels a vague uneasiness, a subconscious awareness of the hazards. So you'll find many companies that pay lip service to high growth, but back off whenever they get too close to actually making the transition to the next size range. Unfortunately, some companies fail to turn back in time and involuntarily find themselves shooting through rapids that they are not qualified to handle.

THE RIGHT SIZE FOR YOU

What is important is making a conscious, rational decision about the size goals of your company. In the previous chapter we dealt with identifying your personal aptitudes and goals. Now you must decide what kind of company will satisfy your needs. *Your* needs. Don't start out with a preconceived notion of what the company "must" be to satisfy investors, partners, customers, or anyone else. First define what the company should be to satisfy you; then look for investors, associates, and markets that are compatible.

If you don't like supervising other people, want maximum flexibility, and detest hassles, stick with a microbusiness. If you believe in keeping a close eye on every detail and feel uncomfortable delegating authority, you can have a prosperous minibusiness—but trying to grow beyond that will probably be disastrous. On the other hand, perhaps you enjoy team play and like to work in a structured environment on well-defined problems. You may do well in a mesobusiness—but will you enjoy running a start-up? Very few entrepreneurs have the ability or, for that matter, the desire to run a mesobusiness, let alone a megabusiness. If you're one of them, great—but if not, don't get yourself into that situation. If you decide to let your company grow beyond the size you can run—and enjoy running—plan *from the start* to step aside at that point and bring in professional big-company managers. It will be better for the company, and better for you.

HOW MARKETS GROW

You probably already have an idea, perhaps a very specific idea, of the market area you want to enter. You should examine it carefully. Markets have their own growth dynamics.

As shown in Figure 2–1, the growth of a typical market (or industry) may be divided into four phases.

The *primitive phase* involves a product or service that has not yet really found a market. A few customers are tentatively trying it; often they are unsure whether it's really useful or desirable. Quite likely there is no clear-cut idea of what use it

Figure 2–1.   A typical market-growth curve.

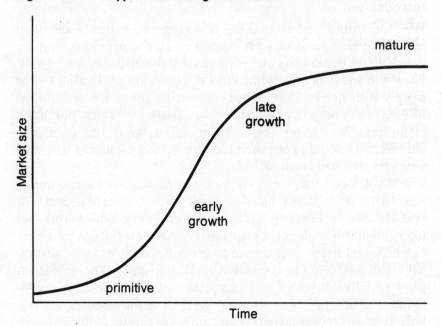

should be applied to. A good example of a market in the primitive phase would be microcomputers in the early 1970s. At this point tiny companies like MITS and Imsai were selling a few computers, mostly as kits, to hobbyists and computer professionals. Other examples: automobiles around 1900; air travel in the barnstorming era. Note that customers in this phase are limited to professional experts in the product area, or at least very enthusiastic amateurs.

   An industry in the primitive phase will typically be populated by microbusinesses and relatively small minibusinesses. Entry is generally very inexpensive; this is the kind of start-up that is financed with personal savings or a second mortgage on the founder's house. That's fortunate, because professional investors will seldom even consider backing a business in such a tiny market. Production methods range from handcraft to small-scale systematic assembly.

   An industry enters the *early growth phase* when its product acquires a clearly defined use and thereby gains access to a significant customer base. By this time one need not be an expert to use it; still, it is not for everyone. The microcomputer industry might be said to have entered this stage with the introduction of the Apple II. Other examples: automobiles when the Model T was in production; air travel in the days of the first airlines.

During the early growth phase, the industry is dominated by minibusinesses. Some of these, but not many, will be grown-up microbusinesses, survivors from the primitive phase. Most will be new entries. Entry is still not too expensive, but most start-ups must be financed by professional capital—typically venture capital. At first investors are skeptical, but since the rate of market growth is accelerating they gradually become enthusiastic.

The *late growth phase* of a market is characterized by increasing standardization of the product. There is widespread agreement about how the product should be designed and how it should be used. Paradoxically, it is during this same phase that the product splits into specialized versions. Thus the microcomputer market, in the early 1980s, split into "personal" computer and "home" computer segments—not to mention video games, word processors, and portable computers. To take another example, by 1940 the automobile was rapidly standardizing—for instance, the accelerator, brake, and clutch were now in the same configuration in virtually all makes. At the same time, such subspecies as the station wagon, pickup truck, and convertible were becoming clearly defined.

By this time, the industry is consolidating into a relatively small number of mesobusinesses—the notorious "shakeout" is beginning. A few minibusinesses still survive by devoting themselves to specialized niches, and megabusinesses are elbowing their way in, attracted by the now substantial size of the market. Entry, however, has become very expensive. Many millions are required for a seat at the table. New entries must be financed by a big company, by public offering, or possibly by the larger venture-capital firms. The industry's growth history has excited investors—but, ironically, it is now too late to reap really big returns, since the growth rate is declining.

Finally growth levels off and the industry becomes *mature*. At this point, the product is almost fully standardized and innovations are rare. Every imaginable customer has been accessed; a company can increase sales only by taking customers from the competition. The highly standardized product provides little opportunity for major changes or improvements, so competitive maneuvers consist mostly of marketing ploys and advertising campaigns. Among our examples, the automobile and air-travel industries are currently in the mature phase; the microcomputer industry is still in late growth, but the entry of IBM is a portent.

In the mature industry only a few players remain at the table, almost all of them megabusinesses. Entry is now so expensive that it is for all practical purposes impossible.

These growth stages may be considered the "normal" sequence. One should keep in mind that some industries follow a "pathological" sequence, for various reasons. Consider, for instance, the "biotechnology" industry. This became an investment fad while it was still in its primitive phase, and vast amounts of money were pumped into it. As a result, it has come to look like a child recklessly injected with growth hormone, a collection of mismatched parts. The industry is dominated by a few large companies, uses mostly handcraft production methods, is considered a hot growth area, but still has no clearly defined product. There are other pathological patterns.

Before you enter an industry, you should be sure you understand the dynamics of its market. Is it following the normal growth sequence? If so, what stage is it at? If not, what accounts for the abnormality, and how will it affect the future?

MARKET TIMING

If your start-up is to be successful, you must enter the market with good timing—which means at a stage appropriate to your company's size and resources. Once you have decided what kind of company you want to run, ask yourself: Will this kind of company do well in the market as it is now? As it will be in the future?

An error sometimes made by entrepreneurs, and frequently by investors, is *tardiness*. They wait until success has been clearly demonstrated by the pioneers, then try to imitate them. Apple Computer started in a garage and grew to a $100 million company in a few years. You can start a microcomputer company in a garage and grow the same way, right? Wrong. Conditions are different now; the market has changed. For one thing, Apple could achieve fantastic growth because it didn't have to compete with Apple. You won't have that advantage. The market is crowded with companies; distributors are short of shelf space and trying to decide whose machines to drop. Nobody needs a new microbusiness or minibusiness in this area.

Starting a new business is risky at best. Starting too late and too small lengthens the odds against you disastrously. Yet this mistake is made amazingly often; apparently, the temptation to imitate someone else's success is hard to resist. One even finds people like Bricklin and DeLorean who try to start new auto-manufacturing companies.

Starting too early or too large is another mistake. Entrepreneurs sometimes see a little too far ahead and try to hurry a market that isn't ready for their product. Investors often try to obtain greater safety by overfinancing a company. (Yes, it does happen!) But no amount of capital can make a company grow faster than its market can make room for it. Pouring in excess money is like giving too much water to a plant in a small pot—it merely sloshes over the edge and is wasted. And—sometimes the plant is killed by mildew.

WHERE DO YOU FIT IN?

Some of this may sound a bit alarming. What if it's not your ambition to found the next IBM or Xerox? Is it really necessary to plan for growth to megabusiness size?

The answer, obviously, is no. There are markets that grow very slowly. There are markets that hardly grow at all, that stay in the primitive phase indefinitely. Many markets are dwarfs that level off into maturity at a size too small to attract megabusinesses. And even large markets usually have small but potentially profitable niches where a small company can survive and prosper. You can pick any size and growth strategy you like, as long as you select a market that fits.

TECHNOLOGY-DRIVEN VERSUS MARKET-DRIVEN

If your product involves technology, there's another issue you should consider. According to Emerson, if you build a better mousetrap the world will beat a path to your door. Venture capitalists love to refute this famous quotation. And they're right; very few products will sell themselves, and innovative products *least of all*. The more radical your improvement, the harder it is to get customers to try it. Unfortunately, many venture capitalists have taken this insight to an unwarranted conclusion. They abhor companies that are "technology-driven." By this they mean a company that is committed to and motivated by its technological innovation and attempts to persuade customers to adopt its new products. Instead, they prefer the "market-driven" company, in which technology is completely subordinated to accommodating customer preferences.

It's hard to deny the importance of being attentive to the needs of your customers. But in practice, the preference for market-driven companies results in funding a lot of passive, imitative start-ups that wither helplessly when they encounter vigorous competitors. It's true that a technology-driven start-up is attempting a desperate gamble, and the vast majority fail. But it's also true that most of the great success stories of American business have been technology-driven. Consider Bell Telephone, Ford Motor, Xerox. These and other big winners did not adapt themselves to customers' traditional habits; they aggressively pushed entirely new types of products in defiance of customer resistance. By their fierce commitment to new technology they *created* new markets. So keep in mind that there is nothing inherently preferable about either the technology-driven or the market-driven approach. They are simply different approaches, each with its own risks and opportunities.

ANOTHER FACTOR

Here's another small but very fundamental factor: How big will a typical sale be for your company? Will you make a lot of small sales or a few big sales? A company that makes a million ten-dollar sales each year is going to be totally different from a company that makes ten million-dollar sales—even though they may be classified in the same industry. For one thing, the latter company is going to be in continual danger of being dominated, or even exploited, by its customers. On the other hand, it may be able to build sales much more quickly, because it does not take 100,000 times as long to make a million-dollar sale as a ten-dollar sale. You have to consider and balance these and similar trade-offs.

Exercise 2–1:
Classifying Your Business and Market

A. What type of business do you want to run?

☐ Microbusiness
☐ Minibusiness
☐ Mesobusiness
☐ Megabusiness

B. How large do you want your business to grow?

Sales:	*Employees:*
☐ Less than $100,000	☐ Just you
☐ Under $1 million	☐ Five or ten
☐ Under $20 million	☐ A few dozen
☐ $100 million or so	☐ A few hundred
☐ $1 billion or more	☐ Thousands

C. What growth rate do you prefer for your company?

☐ High growth
☐ Moderate growth
☐ Steady state

D. Will you stay with the company until you retire, or step aside at some point?

E. Write a brief description of the market you intend to enter.

F. What growth stage is this market currently in?

☐ Primitive
☐ Early growth
☐ Late growth
☐ Mature

G. Is this a normal market? If not, what unusual features does it seem to present?

H. Do your company's preferred size and character fit the market's growth stage?

WHAT'S NOT CRUCIAL

Before we discuss the critical ingredients of your business concept, let's discard some items that are *not* crucial.

Money. Surprised? Entrepreneurs spend a lot of time bemoaning their shortage of capital. They are seldom justified. Yes, money is very useful, but it is rarely the limiting factor. If your business possesses the crucial success qualities, people will come and stuff money in your pocket. If it doesn't, having a Rockefeller for a father-in-law won't help. So don't worry too much about the money. If you do the other parts right, the money will be there when you need it. And, as we'll see when we discuss financing methods, you may not need anywhere near as much money as you initially think.

Experience. As we've already pointed out, statistically, entrepreneurs are young. Usually they haven't lived long enough to get a lot of experience, but it doesn't seem to hurt them. Being an entrepreneur is a complicated job, and each start-up is different anyway. There's only one way to really get experience in entrepreneuring, and that's to start a company.

Prosperity. It's a common excuse: "The economy is in such bad shape right now; maybe when things start to look better . . ." Fact is, as we'll discuss later in detail, the bottom of a recession is the ideal time to start a company. And a lot of companies do get started in hard times. People who are out of work turn to self-employment in desperation; others moon-light in a microbusiness to make ends meet. Often they're surprised by their success.

TRULY CRUCIAL INGREDIENTS

What *do* you need? There are three factors that are absolutely critical to starting a successful company: market, management, monopoly.

Market

You might think it would be obvious that a company can't exist without sales, and that it won't have sales unless there's a market for what it's selling. Yet many entrepreneurs are so dazzled by the brilliance of their ideas that it doesn't occur to them to ask whether customers will buy. The first step to success is the recognition that just because *you* love your product, it doesn't mean it will sell. No matter how good it is, customers may be unable or unwilling to recognize its super-iority. Scientists and engineers are particularly prone to fall-ing in love with their products. This is one reason technology-driven start-ups have such a bad reputation.

If people are buying a product like yours already, at least a market exists. But you must establish this fact, prove it, not merely assume it. If a market does not currently exist, you may be able to create one. But you must plan how to do so, not just assume that it will happen somehow.

Let's be very clear on what a market is. A market is an ongoing demand for a particular product or service. The criti-cal word here is "demand." Desire is not demand. Customers must not only *want* your product—they must be willing and able to *pay* for it.

When the People's Republic of China began to open its markets to U.S. companies, many rushed in to fill the "demand" of a billion new consumers—and got badly burned. Sure, the Chinese *wanted* Western consumer goods; but with a per-capita income of less than $250 per year, they couldn't afford them.

You must be able to look at this question objectively. Don't assume that your customers are just like you. You must find out what their likes and dislikes really are, not just extrapolate from your own. In later chapters we'll discuss market research and marketing in more detail.

Management

Most people think of management as synonymous with supervision. They aren't at all the same thing. Management is organizing work. Whether you organize the work of thousands of employees or only your own, it is management.

You don't have to have experience to be a good manager. There are plenty of experienced "managers" who can't manage at all. You've probably had at least one of them for a boss.

There are three qualifications for management competence. First, you must know *what* to do; this is effectiveness. Second, you must know *how* to do it; this is efficiency. Third, you must be *willing* to apply your knowledge; this is objectivity. Effectiveness and efficiency are skills—rather simple skills, really—which can be learned. Objectivity is a character trait which can be acquired, though with great difficulty. Good managers are rare primarily because the willingness to face facts is rare. Does this seem exaggerated? We can assure you it isn't. You have only to read the business press to confirm what we've seen over and over again in our experience with small companies. You'll find one example after another of businesses—small, medium, and large—that have failed because their managements were guided by emotions rather than reality. An incalculable amount of capital has been destroyed by CEOs who rejected facts because they were unpleasant, uncomfortable, or simply unfamiliar.

When prospective investors consider your start-up, they will look carefully at top management—you. Do you understand business management in general? Do you understand the management needs of your particular industry? They may accept either experience or study as qualification. But above all they'll want to know if you are objective, if you can think about your company clearheadedly.

Monopoly

No business can be successful unless it has a monopoly. Got your attention, didn't we? Let's hope so, because this is a point that can't be stressed enough.

"Monopoly" is not used here in the usual invidious sense. In fact, having a monopoly in the usual sense is generally counterproductive. The point here is that your product must be distinctive and unique. You must offer your customers something that they want and that they *cannot* get elsewhere. Otherwise you will not make money.

Wherever this principle is ignored, one finds industrial disaster. Competition becomes price war. Nobody makes a profit. And once everyone is selling at or below cost the customers are the ultimate losers, for an unhealthy, malnourished industry cannot properly serve their needs.

Your business *must* have some unique appeal to the customer. What? There are many possibilities.

An obvious approach is to be the only one who sells the product at all. High-technology companies often seek this position. If you can make a widget that nobody else can make because you have proprietary technology, your position may be very strong—as long as you can protect your know-how by patent or secrecy. On the other hand, in this situation you are all alone in the market. The only customers are the ones *you* create. You have no direct competitors to assist you in developing the market. And customers may be especially reluctant to buy an innovative product if they are restricted to a single source.

A less demanding approach is equipping your product with a unique feature of some sort. This can be very effective, but the unique feature must be not just an arbitrary add-on but a real benefit to the customer.

Perhaps you should make your price unique. If—*and only if*—you have a superior production process so that your costs are lower than the competition's, then you may want to set a distinctively lower price.

Just be damned sure you're prepared for a price war. I don't know how many times I've seen business plans projecting a quick grab of market share by setting a lower-than-market price—invariably assuming that competitors will *not* drop their prices in response.

Remember that your price can be unique in another way: It can be *higher* than everyone else's! Naturally there are certain risks involved, but if you can pull it off this is a very nice way to develop an image of unique quality for your product.

You can have a unique location. Retail establishments make heavy use of this. Why do you patronize your neighborhood dry cleaner? Probably not because it's better than some other cleaner but because it's in your neighborhood. This strategy can also be applied on a larger scale; a good example is the commuter airline that provides service to small airports ignored by its transcontinental competitors.

Closely related is the approach of unique market outlet. You can try to make it more convenient to buy your product by using market channels ignored by your competitors. Sell in retail stores an item previously available only by mail order. Or *vice versa*. (This is how Sears Roebuck became successful.) Sell in a different kind of store; L'Eggs pantyhouse got a leg up on the competition by pushing its product in supermarkets instead of clothing stores.

Still another strategy is unique service. When you go to a restaurant, why are you willing to pay a high price for food that may taste no better than what you get at home? You pay for the service—romantic atmosphere, being waited on, entertainment, or perhaps just not having to cook. There are a million ways in which a business can make its product unique by adding service.

One summer, while in college, I worked in a computer operation of the telephone company on night shift. We had only IBM equipment. I soon learned why. When a machine went down, a "customer engineer" was always there within half an hour to fix it—and he did fix it, no excuses or delays. When a billing program failed, we called the IBM programmer who'd written it, long distance. He got out of bed, wrote a patch on the spot, read it to us over the phone, and got us running again. By emphasizing this kind of service, IBM has repeatedly pulverized competitors, who often had superior products.

One last suggestion: Consider making your business unique by giving the customer a new way of paying for the product. For instance, there was a time when big-ticket items like cars and houses had to be bought for cash on the barrelhead. The development of installment financing and the standard mortgage revolutionized these markets, and many others. The gasoline credit card had a similar effect.

> Sometimes even a very artificial distinction can be effective. A famous marketing story involves the early days of gasoline merchandising. One of the oil companies developed a new refinery process, which greatly lowered costs. However, the gasoline came out green instead of colorless. Since in those days gas was sold from pumps with glass bulbs, this was a serious drawback. The marketing people discussed the problem. How much would they have to lower the price to make people accept the apparently less pure product? Finally some genius said: "Advertise the color." By deliberately bragging about its green gas, the company was able to charge a premium rather than lower prices.

DON'T REST ON YOUR OARS

Before we leave the subject of monopoly, we should consider the question: How do you *maintain* superiority? Competitors have a nasty habit of imitating your successes. It's not enough to be unique—you must stay unique.

No matter what your advantage is, there is only one way to maintain it: continuous effort. The only exception is the very tiny market niche—so small it's not worth fighting over. Wherever there's money, there'll be competition. No matter how great your initial success, you can't get away with resting on your oars. You must think ahead, plan for the next step.

If you rely on technology to give you a superior product, you must worship at the shrine of R&D. Sooner or later your patent will expire, your secret process will be sold to the competition by a crooked employee, or your method will simply become obsolete. *Somebody* will eventually find a way that's even better than what you're using now—it had better be you. Many an engineer has become so proud of his brilliant

invention that he . . . never made another. When your Model A
has had a tremendous success and is sweeping everything else
off the market—that's the time to be hard at work designing
Model B.

If your edge is marketing, it's even more precarious. Competitors can easily imitate your advertising, invade your distribution channels, and even move right next to your location.
You must anticipate their response and have a plan to keep one
step ahead.

An advantage based on service is hardest to get but easiest
to defend. You can produce a superior widget with little more
than a single bright engineer. One hot-shot marketing maven
can develop a masterful sales campaign. But to provide truly
superior service requires the active participation of virtually
everyone in the company. This means building a whole company culture, which is hard work, and maintaining it, which is
also hard work. If your competitors try to imitate your service,
they'll have to follow the same path, and it's slow going. In
fact, this is one way in which a new company has an advantage. As we'll see in the next chapter, it's much easier to build a
company culture from scratch than to change one once it's in
place.

DEVELOPING THE BUSINESS CONCEPT

Having dealt with these issues, you're now in a position to
develop your business concept.

First, you must define your company's objectives. Start
with your personal objectives. The more specifically you defined your personal goals, the more specific you can make your
company goals.

Then decide what kind of company can meet the objectives
you've chosen. The characteristics of your company—its size,
its market, its product, its culture, its organization—must be
in harmony with its objectives and with each other.

Finally, you must come up with a way to make your
company unique. As noted, it could be new technology, an
unusual marketing approach, a perfect location, exceptional
service—perhaps some entirely new twist. You needn't limit
yourself to being unique in just one way, of course!

Exercise 2–2:
Your Company Concept

A. In 25 words or less, describe the product or service you intend to sell:

_____

_____

_____

B. What approach will you take to the market?

☐ Market-driven
☐ Technology-driven

C. In 25 words or less, explain why there is a *need* for your product:

_____

_____

_____

D. Who will buy your product? _____
Why? _____
Will they be able and willing to pay for it? _____

E. What are your management qualifications?

☐ Experience—general management _____
☐ Academic training in management _____
☐ Experience—your industry _____
☐ Evidence of objectivity _____

F. What will make your company unique in the marketplace?

- [ ] Unique (proprietary) product
- [ ] Unique (proprietary) feature
- [ ] Superior technology
- [ ] Location
- [ ] Market outlet
- [ ] Service
- [ ] Low price
- [ ] High price
- [ ] More convenient purchase
- [ ] Other (specify)

G. What approach will you take to maintain your unique advantage in the future when competitors try to imitate it?

CAUTIONARY TALE: POWERFUL PROFITS IN PRIVATE PRODUCTS

A few years ago, I was approached by a salesman who specialized in the sale of private-label products to chains on the East Coast. A private-label product is a copy of a national-brand product that is sold under either the name of the store itself or a "house" name. It is presented on the shelf right next to the national brand; the packaging is similar in color and shape, and the product is often exactly the same. But there is no advertising cost attached to the private-label product, because it is sold by the manufacturer directly to the store that puts its name on it. Since advertising and promotion account for a large part of the cost of a national brand, a private-label product can be sold at a substantially lower price. Commonly, a successful private-label brand will achieve a 15- or 20-percent market share—partly by eating into the national brand, partly by expanding the market to include some people who can't afford the big-name brand.

In this particular case, the salesman showed me a product called Wet Ones, manufactured and distributed by a company called Lane & Fink (a subsidiary of Sterling Drug). The product is a moist towelette in a cylindrical package. You pull them out one by one, like

Kleenex, to clean hands or various other things—largely one end or the other of a baby—when sanitary facilities are not available. He pointed out that this item was extremely successful and that it provided a real opportunity for a private-label imitation. He was sure he could sell millions of them if we could find a way to manufacture them.

It sounded interesting, so I did a little market research. The world is full of salespeople who are sure they could sell a million of something or other. With experience, you learn to be skeptical of such claims. I went around and talked to representative chain stores and found that, sure enough, this type of product was one of the fastest-growing categories in nonfood items sold by supermarkets and drugstores. So I set forth to run down the cost of manufacturing the product.

There were a number of elements. First there was the plastic container; this consisted of two parts, one of which had to be blow-molded and the other injection-molded. Then there was the fabric for the towelettes, which had to be cut from large rolls and prepared to be placed in the containers. There was a liquid that was used to moisten the towelettes, made up of a number of different chemicals, which had to be formulated in a certain way. There was assembly, of course, and there was packaging.

I traipsed around New York lining up subcontractors, getting costs, and adding them all up. Lo and behold, they came in—on paper, at least—substantially below what would be required to sell this product at 30 percent off the cost of the national brand and still make a very nice profit.

My next step was to make some samples. The salesman went around to his accounts, showed them the samples, and asked if they would buy the product if we could deliver it. The response was immediate and overwhelming. Before we contracted to build the molds for the manufacture of the plastic container—which was the main up-front cost—we already had substantial initial orders from several chains.

I decided that it was time to finance and organize this project. Fortunately, at this time I had a partner in another business whose company actually printed labels for private-label manufacturers. So he was a natural to help me in this effort. I put up a couple of thousand bucks and he put in some more to provide initial inventory financing and get the business off the ground. He also agreed to run the business from his existing office. That way, accounting procedures were already in place and the people who would order the materials were already hired. We did hire one young man directly, to worry about the day-to-day running of the business. He was fresh out of business school, but he acted as an extremely effective foreman, making sure that all the subcontractors performed effectively, with quality products, and in a timely fashion. He spent a great deal of time in the packaging plant checking out the final product. He also kept an eye on inventories, processed orders, answered complaints, and so on.

The overhead of the entire operation was less than $4,000 per month. This approach, moreover, was not only cheap but fast. Within a few months we were in business, we had a product, and we were ready to ship.

It took us only seven months to sign up almost all the major drug chains and food chains around the country. People who had been in the private-label business for years told me they had never seen anything move so fast. It was an extraordinary performance.

In fact, it was a little too much of a good thing. Before very long I could see that this business was getting out of hand. We needed working capital to finance inventory and receivables, and with this spectacular growth the amount needed was quickly exceeding the means of my partner and myself. The banks were unwilling to finance the business without personal guarantees, because we hadn't been in business that long. Receivables financing wasn't a big problem, because our accounts were with major chains around the country, household-name companies. But the banks had no confidence in our inventory, because we'd turned it over only three or four times since the business had started. So within eight months of the start-up, my partner and I had personally endorsed notes to the tune of $3 million for inventory. This was something that made me extremely nervous.

By the fifth quarter of the company's life, we were operating at a level of $8 million dollars a year. This is what you call fast-track growth. We'd obviously found a good thing—so good that it was attracting a lot of competition.

Major companies began to sniff around. Weyerhauser, St. Regis Paper, and Coca-Cola were clearly intending to come into this market. We had to consider our next step. To stay in the business and be competitive, we would have to raise a lot of capital. So far we had put next to nothing into the plant—just some chicken feed to buy the molds for the plastic parts. But to compete with big players, we would have to set up our own production line and automate; this would require a big chunk of fixed capital. On top of that we would need massive amounts of additional working capital.

So when the three companies mentioned above put out feelers about acquiring Private Products, Inc., we very intelligently decided to be receptive. We identified Coca-Cola as being the strongest suitor, and toward the end of 1981 we sold the company to them for a very substantial return on the meager equity that we had put into the business.

Some of the other stories we've told about me in the rest of this book are real bummers, so I'm happy to say that this little project demonstrated my capacity for brilliant timing and implementation.

Private Products was a company with a very distinct business concept. We set out to sell a single, well-defined product to a single, well-defined market. We verified the existence of the market and our capability to make sales before putting in a lot of investment. In fact, by subcontracting the entire manufacturing operation, we were able to avoid ever putting in a lot of investment. We moved promptly to take advantage of a major opportunity in the market, but we didn't skimp on preparation or cut corners. And we kept our overhead low.

But. We also recognized the major limitation of the business concept. What did we have that was unique? Just one thing: price. We didn't have a patent, or manufacturing know-how, or a reputation built up over the centuries—we had nothing that could not be imitated by competitors. Our pitch was simple: "Here's a hot-selling item, 30 percent cheaper than the national brand." Anybody could take this approach; we just happened to be shrewd enough to take it first. So the smartest thing I did with this company was to sell it when the selling was good. I had taken my business concept to its logical conclusion.

HDS

3
BUILDING A TEAM

Two resolute men, acting in concord, may transform an Empire, but an ordinarily resourceful duck can escape from a dissentient rabble.

Ernest Bramah
Kai Lung Unrolls His Mat

Only the very tiniest businesses can operate with just one person. If you undertake anything much larger than a micro-business, you'll find that success will require adding other people to your team. And if you've chosen ambitious objectives, you should consider starting out with a substantial group of cofounders. Experience has shown that start-ups with large founder teams do better than those with small teams, which in turn are more successful than single-founder companies. In fact, these days it's hard to find professional investors who will finance a one-person show. They strongly prefer to invest in a group of managers who can pool their talents.

As you bring on cofounders, advisors, directors, employees, and all the other people that your growing business needs, you'll be faced with a continuous stream of personnel decisions. You'll soon find it necessary to develop personnel policies, and if you're wise, you'll integrate these into a complex of goals and attitudes that is sometimes called a "company culture."

Entrepreneurs tend to focus on technology, production, marketing. The gritty details of personnel manuals, compensation, benefits—these seem boring and routine compared with the excitement of landing that critical sale or getting the first widget off the assembly line. You may feel, "We can worry about that stuff later, when we're big enough to have a personnel department."

In fact, though, you need to give careful attention to "people matters" right from the start, for two reasons. First, the founder or founders can't do it all alone. Your company can succeed only if its employees, from top to bottom, are motivated to produce results. Every business success story, from DuPont to IBM to Apple, has involved developing a company *esprit*. Approaches differ; the methods that work for Toyota may not be suitable for Digital Equipment, and vice versa. But no company succeeds without attention to its people.

The second reason you must think about personnel issues early is that decisions in this area tend to be irreversible. If your product isn't working right, you can redesign it. If your marketing plan fails, you can switch to a new approach. If an R&D project is unpromising, you can abandon it. But when you deal with people, decisions are much harder to change. People resist arbitrary action. They resent sudden changes in policy. They revolt if they perceive you as taking away benefits they've been promised. The day you hire your first employee your organization will acquire an inertia, a momentum, in its personnel policies, which will make it increasingly hard to change them. While your company is still on the drawing board, you can establish any policies you choose. Make sure you choose the right ones, because your employees may not allow you to change them later on.

CAUTION IN HIRING

You'll find that in the early days of your company, you and your cofounders may have a tendency to hire too freely. At this stage, you should be very conservative. Think twice, think three times before you establish a new position. Be sure you insist on quality. When you're working a 90-hour week, it's tempting to compromise, to take on somebody who really isn't up to your standards. You're desperate for help, and you don't want to take time to search for the best. Resist the temptation to settle for second-best; you'll soon regret it if you give in.

Later, when the company is successful and expanding, you'll need to set up controls to keep from loosening up. At this stage, the motive for careless hiring will be different: managers will feel flush. By this time, though, you won't be able to personally vet each candidate to keep things under control. You'll have to establish—correction: you'll *have to have established*—a set of rules.

DELEGATION

Beware, incidentally, of a different error. An endemic disease of entrepreneurs is the reluctance to delegate. You'll want to keep everything in your own hands, under your personal control. If you find it mysteriously difficult to find the right person for that responsible position—the one that you need to relieve you of some heavy operating burdens and let you spend more time on planning . . . well, examine your motives.

Delegation of authority is a subject seldom understood. It used to be said, "If you want something done right, do it yourself." This is a very old-fashioned attitude. It may have applied to the workers of fifty years ago, but these days a more appropriate saying would be, "If you want it done at all, do it yourself." People who can be relied on to do the work, and do it properly, even when the boss is not watching, are increasingly rare—indeed, almost an endangered species. Paradoxically, this is the reason that effective delegation is more important than ever.

The simple fact is that almost any business nowadays is so complex that you *can't* do everything yourself. If you hire very carefully and have some good luck, you may have a few of those rare truly reliable people on your staff. But if your business is to grow, sooner or later you must rely on more or less "ordinary" people.

Since you cannot do everything yourself, and you cannot rely on your employees to do properly the things that you do not do yourself, you must be certain that the tasks you perform personally are the critical ones. Let us put this differently: If you head a growing company, you *will* delegate—the question is, *what* will you delegate? If you're smart, you will arrange things so that you are doing only the critical jobs *and nothing else whatsoever*.

The key to effective delegation is to emphasize horizontal rather than vertical delegation. Most CEOs indulge in vertical delegation; they do tasks that are unessential, even menial, in certain management areas and neglect tasks that are highly important in other areas. The "perfect" entrepreneur would use perfect horizontal delegation: perform all the high-level tasks in every area, and delegate the lower-level tasks. Of course, nobody is this well-rounded, and nobody should be. But you should make an effort to plan your delegation with this principle in mind.

Exercise 3–1:
Planning Delegation

Go through the matrix below and mark off the sectors (tasks) that you plan to handle personally for your start-up and those that you plan to delegate. (If you expect to take a position other than CEO, you need to develop your own matrix, breaking down the tasks in your chosen functional area.)

	Admin. & Finance	*Production*	*R&D*	*Marketing & Sales*
Set objectives				
Select approach				
Monitor results				
Supervise work				
Perform work				

THE PRESENT VERSUS THE FUTURE

A major problem for any growing enterprise is the match between increasingly challenging jobs and people who may not be able to grow as fast as their jobs. Suppose you hire a production manager to supervise the 10 assembly workers you have now. In a couple of years you may have 500 workers. If this woman doesn't have the ability to handle 500, you'll have the embarrassing and unpleasant task of replacing her. If she does, she may go crazy with boredom working with only 10 people—and you may go broke paying her the market price for her credentials.

There is no good answer to this dilemma. No matter how you handle it, sooner or later you'll face some distasteful options. We feel the best approach is to bring in fresh talent who can handle your present needs and who are ambitious. Make it very clear right from the start that they must grow with the job or see newcomers brought in over their heads. Monitor them carefully, and if they start to fall below your expectations, let them know at once. Those who can't measure up may be unhappy, but you'll find that many are relieved to be eased into a subordinate position, provided they aren't publicly humiliated.

NEPOTISM

If you're running a family business, nepotism is unavoidable by definition. But nepotism, broadly defined, occurs almost everywhere in the business world; big business or small, people get hired—or don't—because of their family, friends, race, religion, or old school ties. It's been said that since nepotism is unavoidable, it's better to be the nepoter than the nepotee. And as a practical matter, most entrepreneurs choose their cofounders and early employees from their families or friends.

But there are real dangers in nepotism. First, there is the obvious objection that your son or sister-in-law or whoever may not be competent to do the job. Second, nepotism is violently opposed by the nonfavored workers, and most especially by your best workers. Third, nepotism results in new conflicts in your personal life, because business disagreements now become family matters.

So what do we advise? It's best to avoid nepotism if you can. Sometimes you really can't. In that case, put specific limits on it.

> In some Japanese family-owned businesses that have grown large, there is a rule that members of the family sit on the board of directors but are absolutely forbidden any role in active management. Many family businesses have made it a rule that scions of the founder must start at the bottom and work their way up. Others require family members to work for another company for a few years before coming into the family business. Some reserve certain management slots for family members and others for outsiders.

The key point is to have firm, written rules, established in advance, that will delimit the employment of family members in some way. Other workers may tolerate nepotism if they know just where they stand and have some protection from arbitrary treatment.

THE HIRING PROCESS

Once you've decided that you really do need to hire somebody, how do you go about selecting the right person? Most managers think they know how—until a candidate comes in for an interview. Then they find themselves wondering what to say, what to ask, how to fill up the scheduled time. Successful hiring, like so many other aspects of business, is a matter of preparation. If you do your homework at the start, you'll have no trouble when it's time to interview candidates.

Here is a simple five-step procedure for personnel selection. We've put it in terms of hiring an employee, but the same method will work for selecting a cofounder, a director, a lawyer, or anyone else who will have to work with you on a regular basis.

Step 1: Write a Job Description

It's hard to believe, but an amazing number of managers hire without having a clear idea of the nature of the job they are filling. Frequently they just have a vague feeling that they're understaffed and that having more hands would be helpful. Get down on paper a *complete job description.* Exactly what will be this person's responsibilities? To whom will he report? Who will report to him? Title? Salary? Make it very explicit. Make sure to avoid evasion words like "assist,""supervise," "handle." Not "will assist me with the bookkeeping" but "will make all journal and ledger entries and do the trial balance every month." Not "supervise Station Two" but "monitor output quality at Station Two, make sure preventive maintenance is done, and keep operators supplied with parts." Not "handle routine correspondence" but "compose and type letters in response to credit inquiries and accounts-payable disputes."

The more detailed you can make the description, the better. If you have trouble coming up with this kind of specification, recognize that you have a problem. Maybe you don't need anybody after all. Maybe you do, but you're reluctant to delegate the tasks involved. Maybe you've failed to organize the work properly and don't have a good idea what needs to be done. Back up and rethink your needs.

When you're looking for a cofounder rather than an employee, it's even more important to define the "job" strictly. Decide what *specific* tasks you will expect these people to accomplish.

Step 2: Define Job Qualifications

Now that you know precisely what job needs to be done, you can decide what qualifications are needed. What does the candidate need in order to be able to do the job? Again, be very specific. Most qualification factors fall into one of the following categories.

Credentials. These include college degrees, educational certificates, licenses, certifications, and so on. Though often a legitimate requirement, credentials are frequently overemphasized. Where they are required by law, by contract, or perhaps by custom, they may be necessary. Otherwise, why pay for them?

Experience. If you are currently doing the task yourself and you plan to show the new chap exactly how you want it done, why pay a premium for experience? On the other hand, if you need somebody to do gene splicing and you don't know diddleysnaffle about it yourself, better be sure you hire somebody experienced. Again, the key is to be explicit. Not "five years experience in polymer coatings" but "has personally developed new coatings for high-performance electronic components." The idea of an experience qualification is to get somebody who *has done* what you are hiring him to do. How long he's done it, or when or where, is not nearly as important as that he's done exactly the thing that you're looking for.

Knowledge. This is often confused with credentials and sometimes confused with experience. If it's knowledge as such that you need, buy that and not something else. Knowledge might be a significant qualification for, say, a librarian or researcher: "Must know where to locate information on health effects of any chemical pollutant."

Skills. This is very frequently confused with experience or credentials or both. The mistake can be expensive. If you want somebody who can write accounting programs in COBOL, specify that skill. Don't pay a big premium for an M.S. in computer science, or for three years experience with one of the Big Eight. It's useful to distinguish "talent" skills, such as computer programming or playing the violin, from "craft" skills, such as cabinet making. The former don't require experience (though it's certainly helpful), but only certain people can do them well. The latter can be done by almost anyone, but almost everyone needs a long apprenticeship to do them well.

Intelligence. Most jobs require a certain amount; too little and she can't perform, too much and she's bored.

Creativity. This is needed by artists, scientists, engineers, writers. The hiring manager is often reduced to quivering helplessness by a creativity requirement. You needn't be if you remember two things. First, define just what you want created. You don't want a "creative electrical engineer," you want somebody who can design a microcomputer-controlled television aerial rotator. Second, look at past performance. Note that this is not necessarily the same as experience. Often the most creative people are young, fresh out of school. But they can still show you tangible evidence of creativity. An artist who's never had a job may come in with a portfolio of strikingly effective drawings. A freshly graduated scientist may show you an ingenious undergraduate research project he conceived and executed. Never hire "creative potential"; always look for evidence of accomplishment.

Step 3: Get Applicants

With qualifications specified, you're ready to *generate applicants*. There are various routes you can pursue to bring in qualified people.

Advertise. First, select the right medium. It has to be seen by the people you want. If you need a chemist, you wouldn't advertise in *Science*, which is read mainly by biologists. If you want only local candidates, use a local newspaper, or at least specify your location in the ad.

Timing is part of the medium. For instance, in *The Wall Street Journal*, Tuesday is job ad day; if your ad runs on Friday, it will get much less attention.

Second, write an ad that specifies the essential qualifications. A vague ad may bring in a lot of résumés, but that just adds to the burden of answering (and yes, courtesy requires that you answer every one). Don't worry about excluding good candidates; if you developed honest qualifications and didn't overspecify, an explicit ad won't turn away anyone you want to talk to.

Blind ads. Running an ad under a box number is sometimes justified, for instance if you want to conceal a new project from the competition. But you may not get the best candidates. Usually, a blind ad is motivated by fear of a flood of applicants writing, phoning, dropping in. If this is your problem, perhaps your ad is underspecified; consider making the requirements stiffer.

Headhunters and agencies. The former can be useful in special cases. When you want to hunt out top talent, you may need to call in these professionals to handle the tricky task— especially if you're trying to pirate someone from the competition. Employment agencies, however, are a different matter. Though these worthy institutions perform a useful task for society, the fact is that they seldom provide you with really good candidates. Few of the best people use agencies when job hunting; for that matter, the best people aren't often job hunting. And only a tiny minority of agencies are qualified to search for technical or highly skilled personnel. Keep in mind also that using an agency is expensive. The fee usually is roughly proportional to the square of the starting salary. (It's based on a sliding scale, typically 10 percent for an annual starting salary of $10,000, 15 percent for $15,000, and so on.)

The Old Boy Network. Managers usually do poorly with this, for two reasons. First, they fail to work at it. If you use personal contacts to locate candidates, you should take it seriously, not just make a few phone calls. Contact everyone you can think of, and ask each one to suggest additional names. Follow up every possibility your contacts give you, and don't forget to thank them. The second common mistake is careless vetting of candidates from this source. Too often a friend's recommendation is taken totally on faith. This is a form of nepotism—and as such it can be dangerous. Interview and judge candidates from this source just as you do the others. One final point: keep in mind that the Old Boy Network may produce too many boys and not enough girls.

Current employees. These days many companies rely heavily on referrals from employees. This has several advantages. The new people are likely to get a good feel for your company from their friends, so that they will be better prepared. The employee who recruits a candidate will feel some responsibility for her recommendation and will make an effort to help the new person work out. The practice obviously tends to enhance morale and group spirit. Beware, however, of becoming too inbred.

Step 4: Choose Applicants To Interview

That pile of résumés represents applicants. Now you need to *select candidates* for interview. You may find there is a shortage of good possibilities. Try to resist lowering your standards. Consider rewriting your ad, pursuing other media, or sweetening the compensation (or just giving it more prominence). Also, keep in mind that many otherwise good people lack job-hunting skills. Try to look past an unattractive résumé to see if there might be a strong candidate behind it.

Step 5: Interview Candidates

Now it's time for the interview. The purpose of the interview is to give you a chance to evaluate the candidate on three factors: (1) Qualifications—is the candidate *able* to do the job? (2) Motivation—does the candidate *want* to do the job? (3) Character—is the candidate the kind of person you want in your company and in this job?

Judging the candidate's *qualifications* is the easiest part. You should already, of course, have a start from her résumé. Now, with the job description in front of you, dig in and get the details. Go down your specifications one by one and satisfy yourself that she's got what you want. Some items cannot be evaluated from the résumé, or even from probing questions. You can check credentials and experience by calling her college and her former employers. *Always* do so—you may be surprised how many liars there are in the world. A plant tour is another good way to check on experience if you use it shrewdly. Does she obviously know her way around; does she ask intelligent questions?

If knowledge is a criterion, a few well-prepared questions can quickly settle any uncertainty. Judging skills is much harder. Lead the candidate to talk at length about her past work—have her describe *how* she did it. Listen carefully; you'll be able to hear the difference—with a little practice—between the confidence of talent and the hesitation and evasion of bluff. Another good technique is the "what if" question—"How would you handle such-and-such?"

Of course, simple skills such as typing can be subjected to direct test. For intelligence, resorting to an IQ test is seldom necessary (and is likely to be illegal). You should be able to make a rough judgment from conversation. Creativity, as already mentioned, should always be evaluated on past performance. Somebody who comes up with bright ideas during the interview should not be overestimated; look for proof that he can carry through his ideas to a finished product.

The interview also provides you with an opportunity to evaluate some less obvious qualifications. If social skills are part of the job—and they almost invariably are for management jobs—take him out to lunch or dinner. See if he has basic table manners, if he can carry on a social conversation effectively. You may discover that he can't resist a second martini—or even a third. Watch how he speaks to a waiter; if he's curt or rude to this "menial," that may be a hint about how he'll treat his subordinates. Be sure to introduce him to all the people he'll be working with closely if hired (and later ask their opinions).

Motivation can never be taken for granted. Of course, a candidate who seems unenthusiastic at the interview can be discarded as a poor risk. But a gung-ho attitude is hardly a guarantee of real motivation—it's too easy to fake. To judge motivation effectively, remember what it is: first and foremost, motivation is *enjoying the job*. In the long run, even a very conscientious worker will slack off if she doesn't enjoy her work. So ask questions about what she likes. "Do you enjoy your current job? *What* do you like about it? What do you dislike? What part of your work do you enjoy the most?"John Molloy suggests an excellent question: "Describe the last time you got real personal joy from your work."* Note that these questions focus on past or present. Questions about the future ("How would you like . . .?" or "Where do you want to be in five years?") are unproductive. People don't really know their future feelings, so you'll get either a vague generality or a snappy trick answer taken from some "how to get a job" book.

Evaluating the *character* of a candidate has an old-fashioned ring to it, so these days people usually refer to "psychological factors." Call it what you will, but recognize the importance of this criterion.

First you need to know: is this person a winner or a loser? Sometimes you can spot a loser almost at a glance, as he trudges into your office apathetic, sad, obviously defeated by life. Usually it's not so easy, but there are ways.

▪ Winners feel responsible for themselves; they believe that their own actions determine what happens to them. Losers believe that they are controlled by forces outside themselves. In conversation, probe for these attitudes. Bring up the subject of luck. A loser blames bad luck for his failures. The winner, if hit by a meteorite, says, "I guess I should have known better than to be standing right there." Influence is another tell-tale subject. As Molloy points out, a favorite say-

Molloy's Live for Success (New York: William Morrow & Co., 1981), p. 18.

ing of losers is, "It's not what you know, it's who you know." The winner says, "It's who you know—so it's up to me to know the right people." Be wary also of candidates who *complain* that they've suffered because of discrimination. Winners may be victims of prejudice, but they don't use it as an excuse.

 • Winners are energetic. Look into the candidate's hobbies and sports activities. It doesn't matter much what they are, so long as he's clearly active. It may seem paradoxical, but the chap with no outside interests probably won't be a tiger on the job either. The loser can just barely struggle through a 35-hour workweek; the rest of the time he naps or watches TV. The real winner may play tennis and chess, be a miniature-railroad buff, and write *haiku* in his spare time—in addition to a heavy work load.

 • Winners have self-esteem. They never plead or grovel, even when desperate. They project a calm conviction of their own value. Losers, on the other hand, typically slide into the extremes: either self-criticism and supplication, or bluster and bragging.

Never hire a loser. Beware of pity. The guy who had "bad luck" in his previous job will have "bad luck" in your company. If his previous employer was "prejudiced," you'll find him suing you for discrimination. Harden your heart and send him away.

You'll want to check for another quality: integrity. A resort to polygraph examinations or handwriting analyses is seldom required. All you need is a simple psychological principle: people almost invariably assume that other people are just like themselves. In this specific application, it means that a dishonest person, given the opportunity, will treat you as a comrade in crookedness.

A new employee suggested to me a way to cheat the employment agency through which I hired him of part of its fee, to our mutual advantage. It wasn't quite blatant enough to justify firing him, but as I declined, I made a mental note to keep an eye on him. Still, when he left the company, he took $50 of my money with him.

As you converse with the candidate, probe his attitudes with remarks about unpopular organizations. If he expresses the feeling that it's all right to cheat an insurance company, or a bank, or the phone company—watch out. He may just as easily convince himself that he's justified in cheating *you*.

A lot of the traditional rules of interviewing may seem like nit-picking, but they do have some validity. They are based on the fact that at the interview, you are seeing the candidate at his best. A minor deficiency that shows up at the interview may presage a major deficiency after hiring.

I didn't want to be old-fashioned and arbitrary. He showed up for the interview without a tie, but I hired him anyway. He showed up for work without a shave.

When the time comes to make your choice, you may find that you're not happy with any of the alternatives. After all this work, you'll be reluctant to give up and start over—but maybe you'd better. It's easy to hire someone. But if you have to fire him, it's not very pleasant. After you've done a couple of firings, you'll realize that you'd rather go three rounds with a *sumo* wrestler. You'll have to do it sometimes—you can't completely avoid firings—but you can minimize the need for it. Hire carefully—very carefully.

Checklist 3–1: Before You Hire

- [ ] Have you evaluated the candidate on every qualification on the job description?
- [ ] Have you checked with the candidate's references?
- [ ] Have you checked with references *not* provided by the candidate?
- [ ] Is there evidence that the candidate has enjoyed in the past doing the kind of work you're offering?
- [ ] Does the candidate have adequate social skills?
- [ ] Has the candidate been introduced to his potential co-workers?
- [ ] Is the candidate a "winner?"
- [ ] Is the candidate honest even when being honest exposes him to ridicule?

☐ Did the candidate show up for the interview clean, groomed, and properly dressed?

☐ Do you feel really comfortable with hiring this candidate?

MAKING THINGS CLEAR

Make your choice, make your offer, and when it's accepted, make damn sure the new employee knows the score. Give her a job description in writing; you may want to rephrase the one you wrote at the start of the hiring process, but keep it just as specific. State in writing what is expected of her, and also what she can expect: compensation, how much, in what form, paid when; vacation, how much, any restrictions; benefits, what exactly; salary or promotion reviews, how often, when, what criteria will be used.

There's always a temptation to gloss over any uncomfortable questions; and too often the new worker, eager for the job, will refrain from rocking the boat. But any hand waving or "we'll worry about that later" may plant the seeds of later trouble. Keep in mind that the embarrassing question unasked now may mean a lawsuit or a union-organizing drive later.

These days, hiring is also subject to various government "anti-discrimination" laws. Unfortunately, it's impossible for us to give a detailed discussion, because the rules change constantly. There is no substitute for continued study and a constant effort to keep current. *Do not* assume that being honestly unbiased is enough—it isn't. Also keep in mind that *ex post facto* law is not prohibited in this area. The fact that it was legal when you did it doesn't mean you can't be sued for it later. So never tell candidates why they were hired—or not hired. It may come back to haunt you.

COMPENSATION AND MOTIVATION

Once you've hired someone, the question of compensation comes up. Nobody has yet devised a perfect compensation system, and in any case, you'll have to develop something suitable for the specific situation in your business. However, certain principles may prove helpful.

• Compensation must include an irreducible minimum

that will provide basic financial security for the employee. This also applies to cofounders, and to *you*. You may have to take a substantial cut or even skip a paycheck when cash flow is in a fade, but don't try to show off by starving yourself and your family. It can lead to some very bad decisions.

• Compensation should include some element that will motivate the employee. This can be very tricky. Profit sharing, for instance, is overrated. It has two faults. First, it's too dilute—the employee knows his individual efforts have only a small effect on profits. A good motivation system should reward the employee for his results, not the company's. Second, no employee—except the CEO—really has control of, or responsibility for, profits as such. A good system should tie employees' rewards to factors under their control. However, you should be careful to avoid setting up conflicts among your workers. A little competitiveness is fine, but don't set up a system where one worker gets rewarded at the expense of another. Try adding a component based on team performance.

• Another important principle is: *reward in real time.* A year-end bonus waits much too long to tell people what they're doing right or wrong. Any monetary reward should appear in the paycheck immediately following the performance to be rewarded.

• Stock-purchase plans or stock options illustrate another potential problem. What if somebody doesn't work out? You may not want a disgruntled ex-employee as a stockholder. If he's a cofounder, he may own an embarrassingly large hunk of your company. You can limit this difficulty by using buyback provisions, but keep in mind that the cash necessary for a buyback may not be readily available when you need it. Also, various legal restrictions may hamper your ability to buy back stock. Try to avoid awarding stock up front; instead, feed it out as it's earned by performance. Consider a provision that will transform common stock to nonvoting preferred if the owner leaves the company.

• Compensation should be fair. Make a real effort to tie rewards to objective, tangible, indisputable criteria. A bonus based on "attitude" or other subjective, vague standards may encourage favoritism and other abuses. Also, anticipate the need to extend rewards to those who will come aboard later. Don't be so generous with the early participants that you run out of goodies to distribute.

Before you start hiring—before you talk to the first prospective cofounder, if possible—think out the principles of your compensation system very carefully. And before you finalize the details, talk it over with your lawyer and your accountant.

Exercise 3–2:
Your Compensation System

A. Begin by deciding what kinds of personnel you will be needing during the first two years of your company's life. Normally, these will fall into three groups: cofounders, other key managers, and routine workers. Write a brief job description for each slot.

B. Now consider your options for compensation. The major possibilities are: (1) stock; (2) stock options; (3) commissions; (4) cash bonuses; (5) salary or wages. Decide what you feel you can afford in each category. How much stock are you willing to surrender? Are you willing to pay above-market salaries or higher-than-union wages?

C. Now go through your job descriptions one by one. Select in each case the critical tasks, where you wish to motivate maximum effort. Caution: even in a very complex job description, don't try to provide special incentives for too many tasks; choose one, two, or at most three.

D. Complete your system by allocating your compensation as incentives for the key tasks in each job description.

Here are some simplified examples:

VP Marketing:

- 500 shares of stock for each new product that is successfully introduced and meets sales projections
- Monthly bonus of $1,000 for each percentage point of gross margin over 25%

Production Supervisor, Line #5:

- $100 bonus for every month without breakdown
- $20 bonus for every hour reduction in setup time

OUTSIDE PROFESSIONALS

You will need to select certain professional counselors and handle them properly. Many entrepreneurs choose a lawyer or accountant very casually, on the recommendation of some acquaintance. If you're inexperienced, you may never even realize that the person you've retained is a total dud.

You'll want to have a good business lawyer from an early stage. It should be someone familiar with corporate and business law, of course. You're usually better off selecting a lawyer on the basis of a personal recommendation than out of the Yellow Pages, but even if she gets rave reviews from a friend, check her out. Does she have other clients like you? Is she experienced in this type of work? We laymen tend to think of lawyers as generalists, but modern legal practice is extremely specialized.

As you investigate, remember that a lawyer, like a stock-broker, should give good execution. When you need something done, will she get right on it—or dawdle? When Anthony Trollope created his famous fictional law firm, he named it Slow & Bideawhile. Be sure you don't retain them; things move faster now than they did a century ago. You want somebody who is efficient and will give good service even to a small client.

You probably can't afford, and don't want, the services of a top partner in a major law firm. This leaves you with two choices: a small firm, or a junior person in a large firm. There's much debate over the relative merits of these options. It seems likely, however, that the former is the best choice for a small, stable niche company, and that the latter will be better for a growth company.

Legal services can be quite expensive. Here's a useful tip. When you need a legal document—a contract, say, or a patent application—avoid asking your attorney to write it. Instead, draft it yourself, then submit it to her and ask her to suggest revisions. This will save a lot of time and reduce the amount you spend on fees. Even more important, it will help to ensure that your lawyer understands clearly what you want the document to accomplish.

Another tip: call your attorney "counselor" when you speak with her. They eat this up.

You also need an accountant—again, from a very early stage. It is possible for a layman to set up and operate the accounting system of a small business, but only a masochist should do so. Bookkeeping and accounting are easy; it's dealing with taxes that no civilized person should have to endure.

Your accountant, like your lawyer, should be carefully vetted before you retain him. Remember that this fellow is going to be handling all your taxes; you will have to rely on him, and if he makes a mistake the IRS could wipe you out. This is so important we're going to repeat it: If your accountant screws up your taxes, the IRS will not go after him, they will go after *you*. Again, good execution is critical. Talk to some of his clients. Does he get out financial statements and tax returns *on time?*

Also be sure he is familiar with small-business accounting and with your industry. Accounting has become just as specialized as law.

A cross that I've had to bear—twice—is explaining to an accountant that a chemical manufacturing company does *not* at all resemble the textbook examples of manufacturing companies. In particular, inventory management raises some very difficult and unique problems.

Accountants, like lawyers, prefer to use "canned" systems, because they're easier and cheaper. Unless your company is very typical and average (in which case you'll probably fail in the market) this sort of accounting system will not fit your special needs. We therefore advise you to learn elementary accounting and bookkeeping yourself, if only so you can discuss your needs with your accountant in an intelligent manner. Insist on statements that provide you with the information *you* need; your accountant will prefer a format that simply rephrases the contents of your tax return and is totally incomprehensible to nonspecialists. Go into all this *at the start;* if your accountant is unwilling to cooperate, switch before it's too late.

If you are already using an accountant to help you with personal financial planning or taxes, the instinctive course of action is to retain him for your company's accounting too.

Beware! This can get you into trouble. It is true that as long as your company is closely held, your personal and corporate financial affairs will be intimately linked. But your personal financial adviser may be totally incompetent to handle your business's needs—and, if this is the case, he probably will not inform you of his deficiencies. It is quite possible to have two accountants, one personal and one corporate, and have them work together effectively. Usually this is advisable; it allows you to have competent help at both ends, and can save you from some nasty conflict-of-interest hassles too.

A third important professional is your insurance agent. You will need many different kinds of insurance for even a very tiny company, ranging from workers' compensation to liability. A good agent can simplify your life amazingly by handling all these needs in one package.

A small company usually has a special need for expert assistance in selecting insurers, because of what might be called insurance red-lining. Many insurance companies exclude certain types of customers—often small companies—from coverage.

I'll never forget an incident that occurred when I had just started Reaction Design. We wanted to buy liability insurance. I made an appointment with an agent from one of the nation's top business-insurance companies. He walked in the door and looked around the laboratory. His first words were, "This is a chemical company." I said, "That's right." He said, "We don't insure chemical companies." Then he turned on his heel and walked out.

We've discussed the insurance problem in a bit more detail in the Appendix. In the meantime, our message is: choose an agent with care.

THE BOARD OF DIRECTORS

If you use the corporate form, you'll be legally required to have a board of directors. The minimum makeup of the board varies from one state to another. Your board should be selected with care. In legal theory, the directors run a corporation. In practice, the board is usually a rubber stamp for the management.

The rubber-stamp approach may be very tempting, but a strong board can be a tremendous asset, especially for a growing company.

The directors should perform four functions.

1. They select, and if necessary fire, the CEO and other members of top management. This responsibility implies someone will monitor and evaluate management performance. Also, the directors should be involved in the development of new members of management.

2. They represent and protect the interests of the stockholders. Specifically, they are responsible for watching over the corporation's financial affairs to make sure no hanky-panky is occurring. They also must make certain decisions where management could have a conflict of interest—setting management compensation is an obvious example.

3. They formally decide major questions. There's no consistent rule as to what is a "major" decision. Usually it's a decision where the stakes are high enough that the CEO is afraid to face the music alone if something goes wrong. It is desirable, however, to establish a more objective standard.

4. They pitch in as general high-level handymen whenever their specific talents are needed, giving advice, providing contacts, helping with negotiations.

The personnel policies for your board of directors are the corporation's bylaws, which spell out how many directors you have, how they're selected, what powers they'll have, and so on. When you incorporate, your lawyer will probably suggest using a set of standard, "canned" bylaws. Don't do it. Although bylaws can be revised later, it's rather tricky—and it may require the cooperation of the directors or stockholders who are the problem that makes you want the revision. Before you approve a set of bylaws, try to foresee problems that may come up. Often an entrepreneur prefers bylaws that give the controlling stockholder (himself) almost unrestricted power; this is feasible in many states. Sometimes, after his holdings have been diluted by later financings, he is ejected and finds "his" bylaws now work against him. It's best to have rules that protect the interests of the minority stockholders—you will probably be one someday if your company is successful. Besides, prospective investors are likely to insist on such protection anyway. Try to find a balance between restrictions so tight that flexibility is lost and looseness that results in vagueness and conflict.

Checklist 3–2: Bylaws Traps

☐ The scope of your corporate charter should not unduly limit your future options. (It can be very embarrassing to stumble on a lucrative variation of your initial business and then discover that you legally precluded yourself from entering it when you incorporated.)

☐ The size of the board of directors is five or seven. (A small company seldom needs a larger board. Some states will let you get away with two, or even one. But be careful—what if you desperately need extra members in the future?)

☐ Make provision for removal of directors. The time may come when it is crucial to get rid of a dissident without waiting for the next annual meeting.

☐ Officers should be specified carefully and their duties taken seriously. *These are legally meaningful titles.* The people who hold them are responsible for the assigned duties and can be sued if they fail to perform them properly. If you make your spouse Secretary or Treasurer, you may not be doing him or her a favor!

☐ Make absolutely sure the minutes of your board meetings are properly kept. They may figure later in an IRS audit or a lawsuit.

SELECTING THE BOARD

Choose strong people for your board. They will fall into three groups: members of management; major stockholders or their representatives; and outside directors. One good policy is to have roughly equal numbers of these three types. You, as CEO, will have a strong voice in the selection of directors, but as the company grows you will come under increasing pressure, especially from investors. One way to maintain control is to take the initiative in bringing in outside directors. Don't wait until the venture capitalists force their candidates on you. Find people you have confidence in, preferably other entrepreneurs with strong credentials.

Never take the board of directors for granted. Select directors with care, keep them informed, stay close to them. Big investors will expect to name their own people to the board. That's fine, but insist that their candidates meet your standards. Put up a fight, if necessary, but don't let Mr. Moneybag's incompetent brother-in-law sit on your board. All directors must bring with them useful talents, knowledge, and if possible, prestige. Every director must have integrity. Every director must be compatible with the rest of the team—don't ever allow your board to split into factions. And above all, every director must be *willing to work*. Expect each member of the board to take an active interest in the company; to visit, investigate, question, advise; to be continually on the lookout for ways to help.

COFOUNDERS

Your earliest and most crucial personnel decisions will involve cofounders. Much of what you need to know to select the other members of your initial management team has already been covered. However, obtaining cofounders does present certain unique problems.

If you did the self-analysis recommended in Chapter 1, you should have a list of tasks that you don't want to do, either because you're not good at them or because you don't enjoy them, or both. Many of these tasks may be the sort that relatively low-level employees can handle. Some, however, will probably be of a nature that demands top-management attention. Look for cofounders to take on the important areas that you don't want to deal with. Don't accept cofounders at random, people who are friends or relatives or who are just looking for a good thing. Write job descriptions and go through the five-step hiring process described earlier. Never forget that the *only* valid reasons to take on a cofounder are to relieve you of work that you don't want and to provide essential talents you don't have.

It's quite common for a new entrepreneur to take on partners she doesn't actually need simply because she's unsure of herself and feels insecure. Watch out for this tendency.

You may feel guilty about taking the good stuff yourself and making someone else do the unpleasant parts. Don't. The right person will *like* doing what you consider the unpleasant parts. This principle is the key to forming a compatible top-management team. Good people seldom fight over money or recognition, but they'll fight like minks over responsibility. The only way to keep the peace is to eliminate or at least minimize areas of overlap between cofounders' interests. Clearly define each one's domain.

You'll probably find that a person who likes doing things you hate has a personality different from yours. Welcome this. Too many start-up teams are overly homogeneous in attitude. A bunch of engineers can definitely use a marketing type to remind them that their better mousetrap won't sell itself. A group of high-flying salespeople will do much better if augmented with a controller who can bring them back to earth on occasion. If you're an optimist, be sure there's a pessimist on your team. If you're a pessimist, be sure there's an optimist.

Another area of concern is commitment. There are a lot of people out there who *think* they are eager to get in on the ground floor of a new business. Your selection process had better filter them out. Each cofounder should be competent to do his job, and he should also be an entrepreneur. Test the commitment of each cofounder in three stages. First, will he work? As you develop your business plan, be sure each cofounder is given tough assignments as his contribution. Slackers should be politely excused and replaced. Show no mercy. Second, will he invest? Pay all expenses yourself during the planning phase, but make it clear that your cofounders will be expected to chip in at incorporation. Each should contribute roughly the same amount, by the way. Money talks, and a VP who puts in ten times the amount the others do may start talking too loudly. Those who don't write a check at incorporation should be politely excused and replaced. It makes no difference whether they are unwilling or unable to invest. Third, will he come on board? When you actually start operations, it is time for your people to cut the umbilical cord and work full-time for the new company. Avoid making exceptions. The chap who wants to play it safe will leave you in the lurch just when you need him most.

Keep in mind that people who lack commitment are not evil or contemptible. Always drop them kindly and considerately—but be sure you do drop them.

Finally, compensation is especially tricky when dealing with cofounders. In addition to the principles we developed earlier, you should keep in mind the importance of clarity. There is a deadly temptation to come to a rough agreement on touchy questions like stock apportionment and leave the tedious details to be settled later. When "later" comes—especially if a cofounder is being dropped—you may be in for a fight. Right at the start, define what each cofounder's responsibilities will be and precisely how he will be paid. Leave no detail unspecified and *put it in writing*. When verbal agreements are made, people tend to hear what they want to hear. If you have it in writing, you can skip a lot of "I told you last year . . ." "No you didn't . . ." arguments.

Years ago, I began keeping a business diary. At the end of every day I spend five minutes jotting down the events of the day. This is augmented by notes taken at or immediately after especially important meetings. It has proved immensely valuable on several occasions to be able to go back and find exact information on who said what, and when.

Cofounders usually get their major compensation in stock. We pointed out earlier that stock should seldom be awarded up front. Let's reiterate that here, for the stakes are much higher. Each cofounder should purchase some stock at incorporation. The rest should be awarded, by the board of directors, based on the performance of explicitly defined, previously specified tasks. This will probably have to go for you too.

BUILDING A COMPANY CULTURE

There is nothing mystical about a "company culture." A company culture is simply the sum of the attitudes, motives, and policies of your individual employees. Every company that survives develops some sort of culture. If you do not actively define a culture by intention, your employees will randomly define one by default.

What kind of culture your company should have depends on what kind of company you have—or want to have.

Consider, for instance, a company that does door-to-door sales of some household gadget on a one-shot basis, with no attempt at repeat sales. Such a company is likely to develop a culture that emphasizes aggressive selling—get your foot in the door, blast down the customer's sales resistance with a petard of high-pressure sales techniques, and leave him dazed with gadget in hand and thinner wallet. The best-rewarded and most admired people in the company will be those sales-people who can move the largest amount of product each month. On the other hand, having been encouraged to exploit their customers, employees are not likely to show any greater respect for the company or for each other. The company culture will thus include a great deal of disloyalty and infighting.

To understand any company's culture, first ask: What are its employees most proud of? At Toyota, it might be turning out a high-quality product. At IBM, it might be customer service. At Genentech, it might be technological leadership. What do you want *your* employees to be proud of?

Company culture is important because it is the only way to effectively motivate your employees. Experience has shown again and again—in big companies, in government bureaucracies, in socialist economies—that you cannot get real effort out of people solely with carrot-and-stick tactics. Rules, quotas, bonuses, demerits, even the whip will not make them put out 100 percent. To get their best effort you must engage their loyalty and enthusiasm.

How do you do it? There are four things you must do.

First, set an example. There is a simple rule: employees are never better motivated than top management. If you want them to work hard—*you* must work harder. If you want them to drop everything and rally round when a customer has a problem—*you* must take the lead. If you want them to keep costs down—*you* had better be conspicuously frugal.

Second, make sure your management control systems are

in harmony with your company's goals. You should keep in mind that everything you use to make sure things are done properly is part of your management control systems. Vacation policy, accounting procedures, work rules, QA standards—any rule, procedure, or policy constitutes an official statement of what you want your company culture to be. Thus every item should be carefully examined to determine how it fits in with your objectives.

Suppose you want your employees to take the initiative in spotting and correcting quality problems—but your assembly-line work rules require the worker to get permission before going to the bathroom. Suppose you want new inventions from your R&D group—but every new idea must pass a strict evaluation process before getting approval. Suppose you want every employee to be oriented toward solving customer problems—but promotions go to those who are prompt and accurate with their sales reports. If this sort of contradiction is common in your controls, your employees will be frustrated and turn off. Most will serve their time and try to get by with minimum effort. The best will leave.

Third, go and find out. Don't settle for an "open-door policy"—go out the door and actively seek out grievances to resolve. Don't just put up a suggestion box—ask people for suggestions in person. There's only one way to find out how your control systems are working, and that is to examine them in action. Set aside a certain number of hours each month for "inspection"—informal, not the white-glove type. Drop in on the production area, talk to the janitor, ride along with a salesperson for a day.

On these occasions, you must have an open, noncritical attitude. Don't lay down the law, ask questions. Avoid, however, vague queries like "How are you doing?" "How do you like it here?" "Do you have any problems?" This sort of thing makes you sound like a distant, out-of-touch figure. Instead, get down to specifics. "What do you think about this design—could it be made easier to assemble?" "Would you say we're throwing away scrap that could be salvaged?" "When you need a firm shipping date to close a sale, would it help to have a hot line to Production that you could call?"

Fourth, motivate attitude with the intangibles. You'll recall that basing tangible rewards such as salary, bonus, or promotion on attitude is a poor idea. Tangible rewards—and punishments—should always be based on objective criteria of performance. The complement to this principle is that attitude, effort, enthusiasm should be rewarded with the intangibles: praise in front of coworkers, or better yet in front of family; a letter of commendation in the personnel file (with a copy on the bulletin board); an award ceremony; a plaque or trophy; these are the appropriate ways to applaud those who put out for the company. (Often, of course, they will go to the same people who are getting bonuses for specific accomplishments.)

There are, however, two traps to watch out for. First, never use intangible rewards as a consolation prize. If someone deserves a raise, give her a raise—not a medal. Second, beware of the "Employee of the Month" habit. Sooner or later— usually sooner—a month comes in which nobody (or nobody who hasn't had the award already) has done anything outstanding. If you give it to a second-rate worker just once, you make all the previous winners feel defrauded and, by cheapening your reward, destroy its future value. Never make a commendation a routine event; its value lies in being exceptional.

If you follow these rules, your company will have a culture that complements your goals and makes them effective. You'll never have trouble hiring or keeping good people. Union organizers will hit your company and bounce. And your company will be a happy and pleasant place to work—for your employees and for you.

CAUTIONARY TALE: INSECURITY IN SECURITY

Some time ago I was invited to serve on the board of directors of a company I'll call Digitensor. Pat Chroman, the founder, chairman, and president, was an engineer who had developed some technology that could be extremely valuable to the security industry. There is a persistent, ongoing need for methods to check people out before allowing them access to business premises or military facilities or computers and so on. Dr. Chroman's gadgetry used electronic means to determine, very reliably, whether an applicant for admission was authorized or not. Don't ask me how it worked; he often tried to explain it to me but I'm not a technology type, and all I can remember is that it had something to do with determining whether a person was contravariant or covariant.

With all the concern these days about computer crime, terrorism, and security in general, you can see what a tremendous market opportunity was available, if the device could be developed and marketed properly. That was where I came in. Digitensor had made a public offering but was trying to raise even more money to finish development and start marketing.

Chroman's background was essentially pure engineering. He had founded a previous company, which had failed. I didn't hold that against him; on the contrary, I prefer to work with entrepreneurs who have had some acquaintance with adversity. Those who have never experienced anything but success may crumple up when things get tough. Digitensor had a really exciting product and presented an interesting challenge. Chroman had attracted a fine group of engineers, but at this point it was time to build a complete team, for supposedly the product was about ready to come out of the lab and get into the marketplace. Digitensor needed a skilled chief financial officer, to handle the considerable amount of money already involved and to assist in raising more. It also needed to add a sales manager with some extensive marketing experience, and a production manager competent to develop a reliable manufacturing process for a new and very complex device.

Unfortunately, almost as soon as I took my seat on the board, there began to be friction between me and the CEO. Chroman was an engineer's engineer, and for him it all began and ended in engineering. He paid lip service to the need for strong people in marketing and sales and finance and production, but in his heart of hearts he was loyal only to his own god. As an engineer, he felt that if you perfected a fine product, everything else would take care of itself. The market would knock down your door. Money would pour in, and any kind of financial controls or accounting would be unnecessary. Production would be trivial, because the item was so well-designed and easy to manufacture.

In short, product design was to him the creative and important part of a business venture, and the other activities were merely incidental. This sort of attitude makes it difficult to build an effective management team. In fairness to Chroman, I have to say that this "my specialty is the only thing that counts" feeling is not confined to engineers. I've encountered it among sales, marketing, financial, and production people also.

Chroman and I quickly tangled over the selection of a sales manager. I had managed to identify a number of candidates who in my judgment had the background and temperament that would be necessary to fill the job. Chroman refused even to interview any of them. He had been "fortunate" enough to identify someone who had expressed an interest in the product. This individual worked for a major computer manufacturer as a divisional sales manager. He was extremely enthusiastic about the Digitensor security device—and Chroman hired him as sales manager. Well, the mere fact that somebody likes what you've designed and, by virtue of that, likes you is no reason to hire him. But more important, you don't want to hire the first prospect who appears, even if he looks very good, without checking out other candidates.

Our new sales manager, though well meaning, simply did not have what it took to promote a new product in a skeptical marketplace. He was used to working with the resources and support of a big company, selling established products. His task was somewhat complicated, to say the least, because the product was always under redesign. Chroman had great difficulty letting go and pushing the product out into the marketplace. He always wanted to make it more and more perfect.

As chief financial officer he hired an accountant who had worked in his father's accounting firm. This fellow was a perfectly competent CPA, but he simply was unable to cope with the start-up nature of the business. He didn't have any idea of how to manage the finances of a growing enterprise. Eventually this poor chap was replaced, but unfortunately his successor was no better.

Then there was the production manager. Chroman hired a man who had worked for him in his previous, unsuccessful venture. He had pretty much a job-shop background and lacked the experience needed to set up from scratch a full-scale production facility.

What these people and, indeed, the entire management team had in common was weakness—not just weakness in qualifications for their particular jobs but personal weakness. Chroman kept them all under his thumb and ran the company as a dictatorship. He could not brook any opposition. As a result he was surrounded by yes men, and that is the last thing you want in a growth business. Independent viewpoints from all the various disciplines are necessary. One man can never have all the answers, particularly if he has an extremely narrow background and experience.

I began to realize that Chroman, in spite of his real talent as an engineer, was extremely uncertain about himself. He felt fundamentally inadequate because he didn't understand marketing, didn't understand finance—didn't understand business, in short. He was superb in technology, but management issues made him feel insecure. The result was that he felt threatened by anyone who really knew any of these areas.

This insecurity was also the source of the company's persistent inability to get its product design finalized and start selling. In my frustration, I sometimes felt that all Chroman really wanted to do was sit at the bench and make that machine do more wonderful things than it had done the day before, irrespective of whether it ever got onto the market. In fact, that turned out to be pretty much the case. If he got out and actually did business, then he would no longer be relying on his strength as a creative technology person. He would have to deal with all sorts of nontechnology issues that he felt uncomfortable with.

The result of all this was that Digitensor went nowhere. Nobody really knew what to do. The product just sat in the lab, being "improved" and adapted, under various contracts, for specialized applications. Digitensor didn't have a single commercial site. Naturally, this couldn't possibly be Chroman's fault, could it? So he began replacing his yes men with other yes men. Pretty soon the company had a revolving door of key personnel, and it hurt the company badly. The customers lost faith because every time they called there was another sales manager in place. The financial community lost faith because chief financial officers kept coming in and going out.

After about 18 months, I was fed up and left the board of directors. Digitensor is still hanging on as this is written; the stock has bounced up and down as new development contracts were announced. According to a recent announcement, however, the company has finally got a standardized product to market and is starting to move. Apparently, it has muddled through at least some of its personnel difficulties.

I want to emphasize that this is not a case of an incompetent or neurotic entrepreneur. As head of a contract engineering company Chroman would have been perfect. With just himself and a few assistants, working on the leading edge of technology and not needing to worry about manufacturing, marketing, or financial issues, his talents would have been put to ideal use.

Yet I can't really say that the fundamental problem here was a mismatch of entrepreneur and company. Digitensor was based on a very bright idea for filling a very important need in the market. This venture could not have been properly pursued as a contract R&D operation; Chroman *had* to build a growth company. As is often the case, the decision to tackle a certain problem forced certain other decisions about the company.

Given that, what should have been done? First, of course, Pat Chroman should have confronted his own problems with delegation. Next, he should have built a strong board of directors. I probably was a poor choice; somebody with more knowledge of technology might have communicated with him more effectively. And to have a dissident like myself on the board was in itself a serious problem, which should have been resolved earlier one way or the other. Above all, there was a need to have a system—some sort of rules or principles—for hiring top management. It's easy to criticize Pat Chroman for letting his personal insecurity result in poor hiring decisions, but all of us are subject to similar tendencies. That's why you need a *policy* to guide you in hiring.

HDS

4

MARKET RESEARCH

It is a capital offense to theorize in advance of the facts.

Sir Arthur Conan Doyle
The Adventure of the Second Stain*

Most new companies fail. And the most common cause of failure is simple starvation—inadequate sales.

Your new venture is particularly vulnerable. An established company has ongoing sales; you do not. You must build sales from scratch. So the first question you should ask—and certainly the first question a prospective investor will ask—is: Do you have a *market* for your product?

When I look at a business plan, I like to see, right at the beginning, a section dealing with the *need*. No matter how clever the product, how ingenious the technology, how talented the management—if there's no real need in the market for the business, it cannot succeed.

Your estimate of future sales provides the foundation of your business plan. As we'll see when we discuss financial projections, everything will be based on your sales projections. Your estimates of costs, profits, cash flow—all depend on sales

*The Annotated Sherlock Holmes (New York: Clarkson N. Potter Books, 1967), p. 311.

and all will be pie-in-the-sky unless your sales projections are reliable. This is the first (but not the only) reason you need market research. You need to be sure there's water in the pool before you jump off the diving board.

"TOP-DOWN" MARKET RESEARCH

Investors want to know what *evidence* you have that sales will be high enough to make the company profitable. When they pick up your business plan, the first thing they do is flip through it to find the key paragraph that addresses this question. Suppose you do your market research the way it's usually done. Then they'll read something like this:

> According to an authoritative study done by *Mushroom Age* in 1981, there are 10,000 mushroom farms in the United States alone, and each spends an average of $20,000 per year on mushroom-cutting machinery. Thus the total market is $200 million per year. On even a pessimistic estimate, we can take 2 percent of this market the first year, and so we project sales of $4 million . . .

At this point the investor closes your business plan, tosses it into the "reject with regrets" basket, and picks up the next plan. You just blew it.

But, you protest, you're estimating only a 2 percent market share. Surely it's perfectly reasonable to expect that you can attain it—such a tiny percentage!

Is it? Try the following experiment. Go to one of the established companies in the industry, Monolithic Mushroom Machinery. Talk to the CEO. Tell him: "Our new company, Incandescent Fungoid Cutters, Inc., is going to enter your business. That will mean taking away some of your market share—just a *little*—you'll never miss it!" See if he thinks that's "reasonable."

This is why "top-down" market research, performed in the library, is of limited value. It doesn't matter whether it's 1 percent of a $1-billion market or 100 percent of a $10-million market. Either way, you're going to be taking those sales away from someone else who either has them now or would like to have them, and he's not going to give them up without a fight. In fact, he's going to fight like a Tasmanian devil.

The top-down method of market research merely establishes that there *is* a market—people are buying this kind of product, and plenty of it. There are a number of sources you can use. Market-research firms produce studies of markets they consider interesting. If a recent study exists for your market, you can buy a copy—for several thousand dollars, typically. Usually the major results of the study will be published in trade magazines, and you can read at least that much for free. A publication called *Predicasts* provides a summary of these studies every year, indexed by industry (SIC code, to be precise). You can find a copy in almost any college library. If you are planning to sell a consumer product or service, census statistics, available—again, at a hefty price—from the Federal government, can be invaluable in defining the demographic and economic characteristics of a given geographical area. You certainly should familiarize yourself with as much of this kind of information as you can manage to acquire—but *don't stop there.*

In my current activity with Vanguard Ventures, I have looked at a number of retirement centers that have failed. These projects are not inexpensive to construct—they run $30 million or thereabouts. The housing and facilities are designed specifically for the needs of the elderly and can't be easily modified, so if you don't attract your intended market you're stuck with a lot of empty units and a real financial disaster.

Each of these failures resulted from reliance on census information. The developers went to major accounting firms and paid them to do so-called "feasibility studies." These involved getting the census data for the appropriate tracts and determining how many elderly there were in the local population, their incomes, competitive housing available, and so on. After careful analysis, the accountants came out with wonderful studies that confirmed that indeed there was a market and that demand for their units would be strong.

In each case the project, once constructed, went into bankruptcy because the promoters had not bothered to talk to anybody in the community. There was never a face-to-face conversation with people who would actually be buying into these apartments. It was all done by statistics—and goods and services are bought not by statistics but by people.

In one case the promoters arranged for a local Jewish Temple to sponsor the project. Naturally they assumed that every Jewish person over 65 in the area—of whom there were many, according to the census data—would move in. So they didn't bother with little details like asking their prospective customers what size and shape and design of apartments they would like—or how much they would be willing to pay.

In another case the promoters chose to locate the project in a town that had an Italian-dominated city government. Unfortunately the prospective customers, who were almost exclusively WASPs, refused to live under this jurisdiction. Because of this prejudice the project could not be filled. Again, this problem could have been avoided if the promoters had gone out and actually talked to the customers.

In short, statistical studies of your market and its growth are very useful, but you've got to produce tangible evidence that *you* are going to be able to make significant sales.

"BOTTOM-UP" MARKET RESEARCH

The only way to get reliable sales projections is to do "bottom-up" market research. Suppose the investor looks for that key paragraph and finds this:

> We interviewed 100 randomly chosen mushroom farmers (see Appendix C for details) and showed them our prototype cutter. Three of them gave us written purchase commitments on the spot, and five more stated that they would almost certainly buy one of our cutters as soon as we are in production. Based on these results, we believe that in the first year we can sell a cutter to at least 1 percent of the 10,000 mushroom farms in the U.S. At $15,000 per unit, this translates to sales of $1.5 million . . .

This is the kind of market research that makes an investor's checkbook itch. She is going to read on with real interest, because your plan stands out very favorably from most of the others in the stack. Every day she reads and rejects half a dozen business plans with good products but no real market research—just a quotation from *Predicasts*. If you've done bottom-up market research, you've demonstrated that there is a real need for your product, and also that you have some direct contact with the market.

Generating Sales Projections

Of course, the bottom-up market-research approach has a serious drawback—it involves an awful lot of work. In fact, it's even more work than you might think. The intimate details of preparing sales projections are beyond the scope of this book, but the minimum you will need to do is the following.

1. Select a random sample of your market—and try to make it really random. If your research sample consists of your best prospects, you're in for a nasty surprise when you try to sell the other guys. If you talk only to prospects in New York, you may later find—the hard way—that Californians are different. Getting a truly random sample is impossible, but do your best.

2. Interview them. You'll get the best results if you can do it in person. Telephone interviews are adequate. Surveys by mail are not so good but a lot better than nothing. If someone does not respond, do *not* drop him from the sample; count him as someone who will not buy. Use a written list of questions and be sure every prospect is asked all the questions and the same questions.

3. Analyze the results and make a *conservative* estimate of the sales you can achieve. Keep in mind that just because you could "sell" 3 percent of the people you interviewed, you are *not* entitled to assume that you can sell 3 percent of the total market. Will you have enough salespeople even to call on everyone in the market? Will your salespeople be as convincing as you are? Will your sales arguments remain convincing after your competitors have had a chance to counter them? And above all, how many of those "sure sales" will still be sold when it comes time to actually sign a check?

Actually, you may not need to do much market-research work—if there isn't any market! While I was running Sedgwick Printout Systems, I was approached by a man who wanted to start a company in a related area. At about that time, technology had become available that made it possible to print text onto microfilm at high speed directly from computer tapes. He was certain there would be a huge demand for this service, which would put large amounts of information into a small space very quickly.

I looked at his business plan and did some very simple market research.

I called up various computer operations in the New York area to see how much information they or their customers needed to store as a permanent record. It turned out that the vast majority of the data spewed out by their computers using line printers was of strictly temporary value—used for a short period of time and then thrown away. There just was not—at least at that time and place—a significant need for a magnetic-tape-to-microfilm service.

So I declined to participate in this venture. This chap went ahead, got funding, and opened up seven or eight microfilm service centers, and went bust after 18 months. He really should have listened to his market.

Now, the need for realistic sales projections is the first reason you must do market research, but it's not the only reason, or even the most important. Even if you do a good job, your sales projections probably won't be very accurate. In fact, they could be way off. First-rate market-research experts—real professionals—told Ford that the Edsel was just what the American car-buying public wanted. A very good study done for Xerox (then called Haloid) predicted that its first copier would be a flop. Customers don't always do what they say they'll do! You must generate those sales projections—if only to please the venture capitalists—but focus *your* attention on something even more important.

Understanding Your Market

Here is the second reason you need market research: you need to *understand* your market. Getting valid sales projections is difficult, because customers are not good at predicting what they will do in the future. But more important, it's not very informative, because it doesn't tell you *how* to make the sale.

So the most important function of your market survey is to answer questions like the following:

1. Who is your customer? Who actually makes the purchase decision? Be sure you don't end up aiming your sales presentation at someone who is unable to buy. If you're selling a retail item, it's not enough to say, "We're aiming at families in the $15,000-to-$30,000 bracket." Define who buys it—Dad, Mom, Junior, Sis, or the whole family in conclave? Suppose

you're selling to industry. What companies buy your type of product? Who within those companies sets the budgets, writes the specs, signs the purchase order? It may well be three different people, and you may have to sell all three of them—each in a different way.

2. What does the customer want? The key to getting good results with this question is to focus on the past, not the future. The usual tendency is to say, "We're planning on having this feature—would you like it?" This approach produces fuzzy and unreliable responses. Instead, ask what he's bought in the past, and why. What did he like about the unit he purchased last time? What did he dislike? What are his key concerns—price, quality, reliability, service, style?

3. How does the customer buy? Again, focus on the past. How often does she buy? When was the last time? How much does she buy at once? Are there other items that she usually buys at the same time? Did she shop around last time? Whose products did she look at? How did she decide? Did she consult anybody for advice? If it's a retail item, how did she pay—cash, check, credit card?

4. How does the customer like to be sold? Again, focus on the past. What ads did she find memorable or enticing? Did she encounter sales tactics that turned her off? Was some sales argument particularly convincing?

When I was 16, I took $40 that I'd saved up from my job in the Chemistry Stockroom and went to buy a slide rule. I wanted one rugged enough to use in the lab without concern. The salesman selected a K&E Decilon® and threw it across the room. Then he went over, picked it up, and hammered it against the counter. It wasn't even scratched. I was sold on the spot. You probably remember from your own experience a similar case. Look for these highly effective arguments or demonstrations in talking to customers; when you find one, use it!

5. What does the customer think of your competitors? Which ones is he familiar with? What is his image of each? What—in *his* opinion—are their strong and weak points? From whom does he buy now? Does he switch brands readily or is he loyal to one supplier? When did he last switch? Why?

HPLC is a technique for chemical analysis that has become extremely popular in recent years. Many companies have tried to enter the lucrative market for HPLC "columns." Newcomers, however, have found some difficulty due to seemingly irrational customer brand loyalty; even a substantial improvement in performance may be inadequate to induce the customer to switch. The reason is that developing a new analytical method using HPLC is a tedious process—though, once developed, it is fast and simple to do repetitive runs. Thus, the fact that a column is superior works against it; the better performance means that the procedures worked out for the old column are no longer applicable and the method development work must be done over again.

A good market survey may tell you such interesting facts as that you are planning to sell the wrong product—or perhaps the right product for the wrong use.

You know Velcro—the sort of fuzzy tapelike fastener material. The company was founded originally by a Canadian friend of mine named Ben Webster, who came from a very prominent and wealthy Canadian family. He bought the rights to the patent for Velcro, which he considered to be a replacement for the zipper.

I became involved with him in a very minor way, but I remember a conversation we had about the business. He contended that this material would make the zipper obsolete. I suggested to him that he should first talk to people in the garment industry who bought zippers and determine what they required. For instance, would they reject Velcro because it was bulkier and less durable than a zipper? I also suggested that he look at the market in more general terms—not just zippers but buttons and snaps and buckles.

Webster persisted in going after the zipper market, and after some early hardships, he managed to make a go of it. In the end Velcro became a big success, and as we all know it is now being used to replace every kind of closure imaginable—yet zippers somehow are still with us. . . .

The point of this little story is not that I was smarter than Ben Webster but that nobody, no matter how smart, can safely enter a new market without a real knowledge of his customers and their needs and wants. It's all very well to linger in the dining room with a decanter of claret and a fine cigar and speculate about the market, but that's no substitute for the gritty work of getting out there and talking to your customers.

In addition to familiarizing yourself with your customers and their characteristics, you must also understand the dynamics and standard operating procedures of the sales process in your industry. Particularly if you are selling to an industrial market, you must take into account the sales cycle and the purchasing process.

Retail versus Industrial Markets

Individuals who purchase retail goods or services are (usually) spending their own money. This is a natural source of sales resistance. Industrial purchases, whether of paper clips or jet aircraft, are made by people who are *not* spending their own money. So any company that fails to develop institutional procedures to implement an artificial "sales resistance" will quickly spend all its capital and go bankrupt. The standard method of controlling spending involves separation of the buying decision into three steps, with (in all but small companies) three different people involved. First, someone—generally a department manager—must *budget* the purchase, that is, authorize the expenditure and set an upper limit on the amount. Second, someone else—often a technical person—must *specify* the purchase, that is, decide exactly what is needed. Finally, a third person—usually the purchasing agent—will *select a vendor* and carry through the purchase. So, if you are selling to an industrial market, you must know who these three people are in your customer company and how to sell all three.

That's not all. This process takes time. Many promising start-ups have foundered because they failed to determine the length of the *sales cycle* for their product. This is the period from the first approach to the customer to the receipt of the check; it can vary from a few minutes to over a decade. If it's very long, you may quite possibly starve to death while you are waiting. So you must find out in advance: how long will it take a customer to buy this product? The more expensive the product, the longer the sales cycle. Also, the bigger the customer, the longer the sales cycle.

This list of questions is by no means exhaustive; we've

attached a checklist that is more complete. You will have to carefully consider the structure of your questionnaire, to gather the maximum amount of important information without making the subject impatient. This is why face-to-face interviews are better than phone interviews, which in turn are better than mail surveys—people will take more time for a direct interview. You may want to split your questions among two or more groups. In fact, it may be desirable to do two or even three independent surveys so the results can be cross-checked to test for bias. Also, you may want to improve response by thanking your subjects with a small gift; this practice is common, especially when mail surveys are used.

There are a couple of other pitfalls that we should mention. One is the neglect of geographical differences. If you are planning to sell your product nationwide, you should be aware that consumers may have very different tastes and attitudes in various parts of the country. This is true of industrial as well as retail customers. Of course if you have any plans to sell overseas this becomes even more critical. But geography may be significant even on a block-by-block scale for a neighborhood retail store.

You should also consider the timing of your survey. Some markets—such as the semiconductor industry—are extremely subject to the business cycle. During the boom, they frantically race to expand capacity as backlogs build to months or even years. Then, during the bust, they lay off workers by the thousand and sell off warehouses full of inventory at fire-sale prices. If these are your customers, conducting your market survey during the expansion phase may lead to overoptimistic estimates of the market, resulting in an extremely unpleasant shock when the crash comes. Once again we must emphasize that it is insufficient to ask customers what they are doing or plan to do. You must probe their behavior in the past, and if they are part of a cyclical industry be sure you examine their behavior in all phases of past business cycles.

The size of your survey will depend, of course, on the size of the market you are investigating. The number you must sample to achieve a specified confidence level for the results can be calculated mathematically. It turns out that a surprisingly small survey will give good results if the sample is carefully chosen to be random.

The national polls taken by the Harris and Gallup organizations can predict election results to within 3 percent, yet only about 4,000 people are interviewed.

Of course, the size and sophistication of your survey will also depend on your resources, and must be intelligently adapted to the size and complexity of your proposed business. If you're going to start a hot-dog stand, simply standing at the proposed location, counting the lunch-hour crowd, and talking to passers-by may give you as much information as you need. On the other hand, if you propose to raise $50 million in venture capital to launch your new chocolate-coated videodisk recorder nationwide, you'd better budget for a really substantial market-research program.

CALLING IN THE PROFESSIONALS

Lately it's become stylish to have your market research done by a professional outfit. This has certain advantages. Potential investors may be impressed by a prestigious consultant. Very large surveys can be done without drowning in paperwork. It's much easier to maintain anonymity, if you wish.

On the other hand, it's quite expensive; even a lousy survey will cost thousands of dollars, and a good one will set you back quite a bit more. If you are planning to sell a consumer item nationwide, it may well be justified. But if you go this route, be sure that you remain intimately involved with the whole process. Insist on looking over their shoulders. Examine the entire design of their survey and ask them to explain what they're doing and why. Even if you hire the best, you must always remember that there is no substitute for knowing the market yourself.

One advantage a professional market-research firm *may* provide is objectivity. Unfortunately, you can't count on it. Consultants are in business too, and being marketing experts, they have a very strong predisposition to tell the client what he wants to hear. Before you hire a market-research firm, look into its track record. Talk to former clients and ask them how their predictions worked out.

Checklist 4–1: Market Research

A. Choosing a sample
   ☐ Sample covers entire geographical area being addressed
   ☐ Sample contains members of all market segments addressed
   ☐ Sample is chosen randomly (note: the prospects who are easiest to find do *not* constitute a random sample)
   ☐ All members of sample are questioned consistently

B. Data for sales projections
   ☐ Each prospect gets standard presentation of product
   ☐ Purchase commitment is requested
   ☐ Commitments are classified and tabulated
   ☐ Prospect is asked *when* he will buy

C. Identifying the customer
   ☐ Retail or ☐ industrial product
   ☐ Individual, ☐ family, or ☐ group purchase (retail)
   ☐ Customer specifies, ☐ budgets, or ☐ purchases (industrial)

D. Retail sales—most likely customer
   Sex _____
   Age group _____
   Marital status _____
   Income level _____
   Ethnic group _____
   Occupation _____
   Geographical location _____
   Educational level _____

E. Industrial sales—most likely customer
   Company business _____
   Company size _____
   Geographical location _____

F. Customer needs and desires
   Past purchases, likes and dislikes _____
   Benefits desired _____

Features specifically mentioned by customer as desirable

_____

_____

Ranking of concerns:
- ☐ price
- ☐ quality
- ☐ reliability
- ☐ durability
- ☐ service
- ☐ style

G. Customer buying habits
    Frequency of purchase _____
    Date of last purchase _____
    Size of typical and/or last purchase _____
    Seasonal item? _____
    Business-cycle effects on purchasing _____
    Concurrent purchase of related items _____
    Extent of shopping before purchase _____
    Criteria for decision _____
    Information or advice relied on _____
    Payment: cash, check, credit card (retail) _____
    Payment: C.O.D., net 30, discount, etc. (industrial) _____

H. Selling media and arguments
    Media where customer looks for advertisements _____
    Ads customer found memorable or motivating _____
    Sales tactics that offended customer _____
    Sales tactics that impressed customer _____

I. Sales cycle
    Stages in customer's purchase decision _____
    Time involved in previous purchase _____

J. Competition
    Competitors of which customer is aware _____
    Customer's evaluation of competitors _____
    Customer's current supplier _____
    Brand loyalty _____
    Most recent switch: when and why _____

GAUGING THE COMPETITION

Before doing your market research, consider setting up a dummy organization and a cover story to conceal your true identity and intentions. Word of your survey may get back to your competitors, and if they're on the ball, they'll respond. A description of your product prototype may be very useful to them. If they can find out who you are, how you're financed, what your plans are, they are in a position to launch a preemptive strike against you at a time when you are most vulnerable. They can use all sorts of tactics, ranging from predatory price cuts to lawsuits or vicious rumors.

Established companies commonly do anonymous surveys, not only to avoid tipping the opposition but to get an unbiased judgment of themselves and their competitors. Customers may tell quite different stories, depending on whom they are talking to. Consider using this ploy yourself, allowing it to be thought that you are one of the old-line companies in the industry.

Of course, you should make every effort to thoroughly know your competitors. Your market survey is the most important part of this, but you should also use the trade press, industry gossip, and any other method you can think of—short, that is, of industrial espionage.

One valuable technique is to obtain Dun & Bradstreet reports on competitive companies. Your banker or a friend in a large company may be able to get them for you. They provide information not only on credit history but on ownership, employees, quality of their plant or office, officers' names and biographies, and sometimes even a financial statement. Unfortunately, this information frequently contains errors. Incidentally, this should also be considered defensively. You won't be in business long before D&B sends somebody around. Decide in advance how much to tell them—enough to reassure your suppliers, but not so much that you lay yourself naked to the competition.

We were close to starting when we got word that another company was showing signs of interest in the same area we intended to enter. We knew it could be a formidable competitor if it made a strong move into this technology. We got a D&B on it and discovered that the management had recently bought out the previous majority owners. A look at the firm's financials indicated that this burden would preclude any major R&D effort for some time. We concluded—correctly, as it turned out—that we could safely go ahead.

One of the most common mistakes made by new entrepreneurs is regarding competitors as stationary targets. They proudly proclaim that they have thoroughly investigated the competition and found it wanting. Like a white belt in karate, they attack as if their opponents were immobile, waiting to be kicked. In real life competitors move, change, respond.

The Marketing VP's presentation was smooth and professional. He conceded that the start-up's product—a word-processing widget—would face strong competitors like IBM, Wang, and Lanier. However, he pointed out that the company's own product would be technologically far ahead of the others and loaded with new features that prospective customers raved about.

After the presentation I asked one of the venture capitalists who attended what he thought. "These guys are comparing their prototype to IBM's current model," he replied. "By the time they get it on the market, IBM will have a new model out, and it will be at least as good as theirs."

I've forgotten the name of this start-up. So, I'm afraid, has everyone else.

Our discussion so far has dealt with competitors who are (1) direct competition, and (2) current competition. You should also keep an eye on competitors who may not be both. You will always have indirect competitors, for your customers will always have other possible uses for their money. Some of these alternative uses may provide the same satisfactions as your product. Your market research should therefore look into why customers buy your type of product rather than other items, and you should keep an eye on trends in the broad marketplace.

If you sell, say, a home computer, you are competing not only with other home computers but with other electronic gadgets. For instance, your customers will be pondering whether to buy a computer or a videocassette recorder or a laserdisk player.

There are pitfalls even in dealing with simple, direct competition. Companies are always moving in and out of markets. Your competitors tomorrow may be a completely different set from the ones you have today. New players may enter your market without warning, posing a serious danger. Old players may suddenly leave, presenting a major opportunity—if you are alert. You must always keep your market research and market planning up to date, and even ahead of its time.

A final word on this subject: *our experience shows that lack of good market research is the most common single factor that causes start-ups to fail.*

Exercise 4–1:
Assessing the Competition

A. Identify and list *every* competitor, no matter how big or small, that sells into your market.

B. Obtain the basic statistical information on each competitor—size, profitability, whatever information is available.

C. Examine and evaluate your competitors' products. Assess their strengths and weaknesses, and compare your evaluation with that of customers, as shown by your market research.

D. If your industry is innovative, also attempt to predict the most likely improvements competitors might make in their next models.

E. Research the history of the industry. In particular, see how major competitors have reacted in the past to major events. How have they responded to a technological breakthrough? A new entry to the industry? A competitive price cut? Piracy of personnel?

F. Look into likely new entrants to the industry (primarily large companies). What are their habits? Do they tend to start new divisions or buy into the industry by acquiring an existing company? Do they push price, technology, or service?

G. Check into the weaklings of the industry. Who are their customers? How can you eat up their market base and push them out?

H. Develop a written security plan. Decide what information about your start-up would hurt if it got to the competition and make sure you have policies in place to protect it.

I. Assign one of your team to monitor the competition. This person should be required to give you a written report updating your information on competitors at least every six months, and in a fast-moving industry every month.

CAUTIONARY TALE:
A LANDSLIDE DEFEAT

Simulmatics was started by a group of social scientists, political scientists, and computer scientists. In 1960, this company developed a computer model of the American electorate that could be used to test various political strategies and simulate the response of the voters. The company sold this scheme to the presidential campaign of Jack Kennedy. I came in at an early stage because the head of the company, Edward Greenfield, was an old friend. I had known Bobby Kennedy at Harvard, so I made an introduction and sat in on the meetings where the deal was worked out. Simulmatics did a good job for the campaign, particularly in advising them on the issue of Kennedy's Catholicism and how it should be handled. I had played my part by bringing the parties together and had nothing more to do with the company for a couple of years.

With the election over, Simulmatics needed something else to do with its computer model. Management decided to use it to simulate Americans in, shall we say, a consumer mode and sell the results to advertising agencies. The idea was that Simulmatics could predict how many people a given ad campaign would reach, what media would give the best coverage, how the product should be promoted, and so on. Clearly this sort of information would be extremely valuable to advertising agencies.

In the early 1960s, there was a nice new-issues market and it was easy to go public, so Simulmatics did so. It raised $1.5 million and set out to conquer Madison Avenue. It never occurred to management to do any market research because of course the value of the service to the customer was so obvious that any fool could see it.

Somehow, though, the company didn't do so well, and this is

where I came in again, in 1962. I was asked to join the board of directors, since I was the only person affiliated with the company who had any prior business experience. I went on a few sales calls to the advertising agencies with the salespeople, attended some meetings, and soon realized that the agencies simply were not going to buy.

First of all, the advertising community, in spite of all the up-to-the-minute hype, is very conservative. Ad agencies used computers for accounting and payroll, but they had never heard of mathematical models or simulation.

Second, they already had a method of evaluating their results—the Nielsen ratings and other measurement services. These old-fashioned methods weren't very good, but the agencies saw no reason to change. As a matter of fact, they tended to fear that any really accurate measurement technique might inform their clients that their ads weren't effective at all. And Simulmatics had to charge an up-front fee of $15,000 to $20,000 to reprogram for a particular agency's application.

Which brings us to the third point, which is that advertising agencies never spend their own money. They only spend the client's money and they add on 15 percent before billing. No way were they going to pay out of their own pockets to try out a new system and see if it made sense for them.

I went back to the board, reported my findings, and recommended that the company drop the whole approach and fold up the operation as it then existed. Its $1.5 million had already dwindled to a couple of hundred thousand, and it was essential to stop the bleeding quickly. Then we sat down and brainstormed.

There was really only one chance for the company, and that was to sell simulation services to the government. Our personnel included a lot of visible and successful political scientists and social scientists with solid achievements and credentials—they were at Yale, Harvard, Johns Hopkins, names that tend to impress bureaucrats. It was a Democratic administration, and we of course had some very good high-level contacts because of our work for the Kennedy campaign. So we went down to Washington and made some sales calls, and we got some very significant contracts.

For the Department of Health, Education, and Welfare we did a simulation of a water-fluoridation referendum. At that time, districts all over the country were considering fluoridation to reduce dental problems. A lot of them were deciding against fluoridation, and HEW was very upset. We did a simulation and played out various strategies so it could see what ways of pushing fluoridation were most persuasive with the voters.

Another contract was with the Defense Department. We sent a dozen or so people to Vietnam to try to figure out why we were losing. We simulated a Vietnamese village so we could experiment with counter-insurgency tactics.

For a couple of years we did very well on government contracts; we met the overhead and made some money. We got a lot of attention in academic circles and learned journals wrote great articles about us. There was even a novel written about the company. But all these contracts were relatively short-term projects. We had to go out and land another big one every few months in order to feed the programmers and the computer. The Federal government is very large indeed, but even a market of that size can be saturated. There were a limited number of senior people scattered among the agencies who were interested in simulation and wanted to play with it. When they'd had their fun, they went on to other ways of spending the People's money. There was no ongoing routine demand for our services, and eventually it just got too hard to make more sales. That was the end of Simulmatics.

This case illustrates what happens when you go into business without doing market research. Our brilliant academic experts assumed that the value of their work would be as obvious to others as it was to them. In reality, there was no market at all on Madison Avenue—and there was a much more limited market than we thought even in the government. Had we done a real market survey—and done it early enough—we probably could have found a viable market for our services. (Perhaps the marketing departments of the big consumer-goods companies would have been interested.) It's really rather ironic. Simulmatics made a business of asking members of the general public their opinions on any subject under the sun, but never thought to ask its own customers what they wanted and what they'd be willing to pay for it.

HDS

5

FINDING YOUR NICHE

Do one thing at a time, and do that one thing superbly.

Astronaut training rule

The most important purpose of performing market research is to provide you with the information you need to formulate a market strategy. You'll possess a market strategy when you have the answers to two questions. First, to whom do you sell? This defines your market. Second, what do you sell? This defines your product.

It is your market strategy which implements your business concept by providing specifics. Your initial market research may result in information that causes you to revise, or even abandon, your original business concept. Don't hesitate to go back to the drawing board, if necessary several times, until you get a satisfactory response from market research.

Marketing for small business is a subject that is very neglected. Most entrepreneurs seem to feel that a formal market analysis and market strategy are unnecessary. They have some justification for their skepticism, for most professional marketers are trained only in big-business marketing. Small-business marketing is quite different. You might like to hire a hot-shot marketer and turn your problems over to her, but you probably won't be able to find anyone affordable who understands small business. One way or the other, you'll have to have at least a rudimentary knowledge of marketing principles yourself.

MARKETING FOR BIG BUSINESS

Large-scale marketing emphasizes the following principles.

- *Selling the same or similar products in diverse markets.* Maximizing unit volume is critical to the large company, for economy of scale is the primary justification for its existence. Thus each product must be sold in as many markets as possible. Quaker State, for instance, sells motor oil by the quart to consumers through grocery and hardware stores; by the case to service stations; and by the tank truck to commercial fleet operators.

- *Exploitation of each market with peripheral products.* Once a foothold has been gained in a particular market, it should be followed up by the addition of peripheral or even unrelated products for sale to the same customers. Thus Sears, which sells household goods to middle-class consumers, successfully added a completely unrelated product—auto insurance—for the same market.

- *Extensive formal market research and market testing.* The stakes are terribly high in large-scale marketing, and big companies have the resources to conduct extensive studies before making a move. The introduction of a new product, or even the modification of an old one, is preceded by surveys, focus groups, and market tests, and the resulting data are subjected to elaborate statistical analysis.

- *Careful attention to regional differences.* Advertising, packaging, and even the product itself may have to be modified specifically for each geographical market. For mass-market consumer goods, this segmentation may be taken almost to the city-block level. In New York City, for instance, Coca-Cola billboards are an excellent indicator of neighborhood ethnicity: in Puerto Rican neighborhoods the text is in Spanish; in Harlem the models are black; in Brooklyn each Coke bottle cap is marked to indicate that the contents are kosher.

- *Emphasis on image-oriented advertising and consumer brand-consciousness.* Large companies usually operate in mature markets. In such a market, distinguishing oneself from competitors by product innovation is almost impossible; doing so by price cutting is suicidal. The best solution is to develop loyal customers by stressing a favorable image for the company and its brands, using slogans ("You can be sure if it's Westinghouse"), fantasy characters ("Mr. Goodwrench"), appeals to self-image ("the Pepsi generation"), and various other ploys.

MARKETING FOR SMALL BUSINESS

For a small business, marketing strategy is dominated by a different set of considerations. This is not to say that we have nothing to learn from the way large companies go about it— but there is great danger in the unexamined importation of standard methods. Effective small-business marketing generally requires a rather different approach.

- *Strict concentration on a single market segment.* Economy of scale is of limited importance to a small business. Far more critical is the effective deployment of desperately inadequate marketing resources. To sell into two discrete market segments will nearly double marketing expenses, because it is essential to custom-tailor the approach for each segment. You will have to pay for two market-research surveys, artwork for two sets of advertisements, two sales-training programs, and so on. General Motors can afford this sort of thing; you can't. Even more important, your top management will be stretched very thin even if you restrict your selling to a single market segment. If you try to approach several segments at once, none of them will get enough attention.
- *Concentration on a single product* or else a limited line of related products. The only exception is the retailer or distributor in a business where "one-stop shopping" is a customer demand. Even in this case you will frequently find it an advantage to be more specialized than your larger competitors. For the small manufacturer, a diversified product line can be disastrous, because it dilutes not only marketing but also production capabilities.
- *Reliance on close customer contact and intuitive knowledge of the market.* Large companies rely heavily on detailed statistical studies, not because they enjoy doing them but

because it's impossible for their marketing executives to stay in personal contact with the market. Their markets are simply too vast and too complex to be comprehended without statistical analysis. The small business, by contrast, usually sells to a small and relatively simple market. It's possible for one or two marketing people in the company to be thoroughly familiar with the entire market—to talk daily with a broad cross-section of customers. A certain amount of quantitative analysis is still essential to provide objective data, but the small company can and should rely on intuitive understanding of the market to a degree that would be quite unsafe for a mass marketer.

- *Restriction to a single geographical region,* or to a national market with few or no regional peculiarities. Again, the small company simply does not have the resources to handle regional or ethnic diversification.

- *Emphasis on substantive superiority of the product* as the source of competitive advantage. This is not to say that image is unimportant to a small business, but usually it should not be the primary focus. A new company, in a growth market, should concentrate on providing superior value to the customer—and its marketing should concentrate on letting the customer know it. Image-creation advertising, conspicuous charitable deeds, and similar techniques are usually a waste of resources.

YOUR MARKETING STRATEGY

With these points in mind, let's consider the development of a market strategy for a start-up. How should you answer the two interlocking questions: Who is our market? What are we selling? Neither question can be properly answered without reference to the other.

It's important to consider your marketing strategy from the most fundamental aspect possible before you commit yourself. For example, suppose you have a fantastic idea for a new type of widget for making printed circuits. There are at least three ways in which you might try to turn this idea into a company. (1) You develop the widget, apply for a patent, then go to the giants in the electronics industry and license them to make widgets, while you develop an improved widget. (2) You build a factory, start manufacturing widgets, and sell them to companies that make circuit boards. (3) You build some widgets, keep them yourself, and go into the circuit-board business. Any of these three approaches may be viable, depending on the specifics of the case, but many engineers will pick the second without examining the other alternatives, or even realizing that they exist.

MARKET TYPES

We previously discussed market growth cycles and classified markets according to their growth stages. Now let's reexamine market classification from a slightly different perspective: what market strategy is appropriate for each type of market?

The Radical Product

The most primitive type of market is the market that does not exist at all: the customer does not have a need for your product. In order to succeed, you will have to begin by creating a need in the customers—you will have to make them want something that they never wanted before, perhaps that nobody ever wanted before. This task is extremely difficult but not quite impossible. The most prominent recent example is the personal computer. As late as 1970 the idea of a powerful individually owned computer was strictly a science-fiction concept. Who needed his own computer? What on earth would he use it for?

If you wish to tackle this type of marketing problem, the best approach is to experiment; try out the product with the most adventurous and innovative people you can find. Better yet, see if someone else has already done such a test wittingly or unwittingly.

During the 1960s, MIT had a PDP-1 computer, which had been donated by Digital Equipment Corporation for student use. The PDP-1 was the first minicomputer; it filled a room, but only a small room. The most frequently used programs written by MIT students for this computer included: "Expensive Typewriter," a very primitive word-processing program; "Space War," a simple video game that threatened to monopolize the machine until it was forbidden; and a music program that played the Minute Waltz in 57.5 seconds, plus a variety of Bach fugues. Twenty years later, word processing and video games are major uses of microcomputers, and computer ("synthesizer") music is a major and growing factor in rock culture—having been first popularized by "Switched-On Bach."

Bringing out a product that is so radical is comparable to a Marine landing: you face a desperate fight just to get a beachhead. The odds are you'll be pushed right back into the sea; even if you manage to maintain a toehold, further progress will be slow. And, to continue the metaphor, it's very likely that you'll suffer such heavy casualties that the follow-up troops (that is, me-too competitors) will make the big gains and reap the big rewards. This is exactly what happened in the personal-computer industry. Who remembers the Altair 8800 now?

The way to get that first market beachhead is to piggyback in on an existing market. In the personal-computer area, this was the electronics hobbyist. There was an existing market for do-it-yourself electronics kits; hobbyists built their own hi-fi components, television sets—why not a computer? This is exactly how you do it: present your product not as a radical innovation but as a variation in an existing market. More examples? The airplane was initially sold to the military market as an improvement of the reconnaissance balloon—and to the civilian market as a new type of carnival ride.

Only after the initial market has been secured can customers be induced to feel the new needs the radical product can satisfy. At this point you face the real problem: if your company is to grow, you must pick it up, remove it from the initial market, and set it down in the emerging market. And your timing must be perfect—too soon and you'll starve, too late and the competition will have all the best claims staked out. The latter case is the common one. In personal computers, for instance, companies like Apple and Atari, though relative latecomers, took over from the early, hobbyist-oriented firms like MITS. The big market will inevitably be entirely different from the initial market. To jump from one to the other is difficult indeed.

It's so difficult that you probably shouldn't try it. If your product idea is ultra-innovative, it may be best to plan for staying with the initial market—and staying small. But if you want to go for the gold, consider using a two-company strategy. Plan right from the beginning to start a second company later to exploit the growth market when it emerges. That way you'll bring experience and perhaps a little extra capital with you, giving you an edge over the "me-too" newcomers. But you must start a new company to do this effectively, for the first company will have developed a momentum that will make it almost impossible to wrench it into a new direction. You can either sell the first company or make it a division of the new company.

The New Product

Less ambitious and less difficult is the marketing of a product that is new but not radical. An example of this type of product is the pocket calculator. It's interesting to note, incidentally, that this product was marketed initially not as a portable version of the familiar desk calculator—the most obvious approach—but as a replacement for the slide rule. This illustrates an important principle: when introducing a novel item, address a small but adventurous market segment first; then expand into larger but more conservative markets. Hewlett-Packard made a tidy piece of change selling its early calculators to scientists and engineers; had it started with office managers, it probably would have failed. Of course, once the ice was broken and the product was familiar, it easily invaded the much larger office-calculator market.

The new product, as we use the term here, is characterized by its ability to satisfy an existing customer need in a different way. What does this imply for market strategy? One consequence is rather obvious: if there's a recognized customer need, most likely there is an existing market with existing products filling that need. Thus the initial question is whether to annex part of the existing market or to expand it. Consider again the pocket calculator. It actually annihilated the slide rule, and it ate up much of the desk-calculator market. But it also expanded the market; today many people use it for simple arithmetic that would once have been performed with paper and pencil. In fact, it has made it possible for math-phobes to do arithmetic which, without a calculator, they would not have attempted at all.

If you propose to introduce a new product of this sort, you will have to choose between annexing a share of the existing market or developing a new market segment. *Don't* try to do both at the same time; focus your marketing effort.

To access existing customers you must take sales directly from competitive, established products. Obviously, this holds the disadvantage that you will meet with strenuous opposition from competitors who will not willingly relinquish market share. Under what circumstances should you adopt this direct approach?

One important criterion is easily perceived: weak competition. If you're going to slug it out, it's well to challenge inadequate opponents. Competition may be weak in any of several ways. Perhaps the existing products are grossly obsolete, so that your innovation has a decisive advantage. Competing companies may be old-fashioned, stolid, out of touch with their customers—in fact, just going through the motions. Or competing firms may be concentrating their efforts elsewhere, regarding the market you've chosen as a sideline. Of course, it's also helpful if your competitors are small, weak, and in financial trouble.

A second indicator for direct attack is frustration among existing customers. If the people who are buying it don't like it, but can't find anything better; if they're dissatisfied, irritated, or just plain bored—this may be your cue.

A third factor is a market segment of current customers who are adventurous, innovative, willing to try something new. It should be emphasized that your market research must locate people who have a *history* of trying new products. There are always many who merely think that they would try out an innovation if offered, but they usually do not come through when put to the test.

Finally, the direct approach is more likely to succeed if the need you propose to satisfy is classed as a necessity. Almost by definition, the *existing* customers for luxury items are conservative—there is a *cachet* to doing things the old-fashioned way. Furthermore, the benefits offered by an innovative product tend to be economic; "better value" is an argument that sells refrigerators better than it sells fur coats.

Your alternative is to choose an indirect approach to the market. Surrounding many an existing market is a halo of "almost-customers." These are people who have a need or desire for the product but don't buy it. Perhaps they don't clearly understand their need. Perhaps the existing product doesn't quite fit what they want. Perhaps they "can't afford" the product—that is, it doesn't have enough value. Perhaps they aren't aware that the product even exists, or that it can solve their problem. Perhaps there are cultural, religious, or political obstacles to buying the existing product. This marginal or potential market is hard to identify and characterize. But often it does exist, and under certain circumstances it may offer the best entry for a new product.

This indirect approach is clearly indicated if the existing market is dominated by strong competitors. Rather than immediately climb into the ring and take on several strong, fast, and ferocious opponents, it's advisable to say, "Let's you and him fight," while you pick up the goodies they've neglected. After you've developed and served your new market segment, you'll be stronger—and they may have been weakened.

Of course, the indirect approach can be viable only if the potential market exists. There must be people with the need for your product, unsatisfied by the existing products. Your product must fit—it must fill the gap that prevents these almost-customers from buying the old product.

Another criterion is that the potential market should be adventurous. The almost-customer must be willing to experiment.

Finally, the indirect approach is best applied to luxury items. Obviously, you are unlikely to find a halo of nonbuying potential customers for a necessity. By definition, everybody who needs a necessity is already buying it. But for luxuries— well, the *nouveaux riche* we have always with us, and they provide a continuing market for status symbols.

The Improved Product

The introduction of a product that is an improved version of an existing product presents a somewhat different problem. If you take this approach, chances are you'll be entering a market in the late-growth stage. Recall that during this growth phase, a market is characterized by increasing product standardization, combined with the emergence of clearly defined product subspecies. Also, during this period large companies are likely to be forcing their way into the market, while a "shakeout" of the weaker players may be occurring or imminent. In short, you'll be entering a very treacherous environment that will call for some careful footwork—one false step and you're sunk.

One approach to this situation is to attempt to standardize the product by yourself. "Our new improved widget has ten ventricles, and the frammistan is on the left. This is clearly the optimum design, and from now on it will be the widget industry standard." Obviously, it won't be a trivial task to carry off this bold proclamation over the protests of your outraged competitors. As a newcomer, your credibility is unlikely to be sufficient; normally, this approach should be left to megabusinesses that possess the prestige—and muscle—to get away with it. However, it may be just possible to self-standardize the product in a dwarf market; if the market is very small, the competition very weak, and your improved product very superior, you may want to consider this strategy. But it remains high-risk; have a contingency plan for wiping the egg off your face if it fails. A far more viable approach to this type of market is to define and stake out a new product subspecies.

> Epson attempted the standard-setting strategy in the personal-computer industry with its QX-10 computer. Its "Human Applications Standard Computer Interface" design and Valdocs software were loudly proclaimed as the inevitable future of the microcomputer industry. The attempt was a total failure; instead, the IBM PC and MS-DOS have become the standard in spite of their inferiority in user-friendliness. It was just plain old market clout that made the difference.

> Sony, in the 1950s a relatively small, weak company, used a new technology—the transistor—to improve an existing product, the radio. Instead of trying to standardize the console radio on transistors rather than vacuum tubes, it carved out a product subspecies: the portable radio.

Osborne Computer, in the 1980s, tried the "product sub-species" approach in the personal-computer market. It succeeded in defining a product subspecies—the portable computer—but after an initial period of spectacular growth, it suddenly slid into bankruptcy. What went wrong? Business-school students will be analyzing this case for decades, but two problems stand out. First, Osborne had no technological edge. Its product was shrewdly designed to meet an unfilled need in the market, but there was nothing to prevent competitors from following quickly with imitations. If Osborne had not been under such heavy competitive pressure, it might have been able to weather its second major error: underestimating the urgency of the market push to standardization. When Osborne prematurely announced a forthcoming model with IBM compatibility, sales of its current model dried up.

Before trying to enter a late-growth market, you should make sure your market strategy has the following components:

▪ Start with a clear description of a distinct product subspecies that you will try to establish. There are a number of approaches you can take. Make the product more personalized (for example, the executive or corporate jet). Make it more portable (the folding baby stroller). Make it more convenient to use (the auto-dialing phone). Make it more rugged, for heavy-duty use (the Jeep). Make it more fun to use (the sports car). Your concept should be tested by careful market research.

▪ Provide for some sort of high barrier to entry. Commonly this consists of superior technology, but there are other alternatives. Just be sure you have *something* to keep the competition at bay.

▪ Do a detailed study of potential megabusiness competitors that may enter your industry. On the basis of this intelligence, develop a scenario for the next few years. Who will come in? How will they behave? What will be the effect? How will you deal with it?

▪ Also study the weaklings of the industry. When will they be shaken out? How will they behave when they're thrashing around in their death throes? There will certainly be an orgy of price-cutting—how will it affect you?

▪ Plan for industry standardization. It will happen, and

you must go along, like it or not. It may be frustrating if you
know a better way, but you just can't afford to fight too many
battles at once.

The "Me-Too" Product

The most "conservative" strategy is the most risky one for
a small business: entering a mature market with a noninnova-
tive product. To introduce a new brand of soap is a major
campaign even for Proctor & Gamble. For a small business,
and most particularly for a start-up, going head-to-head with
the giants is asinine. There is really only one viable approach
to this problem, and that is the loyalty niche. Note that trying
to carve out a small niche in the market is not *in itself* a viable
strategy. The megabusiness players in such a market are so
competitive that they will shed blood for peanuts. There is no
niche so small that they'll ignore it. Your only chance is to find
a niche that they *can't* get into because they're too big—which
in effect means a loyalty niche.

> Here's an example of a niche that looked good but wasn't.
> When Detroit stopped making convertibles, several small
> businesses sprang up to exploit the opportunity. They
> bought sedans and made them into convertibles, or modi-
> fied customers' cars for a fee. But in the viciously competi-
> tive auto business, even this tiny niche did not last long.
> Soon the behemoths started limited production of convert-
> ibles again.

What is a loyalty niche? It's a market segment that is loyal
to your company for reasons a big company finds hard to
duplicate. This may involve providing a level of service so high
it is impossible to achieve in a large, bureaucratic organization. Or, you can appeal to ethnic, political, or religious soli-
darity with your customers. You can appeal to snobbery;
smallness can provide a guarantee of exclusivity, in which you
make an asset of your inability to produce large quantities.
Another approach is to ask for preference over big companies
on the basis of your smallness itself, either appealing to a "fair
play" or "David and Goliath" image, or claiming that your
business, being small, is morally superior to a big company.

Many small dry-goods retailers sell high-quality but otherwise rather ordinary items—which customers gladly buy even though they could get the same items cheaper at a department store. Image is the key. A piece of clothing with an L. L. Bean or Land's End label may be a trademark for your lifestyle.

Goya canned foods hold a lucrative niche in the Spanish-speaking market. Bigger companies can make the same foods and label the cans in Spanish, but they haven't succeeded in presenting themselves as members of the Hispanic community. Similarly, on a much smaller scale, ethnic grocery stores—Jewish, Italian, Japanese, Korean, Filipino, and so on—have burgeoned at the same time that conventional "Mom-and-Pop" groceries are being wiped out by the big supermarket chains. The chains can easily stock ethnic foods, but they can't provide clerks who can gossip with the customers in their native language.

A bold approach to the moralistic loyalty niche was taken by DeLorean Motors. Its attempt to market an image of moral superiority to Detroit failed, but it might have succeeded if there had been more substance to its claim.

If you choose the loyalty-niche approach, you must recognize that it will probably put a limit on your growth. By expanding too much, you risk losing the qualities that make your customers loyal.

One final pitfall in this strategy: among companies that use it, it's surprising how many focus so intently on protecting themselves from big corporations that they neglect to keep track of smaller competitors.

Exercise 5–1:
Market Strategy—Industry

What kind of market do you plan to enter, and what approach do you plan to use?

- ☐ Primitive market
    - ☐ piggyback on existing market
- ☐ Early-growth market

☐ access existing market
☐ develop new market segment
☐ Late-growth market
  ☐ set industry standard
  ☐ define new product subspecies
☐ Mature market
  ☐ develop loyalty niche

JUST WHAT ARE YOU SELLING?

Let's turn to another viewpoint on market strategy. What is your product? This is a treacherous question. The classical example, which has become a cliché among marketing people, is the small drill press. The company that makes this item thinks it's selling drill presses. But, the marketing expert points out, the man who buys it sees it only as a means to an end—namely, making holes. Thus the company isn't really selling drill presses, it's selling holes.

Or is it? Suppose the company believes this analysis, and decides to satisfy the customer's needs directly instead of indirectly. It approaches him in his basement workshop and offers, for a fee, to drill the holes for his bird-feeder project. What kind of response should the company expect? It seems this chap is not buying holes, he's buying the pleasure of making holes himself. The logical response to this conclusion might be to rent rather than sell the drill press. Yet this approach, too, mysteriously fails. Let's observe the customer more closely. Watch him showing off his workshop to the fellow next door, gloatingly fondling the gleaming machines. Our hypothetical company now has the key to this market: to hell with what kind of holes it makes; design a drill press that *looks* impressive! It is not selling tools; it's not selling holes; it's not selling entertainment; it's selling a status symbol. The company that realizes this can clean up, while its mystified competitors wonder why an "inferior" product sells so well.

The lesson is this: what you think you're selling may not be what the customer is buying. If the customers' behavior seems "irrational," it's because you don't understand their needs. Please note that this applies in industrial as well as consumer markets.

Let's consider what kinds of products might exist. There are as many different products as there are human needs and ways to satisfy them. It's a bit dangerous to limit this array for classification, but the vast majority of products can be fitted into one of seven categories:

> Consumption goods   Information
> Durable goods   Status items
> Services   Social satisfactions
> Entertainment

One must be very careful when using this (or any other) classification scheme. As we've already seen, the customer may classify the product in a nonobvious way. What's more, a single product may be classed in more than one way—by different customers, by the same customer on different occasions, or even by the same customer at one time. Finally, the customer's classification of a given product may shift, either in response to marketing or spontaneously; such shifts can sometimes be surprisingly abrupt.

> A restaurant may seem to be selling a consumption good: prepared food. However, restaurants founded on this assumption almost invariably fail. A successful restaurant generally sells something besides food. Service, obviously. But possibly also entertainment, social satisfactions, or status.

The way customers classify your product has profound implications for your market strategy. Let's consider the possibilities.

The Consumption Good

A "consumption good" is a physical, tangible item that is intended to be "used up" over a fairly short period of time. Many successful businesses have been based on the decades-old trend by consumers to reclassify durable goods as consumption goods. Disposable napkins, disposable diapers, disposable kitchenware are now old hat, but the trend has not run out of steam yet, though it's clearly slowing and in some areas reversing. There are still opportunities. Note also that rather similar products may be classified as consumption or durable goods on the basis of actual duration of use by the consumer rather than total product lifespan, durability, or quality.

> High-fashion clothing is usually a consumption good; "classic" clothes are purchased as durable goods. This is true even though the high-fashion items may be just as well made and durable as the classics. The high-fashion clothes will not be worn—at least not by the original purchaser—when their season has passed and other fads are "in." Note that price has nothing to do with it. A wealthy woman may wear a designer original costing thousands of dollars to one party, then give it away. The day after the party she may be dressed in a tweed suit bought ten years before for a few hundred.

When you are developing a market strategy for a consumption good, your biggest danger is unexamined assumptions. For some reason, people find it especially difficult to analyze this sort of product without falling into preconceived notions. A product should not be ruled out as a consumption good because it has traditionally been considered a durable item. A consumption good, as we've seen, may have a low, medium, or high price. Consumption goods, of course, exist in industrial as well as consumer markets (paper clips, for example). One might think that a consumption good by its nature has an important repeat market, but even this is not necessarily true; consider, for instance, a wedding gown.

One generalization that can be made about consumption goods is that they are usually best marketed by stressing *intensity* of satisfaction. Focus your effort on providing the customers—and letting them know you provide—a strong benefit, even though it may be short-lived. As a corollary, it's well to concentrate on a single benefit rather than spread your efforts over several.

The Durable Good

Perhaps your product should be classified as a durable good. (This term has a specialized technical definition in statistical economics; here we use it simply to refer to a physical good that lasts for a relatively long period of use.) Recently there has been a tendency toward reversal of the trend to disposable products—a return to "quality," durability, tradition. There are opportunities here—not only in consumer but also in industrial markets.

Generally, durable goods should be marketed with an emphasis on long-lasting satisfaction. It's less effective to stress intensity of satisfaction, because it's hard to make a credible claim that customers will experience ecstasy every time they use the product. Ecstasy is a one-shot experience, not an everyday sensation. For a durable good, long product life is a major value by definition. Note that this means not only physical durability but also protection from obsolescence. You should also stress benefit variety; a product that is used frequently raises the specter of boredom.

The distinction between the consumer good and the durable good corresponds roughly to the accounting distinction between the expense item and the capital expenditure. This is true not only in industrial but in consumer markets. Customers not only regard the *products* differently, they regard the *expenditures* differently. Often there are special procedures or restrictions for capital expenditures. A hospital administrator, for instance, may be required to get a formal vote of approval from the Treasury Committee to buy a $10,000 lab instrument—but spend $250,000 per year on laundry, with essentially no oversight. Similar paradoxes abound among retail consumers. A family may agonize for weeks over the purchase of a $300 TV set, yet expend $2,000 per year on beer and cigarettes without a second thought.

Ironically, this distinction sometimes provides a reversed incentive. The thinking seems to be that money spent on a consumption good is gone, but when a durable item is purchased one has "something to show for it." Many businesses, for instance, will prefer to buy a piece of production or office equipment even when accounting analysis shows it would be more economical to lease, or contract out the work. There is something comforting to management—and their bankers—in seeing that they have something "permanent" and "valuable" for their money. Consumers often show the same psychological phenomenon. A shrewd marketer can turn this attitude into a useful selling tool.

The Service

For purposes of this discussion, we define "service" rather narrowly as performing work for the customer—whether changing the oil in her car or flying her across the continent. The concept of a service business can be subtle, and a great deal of nonsense has been written about the United States' "transition from a manufacturing to a service economy." Many, if not most, physical goods are sold in combination with a service component. (Example: again, the restaurant, which sells food plus the services of cooking, waiting on table, and washing the dishes.) The trend in recent years has been to reduce the service component. Sometimes it is simply eliminated (for example, making customers pump their own gas, clean their own windshields, and check their own oil). Sometimes the quality is reduced (compare airline service now with what it was 20 years ago). Sometimes the service is unbundled and charged separately. When these factors are taken into account, the "decline" of the manufacturing sector is seen to be due at least partly to a decrease in its hidden service component. Also, of course, much of today's service sector is devoted to minimizing the effects of high taxes, government regulations, and legal hazards—work that is "productive" only in a negative sense. Another factor inflating service-sector statistics is reverse bundling, the inclusion of manufactured goods with a service. (An oil change, for instance, has the new oil bundled in.)

The important point is that customers can be just as arbitrary and inconsistent as statisticians in defining what constitutes a service. Because services are so frequently sold in combination with manufactured goods, you must be especially cautious.

The key factor in marketing a service is dealing with customer nervousness. A service, even more than a consumption good, leaves the customer with the prospect of "nothing to show for his money." Like a consumption good, once it's "used up" it's gone; unlike a consumption good, it's not visible or tangible even before it's "used up." Thus selling a service, especially an expensive service, requires special attention to reassuring the customer. Your market strategy should take this into account. We have space here only to mention a few approaches.

First, credentials are important in a service business. If you're selling a tangible good you can point to its appearance and quality; as long as it works well the customer needn't know, and doesn't care, whether the engineer who designed it graduated from MIT or Podunk Junior College. It's hard to point to a service, so the credentials of the people who provide it matter. This is why doctors, lawyers, dentists, and beauticians prominently display their framed diplomas.

Similarly, a service business can afford less than any other to look tacky, dirty, or cheap. Everything that the customer sees—your premises, your literature, your advertising, and your people—should convey an image of class, quality, and permanence.

Another approach is to add something tangible to the service. Service businesses often "give away" some item—the house magazines of airlines are a good example. As typically used, this is merely an advertising technique—a calendar, mug, or desk blotter keeps your name in front of the customer. But it's also an opportunity to reassure the customer, if used properly. Consider bundling into your service a related physical good—and make that good very obviously a premium product.

> Organizations that put on expensive "seminars" or "workshops" generally learn to hand out textbooks, course outlines, memo folders, and similar tangible items that the participant can take home—and to make these items at least *look* costly.

Entertainment

Selling entertainment may seem similar to selling a service, but it has its own unique pitfalls. In particular, many companies that ought to know better sell entertainment while believing they're selling something else.

> RCA's videodisk system was a flop—a very expensive flop. It simply could not compete with videotape in terms of the amount of "software" available; the alleged superiority of

RCA's hardware was totally irrelevant. The company wasn't selling hardware, it was selling entertainment. This may seem blindingly obvious, but RCA, a large, successful, and well-managed firm, somehow couldn't see it, in spite of decades of experience in the entertainment business.

In entertainment marketing strategy, one of the most productive approaches is the combination of entertainment with advertising. The typical magazine, for instance, receives more of its revenues from selling ad space than from subscriptions. Broadcast television is supported solely by advertising revenues. Currently there exist major opportunities for shrewd entrepreneurs to extend this principle. Consumers are growing increasingly sophisticated in their ability to screen out advertising—both mechanically, as with videotape recorders, and psychologically. Many advertisers have responded by becoming louder, more aggressive, and more shrill; this approach, however, has proved counterproductive. A few advertisers have learned that it is more effective to make their message entertaining. In view of the emerging consumer revolt against irritant ads, it seems likely that the future belongs to those who incorporate advertising into entertainment. The line between the two is destined not merely to blur but eventually to completely disappear.

> The trend toward combining advertising and entertainment is most visible in television advertising. One might date the beginning to the famous Benson & Hedges cigarette campaign. More recently, a number of children's shows—for example, "The Smurfs"—have appeared that are essentially advertisements for toys.
>
> Note also the increasing prominence of "special advertising supplements" in business magazines—some of them more interesting than the "editorial content."

Information

Although the selling of information is often considered a service business, it may be more productive to regard information as a good, even if an intangible one. As Peter Drucker has been pointing out for years, the U.S. economy has long been shifting its emphasis from dealing with physical goods to dealing with information. Regarding information as a good makes it possible to define the product more specifically. In this analysis, an information product is one that supplies data, knowledge, wisdom, know-how, or the like to the customer.

> Just as important as recognizing information products is knowing what is *not* an information product. Many of the early personal-computer manufacturers failed because they thought software, being "information," was a separate product. They found out too late that a computer program is *part of the computer.* As this is written, software firms are just starting to discover the same fact.

The key to selling information is appreciating the role of the *medium.*

> A mail-order firm sold a self-improvement course on cassette tape. It tried using various mailing lists, including lists of people who had attended self-improvement seminars. Results were very poor. The firm finally achieved an excellent response simply by using a list of people who owned cassette tape recorders.

The media by which information is transmitted include books, pamphlets, magazines, newsletters, newspapers, radio, TV, floppy disks, tape recordings, videotape, seminars—and this isn't an exhaustive list. Selecting the proper medium or media is a crucial decision. Even if the information is extremely valuable to the customers, use of the wrong medium may make it effectively inaccessible to them. On the other hand, the appearance of new media creates opportunities to sell old information to new markets.

> Self-help books have long been a staple of the publishing industry. However, a large segment of the market, lower-class people, was not accessed well. These people tend to be poor readers, not oriented toward buying or using books. The development of cheap cassette players therefore resulted in a major expansion of the self-help market.

Examine your market carefully. What media do your customers use? This variable includes not only the physical medium but also the style of communication. Some people read; others prefer to listen. Some like detailed explanations; others like a simplified exposition with many illustrations. Some customers accept a chatty, informal style; with others, you will lose credibility if you fail to take a portentous, authoritative tone.

The choice of medium also depends on the durability of the information being sold. News, for instance, is similar to a consumption good, and a perishable one at that. Media that are used for news thus tend to appear frequently and be quite ephemeral. On the other hand, information of longer-lasting value, such as reference data, is more likely to appear in a book with quality binding. For information that (supposedly) lasts a lifetime, still other media, such as a college education, may be appropriate.

> Inappropriate medium choice is frequently a problem in magazine start-ups. Undercapitalized magazines commonly lower expenses by publishing on a reduced schedule, for example, quarterly instead of monthly. If customers need the information more frequently, the venture will probably fail. The magazine would have been better off cutting expenses in some other way.

Finally, the medium should be chosen to enhance the apparent value of the content. Information again is an intangible; the customer should be reassured that she is "getting something for her money." She often does judge a book by the quality of its cover or the credentials of the author.

The Status Item

The status item is another product that frequently appears in disguise. Of course, it would be quite correct and reasonable to consider a Mercedes a durable good, a vacation in Biarritz a service, or a Harvard education an information product. But each of these is also, and probably primarily, a status item.

Products that are purchased for the sake of the status they confer on the owner are worth considering separately because of the major part the struggle for status plays in human behavior. It's extremely important to realize that this struggle is not confined to the upper crust; the rich and the poor, men and women, old people and young children, individuals and corporations—all strive for status.

I drive to work through a semi-slum neighborhood. The billboards are dominated overwhelmingly by ads for cognacs, liqueurs, and premium whiskeys—usually featuring a couple in expensive evening clothes. Apparently a bottle of costly liquor is one of the few status symbols the inhabitants can afford.

With the possible exception of some very primitive tribal cultures, every human society provides a variety of possible routes to status improvement. Most of them, however, can be boiled down to four categories.

Power is the oldest and most fundamental source of status. Products that are seen as enhancing power (for example, the notorious dark business suit) sell best to people in structured, authoritarian environments: politicians, bureaucrats, managers in big companies.

Birth is a surprisingly important factor even in the United States. Although constitutionally we have no aristocracy in this country, many middle-class people are willing to pay a handsome price for clothing or other appurtenances that will give them the appearance of belonging to "the best families" or the "old rich."

Wealth is the currency of status as well as of exchange. Money confers status in this as in most other cultures, but it's of no value for this purpose unless it is displayed—though the display may be subtle. There is a very substantial market indeed for products that will discreetly flaunt the owner's wealth—or, better yet, allow him to appear even wealthier than he is.

Talent—superiority in sports, the performing arts, or more intellectual pursuits—is the road to status for those of us who are unsuccessful in the other approaches. Any product that can help the customer to excel and excite the envy of her peers can find a market of this type.

> One of the classic advertisements of all time was based on the appeal to status enhancement by way of talent. It was headlined, "They laughed when I sat down at the piano . . ."

It's important to note that status products can approach the customer from a negative as well as a positive aspect. The obvious status item appeals by its exclusivity: "Buy this; nobody else has it (well, hardly anybody) and therefore it will increase your status." But there are also status items that appeal to the fear of exclusion: "Buy this; everybody else has one, and if you don't your status will be lowered." The latter argument is an even better motivator than the former, and you can sell a lot more units. The really smart marketers start with the appeal to exclusivity, and then, when that market segment is saturated, switch to the "don't be left out" approach!

Social Satisfaction

A final product category consists of items people buy for social satisfactions. Consider, for instance, membership in a hobby club. This product is intangible; yet the customer may get little or no service, information, or status for his dues. He is buying primarily a social benefit—the opportunity to socialize with other people who share his interests. A singles bar, a health spa, a computer dating service—many businesses that seem to be selling services are really selling the ability to better fit into society.

Success in such a business depends on seeing past the obvious product to the true product. The customer's objective is to enhance his social interactions. Some products that contribute to this are: (1) introduction to, or better insertion into, a desirable group; (2) acquisition by the customer of characteristics, appearance, or possessions that will help him join a desirable group; (3) removal of handicaps that prevent the customer from acquiring the friends or lovers he wants.

A typical characteristic of the social-satisfaction business is the nonindependence of the customer class. For other product types, a customer typically will have little if any interest in the identity or characteristics of other customers. But if you are selling social satisfaction, the interactions among your customers may be as important as, or more important than, the relationship between you and your customers. You must therefore give particular care to defining your market. Furthermore, you must clearly understand the customers' social needs—which may be difficult, since they frequently won't understand them well themselves.

Exercise 5–2:
Market Strategy—Product

A. Select one or more of the following categories to characterize your product.

☐ Consumption good
☐ Durable good
☐ Service
☐ Entertainment
☐ Information
☐ Status item
☐ Social satisfaction

B. Cite evidence from your research to show that your *customers* view your product in this way.

_____

_____

_____

_____

_____

_____

C. If you have checked off more than one product classification, examine your market research again. Do all or most of your prospective customers see your product as filling more than one need? Or are there several market segments, each of which views the product differently?

FORMULATING YOUR MARKET STRATEGY

Let's sum up. To develop a market strategy, you must decide on a specific market segment to approach, and decide on a specific product to sell to that market segment. To make these decisions, you must know who your potential customers are, what their characteristics, needs, and desires are, and how to locate and approach them. You must know the history, characteristics, and prospects of your industry. You must define exactly what your product is and understand why customers want to buy it.

Once you've gathered and analyzed all this information, you can develop a simple summary of your market strategy in the form of a customer/product matrix. This format allows you to see at a glance how the characteristics of the customer and the features of your product are related by the benefits your product provides to the customer. As your management team works on marketing and sales tactics and product development, you should refer back constantly to this matrix to focus your efforts and keep on track.

Exercise 5–3:
Customer/Product Matrix

Draw a matrix on a large sheet of paper. Across the top list the features of your product. Down the side list the characteristics of your target customer, as determined by your market research. Now fill in as many spaces of the matrix as you can with *benefits* corresponding to the product features and customer characteristics of that column and row.

Here's an example of how it should work. Suppose your product is a new type of personal computer, and your market is *Fortune* 1000 business executives. Let's say that Feature #3 of your new product is "16-MHz 32-bit processor chip" and Characteristic #5 of your typical customer is "classic Type A personality, driven, always short of time." The entry for column 3, row 5 in your matrix might be "saves time for the user because spreadsheets can be recalculated very rapidly."

CAUTIONARY TALE:
THE WORLD'S SMALLEST CONGLOMERATE

After I failed to get tenure and was cast out of the ivory tower into the cruel world of profit and loss, I became the first employee of a little start-up called Lifesystems Company. One might say I got in on the ground floor—literally—since before this, Lifesystems had been operating in the basement of one of the founders. The company started in 1977, in a very traditional Boston location, an old mill on Route 128.

The founders were Paul, a young and very brilliant biochemist, and Oliver, who had a background in engineering and project management. Briefly, the concept was as follows.

Every living organism—every living cell—is a complex chemical factory. Thousands of complex chemical reactions go on constantly and simultaneously, controlled by molecular processors called enzymes. Among other functions, enzymes make sure that there is not too much or too little of any particular chemical in the cell. Normally, when one wishes to alter the chemical balance in the cell—say, to cure an illness—one puts in certain chemicals: drugs. Annoyingly, the enzymes immediately try to get things back to "normal," destroying the components they consider in excess.

Paul was aware of recent advances that made it possible to intervene in living systems much more selectively and much more efficiently. This involved designing certain chemical bombs that would destroy specific enzymes. Lifesystems Company was set up to exploit this technology by making new pharmaceuticals.

Now Paul and Oliver were by no means so naive as to think that with a capitalization of under $100,000 they could waltz into the pharmaceutical industry, with its massive R&D requirements and years of testing for each new drug. So they did little practical work on their drug ideas. Instead, they looked for a product that they could handle more quickly and use to grow big enough to become a viable drug company. As it happened, the big drug companies were way ahead of them anyway; it turned out that Merck and Richardson-Merrell had Paul's concept pretty well locked up. But Paul's really brilliant idea was that this same concept could be applied to agricultural products.

When I came on board, they had developed a compound that could alter the nicotine levels in tobacco plants. Currently, low-nicotine cigarettes are made by chemical treatment of the tobacco leaves after harvest—a process that is relatively costly and causes certain problems. Lifesystems' approach was a chemical that could be sprayed on the plants shortly before harvest. By properly timing the spraying, one could harvest plants that contained as little as one-third, or as much as three times, the normal amount of nicotine. They demonstrated this in greenhouse experiments. (Incidentally, though you might think that tripling nicotine levels would be useless, in Turkey and several other countries very-high-nicotine cigarettes are popular.) My job was to synthesize new compounds to test.

Though fairly frugal, the two partners were spending money, and nothing was coming in. They had no clear plan for tackling the tobacco companies and made no particular progress in getting their innovation to market. They responded to the developing cash crunch with a two-pronged strategy: raising more capital, and turning some cash by opening another line of business.

Both approaches were moderately successful. They brought in some more investors—small private investors, not venture capitalists. Meanwhile, the company got into the research-chemicals business, making a line of reagents useful in certain aspects of cancer research. They chose these particular items because Paul was familiar with them from his Ph.D. thesis work. It became my job to make them in the lab.

Unfortunately, sales were not very high, and Lifesystems continued to ooze cash like a lacerated hemophiliac. I suggested expanding our line of research chemicals. However, Paul and Oliver decided to diversify into still another line of business: analytical services. We bought (and leased) some instruments and began doing various sorts of analyses—mostly polymer studies—for various local companies. This also involved hiring some technicians, as well as an expert in analytical chemistry.

Soon the company was bustling. Lifesystems expanded from its original three rooms to take over the whole floor, then part of another floor. Our instruments hummed continuously; we added more so as to be able to handle new kinds of analyses; and there was a rapidly growing flow of customer samples, reports, invoices, and even checks.

Trouble was, the analytical-services business was (and is) quite competitive—a lot of people in it were operating out of their garages, with very low overhead. We were under constant pressure to quote low prices to get contracts. The key to this racket is getting really high throughput from your machines. By this time I was spending all day standing at a chromatograph running analyses—not the kind of work I was trained for—and I exercised my mind by analyzing our costs. It turned out we were selling analyses at a negative gross margin.

I communicated this result to Paul and Oliver. They thought it over for a while, then responded very logically by letting me go. I had to admit that it was not particularly economical to use an expensive Ph.D. synthetic chemist to do work that could be performed quite adequately by a low-paid technician.

The company lasted another year and a half. The two partners were co-equal in their holdings, and as the company's problems worsened, personal friction developed. Eventually there was a rather unpleasant bankruptcy and the company was liquidated.

The story of Lifesystems is depressing because the opportunities lost were so vast. The founders were both very intelligent, very competent, and very pleasant, and initially they got along beautifully. The business concept was absolutely brilliant; if they had followed through on the agricultural-chemicals opportunity, Lifesystems might well have been in the *Fortune* 500 by now. The potential applications were not limited to tobacco; perfume oils, rubber, turpentine, more nutritious grains—the possibilities were staggering.

Why did Lifesystems fail? Quite simply, this tiny company acted like a conglomerate. It was involved in four entirely separate and unrelated lines of business. It ended up successful in none of them. Had they stuck to one product and studied their prospective market carefully, these highly talented entrepreneurs would almost surely have succeeded.

REM

6

THE MARKETING FUNCTION

All progress is based upon a universal innate desire on the part of every organism to live beyond its income.

Samuel Butler
*Notebooks**

The marketing function within the company has five major tasks: (1) market research, (2) market strategy, (3) sales organization, (4) pricing and positioning, (5) advertising and promotion. We discussed market research in Chapter 4 and market strategy in Chapter 5. Now let's cover the other functions.

SALES ORGANIZATION

Sales organization is primarily a matter of choosing your distribution channels and making them work effectively for your company. There are four basic distribution approaches, though they are not absolutely distinct. First, there is *direct marketing*. In this approach, there are no salespeople, just

*As cited in *Familiar Quotations*, John Bartlett (Boston: Little, Brown and Company, 1980).

order clerks. The sale is made by the advertisement, which may appear in various media—"junk mail," catalogs, magazines, television, and so on. Customers then place their orders by phone or mail. (In the future, other methods, such as computer transmission, may become important.) Second, there is the *in-house sales force*. In this case, you use salespeople who are employees of your company. Third, you may use *sales reps*. In this case, the salespeople are not your employees; they are, or work for, independent brokers or agencies. Fourth, there is *systematic distribution*. This involves companies that specialize not only in acting as sales intermediaries but also in carrying an inventory of various products.

No law requires you to confine yourself to one marketing avenue. You may, however, be restricted by custom; in some industries, customers have a definite prejudice as to whom they will deal with. Another consideration is competition between sales channels. If you use both reps and in-house salespeople, for instance, there may well be considerable hostility between the two groups.

Direct Marketing

Direct marketing (which used to be known as "mail order") is an extremely powerful selling technique that is now very widely used. It offers several important advantages. First, the sales process is under the direct and immediate control of your marketing management. The whole problem of motivating, supervising, and monitoring field salespeople is bypassed. Second, direct marketing is very fast and flexible. To hire and train a sales force takes months; a direct-marketing campaign can begin as quickly as you can do the artwork and get it through the printers. What's more, if you decide to change your sales pitch, you can turn on a dime—you have no salespeople to reeducate. Third, with direct marketing it is easy to test your sales approach and improve it. By measuring the response to different ads, you can find which is most effective. (Of course, in principle, you could do this with a field sales force. However, in practice, variation in the personal selling effectiveness of the individual salespeople makes it almost impossible to get valid quantitative data.)

136 The New Venture Handbook

The disadvantages of direct marketing arise from the lack of close customer contact. It's not possible to tailor the sales pitch to the individual customer. Furthermore, in the absence of face-to-face contact, it's very difficult to keep in touch with your market.

There is a persistent canard that direct marketing is unsuitable for expensive products, though Sears Roebuck disproved this decades ago. Selling a yacht might be difficult, but even a very costly product can be sold by direct marketing if it can be delivered. However, there are a few product categories that are inappropriate for this approach. Obviously a service, or any product with a strong service component, is likely to present problems. A very complex product may need a salesperson to explain it. A product that requires careful customization to the specific customer can be difficult to handle by direct marketing. And a rapidly changing market may be unsuitable because it is so difficult to keep up with customers.

Direct marketing has evolved into a specialized science. A detailed treatment of the sophisticated methods used in modern direct marketing would require more space than we have; references to useful works on the subject can be found in the Bibliography. However, we'll try to deal here with some of the essential principles.

Direct marketing is unique in that the advertisement must actually close the sale. You must therefore give the closest attention to your ad and to the media in which it appears. And since you'll have little if any opportunity to meet and talk with customers, you have only one good way to gauge the effectiveness of your approach: testing. Test different offers; test different prices; test different media; test different advertising themes. If you're using mailing lists, test different lists. If you're advertising on television, test not only different stations but different programs. It's been known for a tiny change, such as using a different-colored envelope, to substantially improve response. (However, your priority should be to test the major factors before you descend to trivia.)

Understand the volumes involved. If, for instance, you send out a mailing and get a 5-percent response, you'll have achieved a phenomenal success. One percent is more typical.

Remember that customers are buying sight unseen. They don't get to examine the product in advance, and they don't get to meet you either. Naturally this results in a certain amount of nervousness, especially if you're selling an expensive item. For this reason the "money-back guarantee" is practically mandatory in direct marketing. It's also been shown that quality, "classy" advertising pieces have a positive effect on customer confidence. But above all you must *perform*. You must absolutely keep your promises on product quality and shipping date—to the letter—or you'll be in big trouble not only with your customers but with the government.

> If you're selling a consumer item, give very serious consideration to starting out with direct marketing. The fight for retail shelf space is unbelievably vicious these days, and even giants like Proctor & Gamble have trouble launching a new brand. Direct marketing is a much easier way to enter the market, and once you've established customer acceptance, you can use it as leverage to get into the stores.

In-House Sales Force

The in-house sales force has only one significant advantage over other marketing channels, but it is a very valuable advantage indeed: you can easily maintain intimate contact with your customers. Your own people are out there talking to customers every day. Properly monitored, these contacts can provide you with a continuous flow of timely information about the market.

The big disadvantage to the in-house sales force is its cost. Every salesperson you hire represents a substantial fixed expense: salary (straight commission is rare these days), training, travel, expense accounts—it's surprising how quickly all this mounts up.

Hiring your own sales force is most appropriate for a retail store. Your salespeople are right there on the premises, so you can get the greatest advantage at lowest cost. If you need to cover a large geographical area, the cost of maintaining a sales force explodes. Not only will you be paying for travel, meals, and lodging, but your salespeople will be selling only a small fraction of the time—mostly you'll be paying them to ride airplanes, drive cars, and sit in some purchasing agent's waiting room. Furthermore, though your salespeople may be in close touch with the market, if you have a far-flung sales operation, you may have trouble staying in contact with your salespeople.

With an in-house sales force, the twin keys to success are training and follow-up. Consider this: how many kids do you know who want to grow up to be salespeople? Sales is a unique profession in that most of its practitioners have drifted into it from other careers. Entry is easy, and most salespeople have little or no formal education in sales. If they are to be effective, you must ensure that they get proper training either from you or from outside experts. Be sure they have a thorough familiarity not only with general sales techniques but with the specific methods that work best in selling your product. In addition, they should know your product inside out. Last but not least, they should be trained in the importance and the technique of gathering market intelligence.

But it's not enough to run them through a course—even a very good course—and send them out to sell. You must follow up to keep an eye on their problems, their needs, and their performance. Every member of top management should regularly schedule time to work with the sales force.

Sales Reps

Sales reps, or brokers, or agents, are essentially free-lance salespeople. They sell your product, for a commission, but are not on your payroll and do not carry an inventory. There is one very solid advantage to using reps: the up-front and fixed costs are low. If you need to build a large sales network quickly on a small budget, this is the way to go.

Private Products, the company I started to market private-label towelettes, was a classical case of the ideal situation for using sales reps. (See Chapter 2 for the full story.) We were not relying on high technology or management genius. The whole idea of the company was to get this simple product out and exploit a very substantial market very quickly, before the big boys realized what a gold mine they were missing and got off their plump fundaments.

Speed was everything, and there was only one way to expand sales rapidly enough: sales reps—or, as they're known in the grocery industry, food brokers. We hooked up with a master broker in New York who had been in the private-label business for years, and who had relationships with his opposite numbers in other major cities all over the country. In short order he developed for us an entire national sales force.

Through this loosely affiliated network of sales reps we were able to start supplying 44 of the major food and drug chains within a 12-month period. It was this national coverage that a few months later attracted Coca-Cola and persuaded it to acquire the company.

There are, however, some serious disadvantages to using sales reps. The rep is your "representative" to the customer, and thus he has a major influence on how your company is perceived by the customer. Yet he has no inherent loyalty to you, and you have very little control over his behavior. He is representing not only your company but several others, some of which may be direct or indirect competitors. But worst of all, the rep *insulates you from the market.*

You must realize that anyone acting as a broker tends to be paranoid. The rep lives with the constant fear—sometimes rational and sometimes not—that buyer and seller will get together and "cut out the middleman." He therefore tends to see it as in his interest to minimize your contact with the customer. In fact, if you are selling a commodity product and he thinks he can get away with it, he may try to keep both of you in the dark, by "buying" your product himself and "selling" it to the customer. Not only does this prevent any "conspiracy" between you and the buyer, but it gives the rep the opportunity to cut himself an extra large slice. But such an "order" puts you at substantial risk; if the rep doesn't come through, you have no recourse. He's just pretending to be a distributor; he is nothing but a desk and a telephone, and has no resources to back up his commitments.

Start-ups, which frequently lack marketing and sales talent, often become dependent on sales reps. The rep seems like the answer to your prayers. He, the expert, offers to take all those unpleasant sales problems off your shoulders. It's a tempting idea, especially when you're working 18-hour days trying to debug your production process and you "have no time for sales calls." But this is a dangerous misuse of a

potentially valuable marketing channel. There is no substitute—ever—for controlling your own sales effort.

Sales reps are useful by virtue of their flexibility. It's
unlikely that you'll want to use reps as your major marketing
channel on a long-term basis. Instead, use them when you
want to build a sales network fast; follow with a gradual shift
to your own sales force or to distributors. Use reps for other
temporary tasks: selling products with a short market life,
such as fad items; test-marketing a new product; investigating
a new group of customers; or penetrating a new geographical
area.

Distributors

Most complex of all marketing channels is the use of
distributors. For this discussion, a "distributor" is defined as a
middleman who carries an inventory of your product. It may
be a retail outlet or a warehousing operation; in some industries there may even be several levels involved. The distributor
may actually buy your product for resale (as do grocery stores)
or take your product on consignment (as do bookstores). Also
included is the VAR, or value-added reseller, who enhances
your product or combines it with other products or services
before selling it to the ultimate customer.

The distributor, like the sales rep, gives you the opportunity to develop a large sales network rapidly and with minimal
up-front expenditure. Unlike the rep, the distributor offers a
relatively permanent sales channel. Another advantage is that
a top-rank distributor can provide your product with instant
credibility. If your product is selected by Sears or Safeway, it
will benefit from the prestige of the outlet that has thus
endorsed it.

On the other hand, the distributor's cut is usually very
hefty and will mark up the price of your product dramatically.
The distributor, like the sales rep, tends to insulate you from
the market. Selling becomes complicated—you now have two
customers, the ultimate buyer and the distributor, both of
whom you must satisfy. And a large distributor, like any big
customer, may develop too much power over your business.

When should you use distributors? Normally you should

use distributors if, and only if, carrying a substantial inventory at the point of purchase is essential to sell the product effectively. In selecting and negotiating with distributors, never forget that you are paying them, and paying them handsomely, to carry an inventory of your product. That, and only that, is what entitles them to mark up your product 100 percent or more and resell it. (Incidentally, if *your* company is a distributor, you may benefit by keeping this principle in mind.)

An important issue that often comes up in dealing with distributors (and sometimes with reps) is exclusivity. You may be offered a temptingly large order—on condition that you sell your product solely through one outlet. This is a tough decision. Often that one big order is the break you've been waiting for. However, the exclusivity deal can enslave you to your distributor, and quite possibly destroy you.

It's best to resist the exclusive distributor arrangement if you possibly can. But if you feel you must go this route, you'd better make two nonnegotiable demands. First, don't get locked into option agreements on future products. Negotiate exclusivity on one product at a time. Second, don't settle for a single big purchase order; insist on guaranteed, regular future purchases. The customer must agree to buy a certain amount every year, or better, every month. Though you demand this as *quid pro quo* for exclusivity, do not tie them together in the contract. Don't accept an agreement that says, "We agree to buy 100 units per month until we decide to let the exclusive lapse." If you do, you give up the option of developing other customers and make yourself totally dependent on a single one who can unilaterally terminate his purchases at any time. He's quite likely to pull the rug out from under you just when you need him most.

Exercise 6–1:
Your Market Channel

A. What marketing method (direct, in-house sales force, reps, distributors) is currently used for your type of product by competing companies? If more than one route is used, which has proved most successful?

B. Develop a sales-expense projection. Begin by defining a "sales presentation": this is a sales pitch and close attempt to a customer. In direct marketing this is the advertisement; otherwise it is a salesperson's pitch. For your product, and for the marketing channel you propose to use, estimate the effort and expense required to carry through a sale. *Don't guess.* Base your estimate on actual experience or observation. Example: you plan to sell a home computer. If you haven't sold this sort of item yourself, go into stores that do and discreetly watch. You might find that the salesperson has to work with the customer for, say, about 45 minutes on average before closing the sale. You can now estimate that a sales presentation for your product will require 45 minutes of sales time plus, of course, the cost of maintaining a demonstrator model.

Once you have a number for the cost of making a sales presentation, you must estimate the fraction of presentations that will result in a successful sale. Again, avoid guesswork. Find a competitor or someone in a very closely comparable business and observe its results. Then assume that you'll do half as well.

Now it's a matter of simple arithmetic to calculate projected direct sales expense. To make X sales, you will have to make Y presentations, which will take Z salesperson-hours plus a certain amount of operating expense.

C. If you are going to use direct marketing or an in-house sales force, you can plug the figures you have just generated directly into the financial projections for your business plan. However, if you are going to use reps or distributors, you must also estimate what proportion of their selling effort will go into your product in comparison to other products in their line. In this way you will have an idea as to their costs, which you then use when you negotiate with them.

Checklist 6–1: Direct Expense of Sales

A. Direct marketing:
- [ ] Cost to buy or rent mailing lists
- [ ] Cost per name to develop your own list
- [ ] Cost to clean your list
- [ ] Cost of ad composition

☐ Cost to run ad (magazine, TV, and so on)
☐ Cost to print ad (direct mail)
☐ Postage costs (direct mail)
☐ Reception medium (post office box, 800-number phone line)
☐ Reception personnel (order clerks)

B. In-house sales:
☐ Salespeople's salaries
☐ Salespeople's commissions, bonuses, and so on
☐ Sales training
☐ Point-of-sale advertising and literature
☐ Demonstrator models
☐ Travel, meals, lodging
☐ Telephone expenses
☐ Management time and travel to close major sales

C. Sales reps:
☐ Rep commissions, bonuses, and so on
☐ Product literature and training aids
☐ Point-of-sale advertising and literature
☐ Management trips to assist and monitor reps

D. Distributors:
☐ Costs of acquiring and negotiating with distributors
☐ Distributor markup
☐ Point-of-sale advertising
☐ Management time and travel to monitor distributors

PRICING AND POSITIONING

What about pricing your products? Deciding how much to charge is perilous if you are bringing a new product to market. Here's a simple rule of thumb: if a proposed price seems reasonable to you, it's way too low. Consider doubling it.

Anybody who works much with new companies quickly discovers that there's one mistake they make more often than any other, and that is underpricing their product. The founders, for all their brave talk, are very nervous about sales and seem to view a low price as a sort of insurance policy. There's also a common tendency—particularly among engineers—to adopt a "cost-plus" policy: figure the costs and add a "reasonable" profit.

It is critically important to understand that *your costs are utterly irrelevant to your price.* The customer will pay what your product is worth to him. He will not pay more than it is worth to him just because your costs are high. Why should you let him pay less than it's worth if your costs are low? This point is so important that we'll repeat it: **Your product's value is what it is worth to the customer; your costs and your profit margin have nothing to do with it.**

I made the mistake of setting a price that was too low when I set up Private Products. You'll recall that we jobbed out all the production and packaging. I went around and got the costs, added them up, added a factor for profit, crossed my fingers, and set a price.

What happened of course was that I underestimated our costs. In spite of my care I didn't account for mistakes in production, loss of product, certain overhead costs—it turned out to be just about enough to wipe out most of our projected profit.

The guy who put together our sales force, the food broker, told me that we had to come in at 35 percent under the name brand. Looking back on it, we could have come in at 20 percent or even 15 percent under and done very well. But the salespeople wanted low prices to make their job easier. Letting Sales set prices equals trouble—it's a formula you can usually rely on.

As it happened, in this case we lucked out. The low price helped us to expand distribution rapidly, and Coca-Cola came along and bought the company before we had to face the problem of increasing prices in order to keep the company going. Incidentally, *they* promptly began to raise the price, and within eight months they had it up to just 10 percent under the name brand.

You should set your price high: first, to correct for the natural tendency to set it too low; second, because if your pricing decision is wrong, it's easier to lower a price than to raise it; and third, because a high price enhances your product's reputation for quality and value.

A virtually infallible symptom of underpricing is persistent inability to meet demand for your product. This doesn't necessarily apply if you run into an unusual production snag.

But if you're running into not one but a series of production or QC problems, or if you just can't seem to expand production fast enough, you should immediately raise your price. Failure to do so can ruin your company. First, because frustrated would-be customers provide a royal road to entry by competitors. Second, because you develop a reputation as a Mickey Mouse outfit that can't serve its market properly. Third, because you're leaving money on the table—money that will be desperately needed later to expand and meet competition. Fourth, because by running flat out at capacity you're raising your costs and risking a major quality fiasco. Fifth, because this situation tempts you to expand too rapidly—leaving you, when the fever cools, with too much capacity, high fixed costs, and a crushing debt load.

Some marketing theorists advocate a "preemptive" strategy for new-product introductions. The idea is that a high introductory price attracts competitors and creates an "umbrella" for them. Instead, one should start with a low price, thus expanding sales and production quickly. This will build a dominant market position and cut costs, because the high unit volume will push the company rapidly down the "learning curve." It should be clear that we don't agree with this analysis. The theory is beautiful, but in practice it has shown an ironic flaw: although the idea is to accept a short-term restriction in order to gain a long-term advantage, the actual result is usually the opposite—short-term success followed by long-term disaster. The preemptive strategy can work only if it succeeds in deterring the competition. But what if the competition adopts the same strategy and attempts to deter *you?*

Henry Ford adopted a preemptive strategy with his introduction of the Model T. He was spectacularly successful— for a while. Soon competitors responded in kind and began to eat him alive. Ford Motor almost didn't survive.

More recently, Japanese semiconductor companies have attempted to preempt the market for memory chips. They succeeded in capturing a dominant market share, but despite their mad race down the learning curve, their costs never caught up with prices. As this is written they are still selling at a loss.

The preemptive pricing strategy is simply a modern, stylish revival of what used to be known as "predatory pricing" back in the days of the "robber barons." Unlike Standard Oil, you as a small company probably don't have to worry about being broken up under the Sherman Act. But you may find, as Standard Oil did, that this method simply doesn't work. One oil man likened it to "trying to sweep back the ocean with a broom so you can have a dry place to sit."

A strategy with a better track record is "creaming" the early market. Start with a high price and don't drop it until you have to in order to meet the competition. The key to making this work is twofold. First, concentrate on raising sales by understanding and satisfying your customers' needs rather than by cutting prices. Second, work continuously at improving your production methods and cutting costs. In reality, you travel down the learning curve by *learning*, not by just mechanically pumping out product; lower costs result not from volume as such but from the effort to manage production more effectively.

Similar principles apply to products that are not new. Perhaps you're trying not to protect your market but to take market share from established competitors. In such a fight there are many marketing weapons you can use. The most powerful of them all is price cutting. Price cutting is a devastatingly effective weapon against competitors; indeed, one might call it the atomic bomb of marketing. Like the atomic bomb, it is a weapon one should try never to use, for a price war, like a nuclear war, is not likely to have a real winner. Instead you should concentrate on becoming the low-cost producer, and letting your competitors know it. Deter them from lowering prices by making it clear that you will respond in kind, and that you can take it better than they can. The threat is stronger than the execution.

Positioning

Price "positioning" is a factor you should consider. In most markets (except for certain commodities) there is a range of products, with "premium," mid-range, and "economy" models. A large company will often try to cover all or most of the market by selling several models; General Motors, for instance, consciously positioned its five divisions to cover the entire auto market. Your small company cannot afford this approach. Instead, pick one position; then make sure that your total marketing approach is compatible with it. If you've decided to be the Cadillac in your market, don't use a Chevrolet marketing approach—and vice versa.

Checklist 6–2: Pricing Your Product

Place a check beside each of the following statements that is true for your company. If there are more than two statements without checkmarks, you are almost certainly pricing your product too low.

☐ Customers complain sometimes that our price is too high.
☐ Our salespeople frequently suggest that we cut prices.
☐ We have developed sales arguments to justify why our product is worth more than our competitors'.
☐ (For industrial products:) We have developed a quantitative estimate of the financial benefit to the customer of buying our product.
☐ Our capacity utilization is in the range of 85 percent to 95 percent.
☐ We are able to ship on time without exception.
☐ Our prices are not lower than the competition's.

ADVERTISING AND PROMOTION

Whether you develop your own advertising or hire an agency, there's one simple principle that is necessary and sufficient to produce good advertisements: *The purpose of advertising is to gain access to potential customers.* There are a few exceptional cases, such as direct marketing, but in general, you should focus on this objective to create effective advertising.

What do we mean by gaining access to potential customers? Quite simply, getting people who may buy into contact with your sales channels. Let's break down how this is done.

1. Target your best prospects. On the basis of your market research, develop a profile of the person most likely to buy your product.

2. Locate the targeted prospects. Choose an advertising medium that will give your ad exposure to large numbers of this selected group—and not to a lot of poor prospects. Whether you're buying magazine space, a slot of television time, or a mailing list, minimize paying for people who aren't prospects—you can't afford to waste the money.

3. Communicate with the targeted prospects. The objective is to let them know that you have a product or service that will satisfy their needs. Aim your ad precisely at the target customer. Don't try to write an ad that will appeal to everyone. Don't try to write an ad that will appeal to the target prospect and also to marginal possibilities. Visualize the person who wants what you have and talk to him or her.

4. Motivate the targeted prospects. This step is where most ads fail. The prospective customer should do one of two things as a result of seeing your ad. Either he should come to you and offer you a chance to sell him, or he should identify himself and invite you to come to him. The corollaries are obvious. First, let him know how to do it—should he come to your store, circle a number on the "bingo card," phone you? Second, make it easy for him—if your shop is hard to find, draw him a map. Third, give him a reason to respond, and to respond immediately before he forgets—whether it's an offer of free literature or an entry in a million-dollar lottery.

> You have to think out very carefully what message you want to get across and realize that your prospective customers are very busy. They're assaulted by all sorts of advertising and other pressures on their time from every quarter and simply are not going to drop everything and spend the rest of their day trying to find you to buy your product or service. You have about a millisecond to arrest their race through the day and catch their attention with your message. It will need to be a very well thought-out message.

Effective advertising focuses on the prospective customers and their needs and desires. The ad therefore should emphasize benefits rather than features of your product. The customers probably don't care that your widget has ten ventricles; they want to know why a ten-ventricle widget will give them better satisfaction than an eight-ventricle widget.

Beware of certain pitfalls in advertising. Don't offend or patronize your customers. Don't imply that they're stupid, ignorant, or irrational. They probably aren't; if you sincerely believe that they are, you're in the wrong business. Don't irritate the customers. Ads that are too repetitive, too aggressive, or too uncandid may demotivate them. In some industries, it's become necessary to reassure the wary prospects that they won't be pestered: "No salesman will call." Don't omit important information. Modern consumers are pretty sophisticated, and if you leave out a key item, they're likely to assume it's because you don't dare mention it.

When I was shopping for a personal computer, I sent for information on the Fujitsu Micro 16s. A beautiful brochure arrived, describing an excellent system in great detail, including the technical specifications—but carefully omitting any mention of the price. So I automatically assumed that it was too expensive for my budget and ruled it out. It was only by accident that I discovered that Fujitsu's price was in fact quite competitive.

If you are using direct marketing your advertising will have to go beyond the model described here, since your ads will actually have to close the sale. We lack the space to deal with this subject properly; you should get Bob Stone's book (described in the Bibliography).

Should you hire an agency or produce your own advertising? If you lack the specialized skills involved, you'll have no choice but to get professional help. Even large companies, for instance, don't try to produce their own TV ads. On the other hand, if you're short of funds you'll have to limit yourself to advertising you can design yourself. In between, the two factors should be balanced; if there's a toss-up, it's well to lean toward the in-house approach, if only because it's so educational. Keep in mind that you have the option of maintaining control but hiring professionals for specific tasks.

To promote my products—catalysts that could perform chemical feats almost magical—I decided to put out a newsletter called "Maxwell Demon." (In a famous paper published in 1871, James Clerk Maxwell illustrated certain arguments about thermodynamics by hypothesizing a molecule-size "demon" that could achieve impossible results.) For the logo I wanted a picture of this mythical creature holding a tetrahedral molecule. My printer referred me to an artist who took my crude sketch and produced a beautiful drawing, just what I wanted. The cost: $35.00. It's really true—the world *is* full of starving artists who will work for peanuts.

Of course, advertising costs money. What about publicity, which is "free"? Yes, it may be free, but usually it's worth what it costs. In seeking publicity, it's not enough to make your company well-known to the public at large. Publicity, like advertising, should be targeted. It's a waste of time and effort unless it makes you known to prospective customers and motivates them to make contact with you. Whatever approach you use—press releases, magazine articles, demonstrations, stunts—ask yourself: *who* will see this?

There's a general misunderstanding of the purpose of advertising and publicity. Many entrepreneurs believe that if they get that story in a major business magazine or place a full-page ad, the orders will flood in. Wrong. Advertising and publicity should be looked upon as Chinese Water Torture on your market. You've got to keep at it continuously.

This I learned in politics. When I was running for office on the Upper East Side of Manhattan, I at first had the idea that the announcement of my candidacy would cause the whole world to stop and listen to me. In fact, nobody even noticed my existence until a constant stream of mailing pieces, radio spots, television appearances, public meetings, and sound-truck tours slowly began to take effect.

I applied this lesson at Sedgwick Printout. (See Chapter 7 for the full story.) As one of my competitors said to me, "Damn it, Sedgwick, every time I turn around, there's your name." It was true. Every time he opened up a trade magazine, there was an article. Every time he opened his mail, there was another mailing piece. Every time he attended a meeting, there I was giving a talk. We were ubiquitous, and it worked.

YOUR COMPANY NAME

It's a shame to take up this subject, because one of the greatest pleasures in starting your own company is selecting the name and logo. All of us feel highly competent to do this and are disinclined to listen to advice. However, there are a few points that should be covered.

In my Enterprise Forum experience I've several times encountered entrepreneurs who stubbornly refused to change company names that were clearly hurting them in the market. The best meeting transcription service in New York is called Rainbow Enterprises and has a very frivolous-looking logo. The founder fiercely defended her choice against the panel's unanimous criticism of its negative impact on her potential customers—mostly *Fortune* 500 corporation executives who probably felt a bit uncomfortable with handing an invoice from "Rainbow" to their companies' humorless and steely-eyed controllers. More recently, a similar criticism of UFO Software (it stands for "user friendly oriented") met with the same sort of defensive response.

The name of your company is its most ubiquitous advertisement. It is really helpful for it to say something about what your company does for a living. This is one good argument against using your own name for the company.

The Julius E. Holland-Moritz Company makes specialized pliers for orthodontists. Would you know it from the name? Does this name help the company get new customers? Incidentally, this company is no longer owned by the founder, so the name doesn't even identify the proprietor.

There are several other good reasons for not using your own name. What if your company goes under? What if it is highly successful, you sell it, and *then* it goes under? It can be rather embarrassing and inconvenient to have people asking, "Are you connected with the Joe Blurpsky Company that was indicted for polluting Lake Michigan?" You can of course explain that yes you were but not anymore and it wasn't your fault . . . but why get into this situation? Why put your name in the control of other people?

Perhaps you are quite sure your business will last out your lifetime and you will never sell. Still, think twice before using your own name unless you're setting up a professional business such as a law firm, a brokerage, a consulting business, or the like. If your name is very well known and prestigious, of course, it's a different matter; it may be of marketing value.

Also of dubious value are names consisting of initials. Such names tell the prospective customer *nothing* about your company or its products. They just aren't appropriate to start-ups; such names must be earned over decades. Once everybody knows who you are and what you do, you may be called by your initials, as IBM is. To try to start out this way is over ambitious.

Also to be avoided is the pretentious name.

> A Route 128 company with a dozen or so employees made a very ingenious little computerized gadget that kept track of vending-machine sales. It provided a good method of keeping the maintenance people who go around to collect the money from the coin boxes honest, and it created valuable data for market analysis. Its name—International Totalizing Systems—was probably more a hindrance than an advantage to this excellent little company; whom was it fooling?

Another pitfall is the Mickey Mouse or cutesy-pie name. Basing your company name on a pun—even a very ingenious pun—will inevitably have you and your employees cringing eventually. Even the funniest joke gets stale after a few years. (One possible exception: if the product you're selling is humorous.)

A name such as "Smith Enterprises" doesn't do much for your credibility. Its cautious generality suggests that you are trying out several different lines of business and lack a clear definition. This may indeed be the case, but you should try to conceal it from your customers and prospective investors. Also to be avoided in most cases is "Smith & Associates." A lot of people who get fired set up as "consultants" under a moniker of this type. It's become so common that nobody is fooled—everyone knows that the "associates" are imaginary.

Finally, be very careful not to arouse the prejudices of your customers—or your neighbors. Sambo's Restaurants ran into trouble with black customers and had to resort to the fiction that their name was not related to the children's story. Again, Colonel Sanders, as it turned out, was not the best image to use in marketing fried chicken to the black community. The founders of these companies may not have been racially prejudiced—but that doesn't matter. If you're perceived as prejudiced, correctly or not, you're in trouble.

Lifesystems Company was occasionally confused with the then-notorious Life Sciences Corp., which had committed serious pollution offenses.

I was careful to avoid the word "chemical" and similar dangers when naming Reaction Design Corp. The name we chose identified us to customers, who were technically sophisticated, but, we hoped, conveyed nothing ominous to the general public. Yet, as it turned out, we occasionally were asked if we had anything to do with nuclear reactors and radioactivity. Perhaps you can't win after all.

On a more positive note, your name should convey to your customers at least a rough impression of what you sell. It's nice if you can make the sound compatible with your company's style. If you're setting up a hot high-tech operation, naturally you should use technology buzzwords. (But try not to overdo it. The market is crowded with "X Dynamics" and "Y Technologies" and "Z Systems.") If you're selling sweaters to preppies, something that suggests yachting or duck-hunting is clearly more appropriate.

Unfortunately, selecting a good name may be tough because so many of the clever ideas have already been used. When you come up with a dozen good possibilities and have your lawyer search them for previous trademarks, you're likely to be shocked at the results.

NBC spent a small fortune having a new logo designed by prestigious consultants, only to find that some obscure independent was already using the same design. NBC had to buy the rights.

In some cases your product needs a name, too. Whether it's a personal computer, a bicycle, or a candy bar, the product name will be even more critical than your company name to selling the product.

> A rather ordinary candy caught on as a fad some years ago by calling itself "Spider Eggs;" somehow this caught the perverse fancy of the younger generation.
>
> The personal-computer market has seen two very good product names. One, of course, was "Apple"—conveying, as was intended, an image of simplicity and accessibility to the nontechnical user. But though less appreciated, IBM's "PC" was an equally brilliant choice, conveying—as was intended—the image of the generic standard which the IBM PC in fact has become.

We don't want to ruin your pleasure. Have fun selecting your name, but recognize that it will have serious consequences too.

MARKETING VERSUS SALES TALENT

Marketing is *not* the same thing as sales. We'll be talking specifically about sales in the next chapter, but for now we want to warn you that good marketing people and good salespeople are entirely separate groups. If you have a good salesperson you may want to promote her to sales manager, but don't put her in the marketing department. The talents, attitudes, and personality required for good selling are entirely different from those needed for effective marketing. You may have some problems with this because "marketing" is a prestigious occupation and "sales" is definitely not. Thus you must make it clear to your top salespeople that they can rise in the company within sales and that it's not necessary for them to transfer to marketing to advance their careers.

A FINAL COMMENT

There are counterexamples to this chapter. You can find small-business marketers who do none of the work and systematic analysis that we have recommended above, yet are strikingly successful in the marketplace. Some entrepreneurs have an amazing talent for intuitive marketing. Somehow, by experience or instinct, they automatically develop and follow a clear market strategy. These natural talents swim in the market like fish, doing all the right things without having to think about it. The rest of us have to use aqualungs. Grinding through the detailed analysis we've discussed is a lot of work—but it pays off.

CAUTIONARY TALE:
THE ONE ABOUT THE TRAVELING SALESMAN

My first business venture began after I had become disenchanted with my lot at the Aluminum Company of Canada. I finally left and then rummaged around New York for something to do. I was introduced to a company called Trig-A-Tape. Its product was a device that put price labels on items in retail stores. I bought 10 percent of the company for $10,000 and became General Manager.

The hand-operated labeling device had been invented by a gentleman who had spent five or six years manufacturing these things in his basement and selling them to local stores. At that time there were various existing ways to label cans and boxes and so on. Some stores used sticks with ink stamps on them. Others ordered preprinted labels, which a clerk would then stick on the items by hand. The Trig-A-Tape machine was a real advance; you could set a price on it, make pressure-sensitive labels on the spot, and conveniently extrude them onto the product. Our approach was to get into serious production of these devices and sell them into what appeared to be a very significant market.

We quickly ran into major manufacturing problems. Nobody had looked into the intricacies of manufacturing this gadget. Up to this time the machines had been put together, one at a time, by the inventor. He did it almost as a craftsman would assemble a fine piece of custom furniture, shaping and fitting each piece individually to make the final product work. When that same piece was put on a production line with 15 or 20 people who had never seen it before, the result was a chaotic mess.

There were not only defects in assembly, in some cases there weren't even drawings for the parts. The inventor, who knew it all by heart after making these things for years, didn't need drawings. Neither my partners nor I had any specific manufacturing experience, and we didn't realize how difficult making this simple-looking device would be. So again and again, machines were shipped out and returned because they didn't work. It was a valuable lesson for me. Since then I've made it a rule that anything with more than two moving parts gets jobbed out.

But this was only the beginning. Our real problem was selling the things. We had selected a distribution channel on the basis of the experience of one of my partners. He had had a very considerable success a few years earlier with a paint spray gun, using what are called specialty salesmen. The specialty salesman is an independent rep, a free-lancer. He drives around to retail stores with sample cases promoting various products; when he makes a sale, the order is filled directly by the manufacturer. This had turned out to be very successful in selling spray guns, so we used it for our new gadget.

We advertised the availability of the product in great detail in a series of full-page ads in a magazine called . . . *Specialty Salesman*, which is devoted almost entirely to such ads. We got a very good response; we "sold" the salesperson a sample kit for $20 or so, which included the device itself, some rolls of tape from which the labels were made, sales literature, order forms, and some nice impressive cards from the Trig-A-Tape Corporation of New York City.

What hadn't occurred to us in selecting this distribution channel was that we had the right customers, and salespeople who called on those customers, but *the customers did not buy this type of product from those salespeople*. The retail-store operator bought all sorts of things from specialty salespeople—hardware, dry goods, gadgets— but all of them items for resale. The Trig-A-Tape machine was not for resale but for use by the retailer—it was a system sale. The specialty salesperson didn't want to make system sales and wasn't good at it. It involved convincing the retailers to abandon their old labeling methods and use a new one. This is not an on-the-spot decision; it takes repeat calls and working with the customer. The specialty salesperson doesn't do that sort of thing. He goes to the customer, shows him something, and the decision is made in 15 minutes. Of course, our QC problems didn't exactly help the sale.

Worse yet, we had zero control over our sales force. We didn't even know who they were; each one was just a piece of paper and a check when he sent in his mail-order coupon from our ad. It might be an old hand, or it might be someone who'd never tried selling before and thought this was a good way to get rich quick.

So what happened was that these couple of hundred salespeople got discouraged, sent their sample cases back, and demanded repayment.

By this time, between manufacturing and marketing costs, plus some considerable overhead, the company had run through its original invested capital, some $200,000, and—not to put too fine a point on it—was broke or perhaps a little worse. At this juncture, my partners approached me with an offer to sell me the other 90 percent of the company for about $100,000, which was a superb piece of *chutzpah*. Happily, I had the wits to sit tight. My partners were already involved in starting a different venture and didn't like the idea of simultaneously going into bankruptcy with Trig-A-Tape; it would not have greatly enhanced their credibility with investors. So I acquired the company for $1.00, and they even paid off the outstanding debt.

Then I had to move fast. We had a monthly overhead of $35,000 and no income to speak of. I took over the business on a Thursday afternoon. By Saturday of the next week I had overhead down to $2,000 a month. I had to let go the entire staff. I sublet the loft where we had been "manufacturing" the gadget. I stopped my own salary, of course. I hired an engineer, offering him a piece of the company, and we moved the operation, such as it was, into his basement. The only other person we kept was the inventor, who still kept rolling out two or three gadgets per day by hand as he always had.

The engineer began redesigning the product from the ground up so that it could be manufactured more easily. First, however, we went out and met with people from some major chains like Sears and Woolworth's. In short, we did a little market research, finding out what they wanted in their price-labeling system and even going into the minor matter of what they would pay for it. Six months later we had some prototypes and took them out for testing.

About this time I was approached by some of the big names in pressure-sensitive labels—Dymo, 3M, and a couple of others. We had a patent not only on the machine itself but on the pressure-sensitive labels it produced, so if these devices got out in any volume, there would be a substantial effect on the demand for pressure-sensitive adhesives. We negotiated over a period of months and finally sold the company to Dymo.

There's a rather amusing anecdote attached to this sale. I had a very clear idea of what I wanted. Dymo had just gone public and was considered a hot stock (this was in the bull market of 1961). Dymo wanted to give me some cash and a royalty, but since I wasn't at all sure it would ever actually get the product on the market, I was unwilling to take it. I wanted a nice piece of Dymo's stock. The negotiations went on for weeks. Dymo was on the West Coast, and periodically the chairman and president would come East to buy another company for $5 million or $10 million—and then come and diddle with me for less than $1 million. Finally, in some frustration, the president of Dymo told me that he had examined the finances of Trig-A-Tape—which of course he had in the course of his due diligence—and he'd also examined my own personal finances. He'd found them both very thin (which they were) and told me that his offer of cash and royalty was the last offer and I could take it or leave it.

I asked him if in his investigation of my background he had looked up my wife's maiden name. He looked at me blankly and said, "No. What does that have to do with anything?" I said, "Well, I'm married to Patricia Ann Rosenwald." Now, Rosenwald to anyone informed at all in business history is a name that bears some clout. Julius Rosenwald founded Sears Roebuck, and his heirs are not poverty-stricken to say the least. I went on to say, "I don't *need* to sell this company. If I don't get what I want for it, I'll just put it in a drawer." That did the trick, and I got my deal. As it happens, Patsy's father was James Benno Rosenwald, no relation at all to Julius Rosenwald.

So I ended up with a tidy sum in Dymo Stock at $3 a share, which promptly rose to about $40 and made me what for that time was quite rich. It took Dymo about two years to get the product out on the market in volume. Now this gadget is a commodity that you can see in action in any supermarket.

Overall, this venture was extremely instructive as well as fairly lucrative, and taught me a lot of lessons that were helpful in later ventures (though I still had something to learn, as you'll recall from the story of FOTO COMP). Most important was the importance of distribution channels. The manufacturing hassles, distracting though they were, presented fairly easy problems to solve. The company's big mistake lay in jumping into the market with the specialty salespeople, a totally inappropriate method of distribution. In the end, I was able to finesse this difficulty by selling out to a large company that already had its own distribution set up. You may not want to sell out, of course. But if you're having trouble with setting up distribution, consider ways of getting a big outfit to do it for you. Often it's a lot better than reinventing the marketing wheel yourself.

HDS

7

SALES TACTICS

With the money he had he was able to purchase a good supply of matches, and when it became light enough he began to vend them.

Hitherto he had not been very fortunate in the disposal of his wares, being timid and bashful; but then he was working for Mother Watson, and expected to derive very little advantage for himself from his labors. Now he was working for himself, and this seemed to put new spirit and courage into him.

Horatio Alger, Jr.
Mark the Match Boy*

Somebody has to sell!

It's amazing how many businesses succumb simply because they forget this simple truth. And not just new or small businesses, either. Big companies, generations old, have gone bankrupt when they took their sales for granted.

Between salespeople and the rest of the human race there is a great gulf fixed. All too often, the chasm is widened by bigotry. Salespeople sometimes regard those outside their profession as "marks" or "suckers." On the other side, "He's a real salesman" usually expresses contempt, not admiration. Scientists and engineers especially tend to regard sales types as a lower form of life.

This communications gap creates real problems for many start-ups. When a salesman becomes an entrepreneur, he com-

*(New York: Collier, 1962), p. 276.

monly assumes that obtaining something to sell is trivial. Production, R&D, and quality control are often neglected, with disastrous results. On the other hand, start-ups run by engineers frequently just starve. The typical high-tech start-up tends to resemble a bevy of Victorian virgins trying to open a whorehouse. The founders "know" that selling is necessary, but they just can't bring themselves to dirty their hands with such degrading labor. It might seem that the best solution is for the founding team to include both sales and nonsales types. This is ideal if it works, but only an uncommon tolerance on both sides can prevent civil war.

Nonetheless, *somebody* has to sell! Don't kid yourself that a good product will sell itself. It won't. Don't think that good advertising will "make it sell." It won't. Don't persuade yourself that a half-hearted, fastidious, arm's-length approach to selling will work. It won't. Somebody—some specific person or persons in your organization—must be responsible for making the product move. If you take direct responsibility for sales yourself, you must be committed to performing the task and performing it well. If you lack the talent or inclination to do so, you must delegate it to someone competent and motivated. And if you hold salespeople in contempt, you'd better learn to get over it, or at least hide it well—because you need them.

SELLING—A SURVIVAL SKILL

In any case, selling is a basic survival skill. No entrepreneur can afford to be without a certain basic competence in sales. Selling, in one form or another, is an ineradicable part of virtually all business activities. Just think of all the people you'll have to "sell."

Before you even start your company, you'll probably have to sell some investors. Unless you can finance your company out of your own pocket, you'll have to sell some company before you can sell product. This is a sales job that doesn't go away. A growing company has a continual need for capital. The CEO must take the lead in raising it.

Don't forget your cofounders and employees. You'll have to "sell" them on investing their time and effort on your new, untried, and risky business concept. Once again, this is a task that won't go away. Whenever you conceive a new project, a special effort, a change in approach, you will have to "sell, not tell" your personnel if you want to engage their enthusiasm.

Customers, of course, must be sold. In the early days of your start-up you'll be desperately short-handed. Developing a reliable flow of sales, starting from scratch, is a terribly difficult job, and everybody is going to have to pitch in. When and if your company prospers and grows, the need will not go away. In any successful concern the CEO and other members of top management get plenty of customer contact. Their active participation is frequently essential to close unusually large or pioneering sales. They must be involved in the sales process in order to motivate—and monitor—the professional sales force. And finally, top management cannot understand or anticipate changes in the market unless it is in continuous contact with customers.

This is so important it needs elaboration. You, as CEO, must balance conflicting claims from the segments of your organization in order to make crucial management decisions. The impact of the various factors on sales is a primary criterion. Production wants to reduce costs by restricting the number of different models; Sales wants even more variety. Finance wants to reduce inventory; Sales wants to increase it. R&D wants to develop a new product; Marketing wants to improve the old one. QA wants stricter tolerances; Purchasing wants a loosening. Sales wants to give easier credit terms; Finance wants to tighten up. *You* must decide such issues. What will be the effect on sales? There's no substitute for getting out and making a few sales yourself. It gives you a real feel for the difficulties your sales force faces. It also makes it harder for the salespeople to give you a snow job.

Exercise 7–1:
Sales Responsibility

A. Who is the person ultimately responsible for sales in your company? Who gets taken to the Tower and beheaded if sales projections are not met? _____
B. Nonsales types may have to pitch in to get your start-up sales going. What proportion of total working time do you

expect each of the following team members to spend on sales? Has each one been informed of these expectations?

CEO	_____%
VP of Sales	_____%
VP of Marketing	_____%
VP of Production	_____%
VP of R&D	_____%
VP of Administration & Finance	_____%

THE SALES PROCESS—A FOUR-STAGE VIEW

Full-time selling is not for everyone, but anyone can learn the rudiments of selling. It doesn't require any mystical endowment or innate talent. Selling is not an instinctive act but a rational procedure. Much of the vast array of books, seminars, and lectures on selling is disquieting to those of us who come from, say, a technical background. To hear the "experts" tell it, selling is a highly emotional fine art of psychological manipulation not much removed from hypnotism. And if you're selling underwater lots in Florida to elderly pensioners, it is. Most of us, however, are offering a real value, and for us selling is much more straightforward. The key to success in selling is remembering that it is an exchange of information that is involved. The customer provides you with information about her needs and wants; you provide her with information about your product.

In the analysis that follows, the sales process is broken down into four stages. Other writers on this subject may divide it differently, but the process remains the same. The steps are simple. First, attract a customer, interest him, get him to consider buying. Second, exchange information with him and deal with his objections. Third, persuade him to buy—"close" the sale. Fourth, follow up, and thus renew the sales cycle.

Stage 1: Attract a Customer

For most businesses, the first stage, attracting a customer, is actually a marketing responsibility. We've already discussed it in some detail in the preceding chapter. But it's worth giving it some additional consideration, for one of the most common mistakes in selling is failure to recognize that this first step is *essential*. The mere fact that a customer happens to be in physical proximity to you doesn't mean he is ready to be sold. If you start at stage 2 without completing stage 1, the prospect will be confused at best, and possibly infuriated. On the other hand, by laying the foundation well when you develop initial interest, you make it easier to apply your sales presentation.

> Many high-pressure sales operations make a point of delib-
> erately skipping stage one. The sucker is told that he has
> "won" a free weekend at a resort. Once there, he is pressed
> to buy real estate in a new development. Or somebody on
> the phone or at the door claims to be interviewing for a
> poll; when the sucker has been enticed into a conversation,
> a canned sales presentation surfaces. Or an envelope de-
> signed to look like an important telegram turns out to
> contain a mail-order solicitation. This sort of approach
> implies a fundamental contempt for the customer's intelli-
> gence, which makes it ineffectual for any ethical business.
> Those who use these techniques are in effect saying: "If you
> knew what I'm selling, you'd walk away, so I'll trap you—
> sucker." The victim may logically ask: "If you're ashamed
> to sell it, why should I buy it?"

How should the customer be engaged in the sales process? To start with, he must become aware that he has a *need:*

> "Only seventeen shopping days till Christmas. Have
> you bought a present for your mother-in-law yet?"

Then he must realize that his need *can* be satisfied:

> "Don't despair! This year you can give her the perfect
> gift . . ."

And finally he must recognize that your product *might* satisfy his need:

> ". . . a vacation in sunny Ulan Bator. Special bargain
> price on one-way fares."

Once he reaches this point, and only then, he is ready to participate in the sales process.

As soon as you encounter a prospect, begin by determining whether she's considering a purchase. You'll probably encounter all kinds of prospects. At one end of the spectrum is the prepared buyer: "I need a personal computer to analyze my stock investments." At the other end, you might hear, "I'm curious about personal computers. What are they good for?" Please note that the latter may be just as likely to buy as the former! The object at this stage is not to cull out poor prospects and chase them away but to find out *where you have to start* with this particular prospective customer.

Stage 2: Handle Objections

Once the prospect is ready to consider buying, you can begin stage 2. At this point, the prospect begins to produce objections to buying—otherwise known as sales resistance. You must find out what these objections are and answer them. *Answering objections is easy—it's finding out what they are that's hard.* Rarely will the prospect frankly state his objections. Instead, he may chatter about irrelevancies; or bring up a problem that actually doesn't bother him while avoiding his real concerns; or perhaps just sit there, refusing either to buy or to state any reason why he won't. Don't be in a hurry to chase him out. Unless he has an obvious ulterior motive, like getting out of a rainstorm, he's probably hanging around in the hope that *you* will state his objection—and answer it.

How can you do this? There seem to be hundreds of possible obstacles to the purchase of any product. But the vast majority of them reduce to one of four basic objections.

Objection #1: "It isn't what I want."

The first key to dealing with this objection is to realize that it says "want" and not "need." Entrepreneurs tend to think in terms of satisfying human needs. They are prone to fall into the trap of telling the customer, "This is what you need." But you shouldn't take it for granted that he wants what he needs. If he doesn't, you may produce a list of irrefutable reasons why he needs your product—and get absolutely nowhere. You must find out what he *wants*, and convince him that your product will provide it.

How? Communicate. Get him talking, and listen. What are his motives, his likes, his dislikes? Your market research should have given you some hints. Now use them as a starting point to analyze this particular customer.

We moved to California and decided to buy a house. The first broker we dealt with just wouldn't listen. We'd told her how much we wanted to spend, what kind of neighborhood we wanted, what kind of house. She proposed one house at 50 percent above our maximum price, another in a run-down area, a third needing repairs. We switched to another broker, Juanita. She made us her study. She encouraged us to talk and quietly soaked up information: our backgrounds, jobs, families, hobbies; our tastes in food, furniture, music. With every house we visited, her question was *not* "Did you like it?" but "*What* did you like or dislike about it?" With this technique—and a thorough knowledge of the local housing market—she was able to zero in quickly on the kind of house we would buy.

By *listening* to the customer, you obtain the key to dealing with this objection. Once you know what he wants—very specifically—you can present your product in a way that will attract him. Stress the features that he wants. Perhaps you can offer him a different model, a customized version, or a special service.

Objection #2: "I can't afford it."

This is the objection that separates the pros from the amateurs in the selling game. The mediocre salesperson is always pressing management for lower prices so she can sell more. But to give away your product, you don't need salespeople. When a salesperson comes to you with a request to drop prices, grasp her firmly by the shoulders, rotate her 180 degrees, and send her out again, with the following advice.

The key to handling this objection is determining which of two forms it takes. Listen carefully to the customer.

The real meaning may be, "It's not worth the price. I could pay this price, but I don't like it that much." If this is the obstacle, don't talk price, talk value—your task is to make the customer like it more. Here is just one technique. The question of price and value can lead easily into a discussion of the "good old days" and from there to the customer's previous purchase of a similar product. Get him talking about the old one that he really liked. Then point out to him the similar features of your product. The association with his memories will make your product's advantages real to him. What if his last purchase was a lemon? Then, of course, you use the contrast.

On the other hand, the real meaning may be, "I love it, but I just don't have the money." If this is the case, don't waste your breath trying to make the product seem even more desirable. Deal with the cost problem. Perhaps he could manage it on credit. Perhaps part of the purchase price is tax-deductible, so it doesn't really cost as much as it seems. Perhaps he could manage a cheaper, stripped-down version and upgrade it later.

Objection #3: "It's not the best value."

If your salespeople complain about Objection #2, be very skeptical. If they complain about Objection #3, however, give close attention. This objection is a danger sign.

Even seasoned sales professionals tend to become defensive when this objection surfaces—and that's a serious mistake. If you immediately start a counterattack by, say, bad-mouthing the competition, the customer may well clam up. Then you may lose the sale; but worse, you will certainly lose some extremely valuable information. If a customer is willing to tell you why he prefers the competition—*listen!* Even if he's wrong, ridiculous, stupid—bite your tongue and hear him out. When he's done, still don't respond. Instead, ask probing questions. Make sure you understand what his objections are, and that you've heard them all. Don't hesitate to give up the sale if necessary to get frankness from him. You're getting priceless information that can pay off handsomely in future sales.

Keep listening until the objection *makes sense*. Even if the customer is wrong, he has a reason for his opinion. You haven't listened enough until you understand why he feels the way he does. Then restate his objections, check each one to make sure that you've understood him correctly, and deal with it tactfully.

How? There are basically two responses. One is, "So sorry,

you're wrong." Obviously, you use this when the customer is mistaken in his *facts*—not his evaluations. (And only then, or he'll get mad—one reason you listened carefully.) With this response, you must bend over backward to be tactful: "I'm sorry, Sir, I should have mentioned that this system *does* include a FORTRAN compiler." (Even though it was clearly stated in the ad as well as in your original sales pitch.) The other response is, "Yes, but." If he's got a point, concede it— concede it frankly and freely. This will enhance your credibility. Then counter in an area where you have the advantage *and* where he has shown an emphasis. Suppose, for instance, that he has previously expressed concern about reliability. When he brings up a competitor's superior convenience, quickly return to favorable ground: "It's true that the five-inch diskettes are more widely used, and I have to admit that it's a nuisance to transfer data to a different medium. But we've found that there are a lot fewer errors with the eight-inch disks."

In general, it's a poor idea to criticize competitors unless their deficiencies are very obvious. It's usually more credible to imply, "They're good, but we're better." Remember that the customer sees you—quite correctly—as a biased party and that anything you say about the competition will be heavily discounted. It's not a very productive use of your time. Any comments about the competition should be confined to non-controversial statements of fact; leave evaluations to the customer.

Objection #4: "I don't trust you."

This is an objection you'll almost never hear made explicit, but it's the deadliest of them all. Even when the product is terrific, the price is right, and you're head and shoulders above the competition, the customer may balk because he suspects that he's being taken.

This objection is best handled with prophylactic measures. Once trust has been lost, it's hard to retrieve it. There are four common ways of inspiring mistrust in customers.

1. *Misbehavior of sales or service personnel.* When the pressure is on to meet quota, a salesperson can be awfully tempted to cut corners. Common sins include making exaggerated

claims or promises, understating the price and hitting the customer with hidden costs, and bait-and-switch tactics. You should set up systems to monitor the sales force. An important point: emphasize attitude. Never let your salespeople speak contemptuously of customers, even in private. Make it known that customers are to be referred to with respect; they aren't "marks" or "suckers" or "fish" to be "landed." Take it for granted that real sales professionals respect their customers.

Be sure that customer service, returns, and the complaint desk get top-management attention. Remember, turning a dissatisfied customer into a satisfied one is the *second* most important thing these people do. Their most important function is to let top management know that there *are* dissatisfied customers—and why.

> A number of CEOs—some with large companies—make it a practice to spend one day a month dealing personally with customer complaints.

2. *Bad reputation of company or industry.* If your company has a bad reputation, you can—and must—do something about it. But what if your whole industry is held in low esteem by the public? Well, it becomes important then not only to differentiate your product from that of the competition but also to differentiate your company from your competitors. Change the terminology if you can get away with it; you're not selling used cars, you're selling "pre-owned vehicles."

3. *The deal is too good.* There's a tendency to be suspicious of the bargain that's too good to be true—to ask, "What's the catch?" If your customers are showing this reaction, there are two possibilities. One is that there *is* a catch. If so, maybe your salespeople should be a bit more frank about it. Then again, maybe there really isn't any catch. In that case, consider raising your price.

4. *Hard sell.* Think back to something you've bought that gave you real satisfaction—high quality, just what you wanted, bargain price. How was it sold to you? Not aggressively, was it? In fact, chances are you had to search it out.

In selling, as in courtship, it's a mistake to come on too strong. The customer has a natural tendency to think that a really good product doesn't need aggressive selling. So the salesperson who appears overeager, pushy, high-pressure, will arouse suspicion.

We know that a better mousetrap does not sell itself. But customers almost invariably believe that it *does*. How to sell effectively without looking too eager?

It is *not* helpful to feign indifference. The ideal attitude is probably one of serene confidence in the product, combined with eager attention to the needs of the customer. This positive approach is highly effective, but not always easy to carry off.

A simple negative rule can readily be applied: Don't trap the customer. Leave him an exit. All high-pressure tactics are based on imprisoning the customer: get him where he can't get away—the "closing room" if you're selling cars, his own living room if you're selling encyclopedias, a resort if you're selling desert lots. Then keep after him until he signs. Don't let him leave, and don't let him stop to think. So the fastest way to disarm a customer who is feeling pressured is to suggest that he go home and think it over.

The key to dealing with any objection is listening. Let the customer talk. Some objections will come out quickly and explicitly. But many will not. Customers can be amazingly shy. He may be embarrassed to admit that he can't afford your premium model. He may feel it would be impolite to tell you he likes a competitor's product better. If you get the impression that he has a hidden objection, try running down a list of plausible objections with him. (You, of course, have a prepared answer to each one.) If even this doesn't smoke him out, you're probably facing a #4—suspicion.

Exercise 7–2:
Sales-Presentation Modules

It's extremely important to be able to present your product to the customer in an organized way, rather than rambling on at random. The first step is to break up your sales presentation into modules. You can then organize a "canned" presentation if needed (though this technique should be used sparingly). Better yet, you can adapt your sales pitch to each customer, without becoming disorganized, by assembling a set of modules suited to the customer at hand.

Go back to the benefit matrix you developed in Chapter 5. Then develop your sales presentation modules as follows:

A. Write down a short sales pitch—not more than 100 words—for each benefit.

B. Be sure the first sentence describes the benefit to the customer.

C. Then go on to tell the customer exactly what he will get—that is, describe the features relevant to that benefit.

D. Briefly back up your claim by citing proof or endorsements.

E. Rephrase and restate the benefit.

F. Now read the pitch out loud; imagine you are speaking to a customer. Ask a friend to listen, or tape-record it. Does it sound too stilted or formal? How effective is it? Revise it until it sounds natural when spoken.

These are your basic modules. They are to be used in conjunction with your benefit matrix. Practice a while with a friend posing as a customer until you can automatically use the matrix to select a benefit pitch for a given customer type or for a given feature question.

If you are selling an inexpensive product this is probably all you will need. For big-ticket items you should prepare the following supplementary sales pitches.

A. Benefits: This time use no length restriction. For each benefit go into detail. Make it as glowing and convincing as you can. Remember, for this one, focus on the benefit. Give examples of happy customers, invoke fantasy images, try to make the benefit real and tangible to the customer.

B. Demonstrations: For many products, the most powerful selling technique is a demonstration. That way the customer can actually see or feel or experience the benefits. But a demonstration is very demanding; don't just wander through the features—plan exactly how you will show them and in what order.

C. Features: Although you initially will focus on benefits, if the product is complex or technological you will have to be prepared to back up your features in considerable detail. When the knowledgeable customer asks for the technical details of a tweeter or a computer you must have them at your fingertips. So go down the list of features in advance and write out a detailed account of each one. You probably won't be able to memorize all this material, but at least you'll know where to look it up.

Stage 3: Close the Sale

Once you feel you have elicited and answered the customer's objections, you're ready for the third step: *closing the sale*. To close a sale is simply to induce the prospect to make a commitment to buy. It can take several forms: giving you a purchase order; signing a contract; handing over cash or a check. The amateur tends to see closing as automatic; answer all the objections, and the customer will go ahead and buy. The sales professional knows better. As the close approaches, the customer and the salesperson both experience increasing tension. This tension frightens the inexperienced salesperson; she tends to back off, to give up the close attempt, hoping the customer will somehow take the initiative and close the sale by himself. She's usually disappointed, for the tension also causes the customer to hesitate, and perhaps withdraw.

There are all sorts of specific sales closes. Some are more effective than others for particular products, or particular customers, or particular salespeople. Every salesperson has her favorite close. However, you should avoid picking out one "best" close. Try to master and apply as many different closes as possible.

Sales closes can be divided, a bit arbitrarily, into four primary types: request, pressure, negotiative, and assumptive.

The *request close* is simple and straightforward: you simply ask the customer for the sale. Scarcely subtle, but it is used quite effectively every day to sell products ranging from Girl Scout cookies to the services of prostitutes.

The request close is easy to master even for beginning salespeople. This straight-to-the-point approach saves time and can often stimulate a hesitant prospect into decision. Even if he doesn't buy on the spot, this close attempt may break loose an objection that you can try to counter.

The big disadvantage to the request close is that if it fails you've probably lost the sale. You've more or less demanded that the customer commit himself, and if he gives you a "no," it's hard to get a second chance. You have put him in a position where, in order to buy, he must reverse himself. Nobody likes to be caught waffling, and in a sales situation it's especially distasteful, because it suggests a lack of sales resistance.

The request close is best suited to small purchases. The customer is more likely to respond positively if the amount at stake is not too large. Also, for a small sale you will often find it uneconomic to spend a lot of time making the sale. The request close is nothing if not fast.

The most valuable use for the request close, however, is the subsidiary sale. After you've closed the main sale, use the request close to add value to the sale. The classic example is the gas-station close: "Fill 'er up?" See if the customer will buy more—or buy accessories, extra features, even an additional main product. This can be especially productive when you've just closed a big-ticket item. Often the customer assumes a go-for-broke attitude and readily buys add-ons that she wouldn't even have considered before she committed to the big purchase. Sales resistance, once neutralized, may be slow to recover—so when you make a big sale, don't take a break but push ahead and exploit your success.

Next we come to the *pressure close*. Like all closes, this approach is intended either to force a commitment or else make the prospect expose her objections. As the name implies, the pressure close involves a direct pressure on the prospect. There are several varieties.

The negative time-limit close tells the customer that if she doesn't buy now, the deal will get worse—or even disappear. Examples: "This is the last day at this price—it's going up 20 percent tomorrow." "This is the last one we have in stock." "They say interest rates are going up, so you should finance it now to keep your payments low."

The closely related positive time-limit close offers the prospect an inducement to act promptly. Examples: "We're having a special sale on it today." "You get a set of batteries free if you buy before Friday." "The author is here today autographing copies."

The famous Franklin Ledger is a highly effective pressure close. Here you sit down with the customer and list the positive and negative factors of the purchase on a sheet of paper. It's the openness and fairness of this objective, judicial procedure that puts pressure on the reluctant prospect. He is faced with the choice between admitting that the positives outweigh the negatives (at which point he has no excuse not to buy) or bringing out his hidden objections and writing them on the negative side (which gives you the chance to deal with them). It takes practice to handle this technique smoothly, but the results can be well worth it.

The *negotiative close* operates rather more subtly. Instead of applying pressure to the prospect, you suddenly remove it, so that her own momentum carries her into commitment. How? The key idea is to open a negotiation—to say in effect, "What should I offer you to induce you to buy?"

One very powerful negotiative close is the judo close. To apply this technique, you must identify the customer's major objection. Deal with the less important objections normally, but withhold your answer to the major item. Instead, encourage the prospect to elaborate on it, to emphasize it. Then, when you're sure you thoroughly understand her problem, state it back to her for confirmation. Get her agreement that this is her real objection—and finally, come back with a complete answer. The sudden disappearance of the problem that she herself emphasized will leave her with little alternative but to buy.

Another variety is the subjunctive close. Again, you must start with a key objection. Use this to ask the customer for a conditional commitment. Example: "Would you buy if I could get you one with chartreuse ventricles?" Note that this is most effective if kept in the subjunctive, even though you of course know that you can perform. Much less effective is: "I can get you one with chartreuse ventricles. Will you buy?"

Most subtle and powerful of the negotiative closes is the Clarkson close. To use this, you must get the prospect asking questions. Then respond with an offer phrased as a question. Example: Customer: "Could I get it in pink?" Salesperson: "Do you want it in pink?" Chances are he'll answer yes—and you've closed.

The whole point of the negotiative close is to give the prospect the initiative. Once he is induced to *make a demand*, he can frequently be closed simply by granting the demand.

Most subtle of all is the *assumptive close*. The idea here is to make buying the path of least resistance. You simply assume that the prospect will buy; in order to refuse, he must then actively object.

One approach is the implied-consent close. Here you simply ask a question that assumes that the prospect will buy. If he doesn't object, you've closed. Examples: "Shall I ship this to your Stockton plant?" "Will you be using your credit card to pay for this?"

Also effective is the agreement close. To use this, when you start your close attempt, you pull out a blank "agreement" form. As you discuss the customer's wants, you fill in the blanks. When everything is specified, slide it in front of him and ask, "Would you check to see that I have everything correct? Yes? If you'll just sign right here . . ."

> Especially in consumer sales, it's much better to use an "agreement" than a "contract." An "agreement" using ordinary English is just as legal and binding as a "contract" strewn with whereases and heretofores. In fact, it may be more binding, because the other signatory would find it difficult to claim that she didn't understand what she was signing.

The assumptive closes sound easy but in practice are the hardest to carry off. Don't try them until you have perfect confidence in yourself and your product.

Again, it's important not to get into a rut. Try to practice a variety of closes. A big sale is seldom closed on the first attempt. If the customer balks, you must back up and try something different. You need to know a number of techniques so you don't have to repeat yourself.

Above all, don't drop the sale because a close fails. Remember that the purpose of a close is *twofold:* either to get a purchase commitment or to make the prospect expose an objection. If either of these objectives is attained, the close has served its purpose. Simply keep trying closes until the customer runs out of objections.

Checklist 7–1: Sales Closes

Have you and each member of your sales team mastered all of the following closing techniques? This means not only knowing how to execute the close, but understanding when each one will be most effective.

☐ Request Close
☐ Negative Time-Limit Close
☐ Positive Time-Limit Close
☐ Franklin Ledger
☐ Judo Close
☐ Subjunctive Close
☐ Clarkson Close
☐ Implied-Consent Close
☐ Agreement Close

Stage 4: The Follow-Up

We now come to the fourth, and most often neglected, phase of the sales process. After you've closed the sale, *follow up*. Every customer should be regarded as an asset to be cherished—not a throwaway disposable.

It's very common, after a purchase has been made—especially if it's a big-ticket item—for the buyer to have second thoughts. Once she's got what she wanted, it may not look as enticing. And once she's committed to pay, the money tends to look larger. You can give sales a real boost by dealing with "buyer remorse" effectively.

Begin by following up your successful close with reinforcement. Congratulate the customer on her ownership of such a fine product. Remind her about the features she particularly liked. Above all, get it into her hands and operational as fast as possible—the longer she has to wait for delivery, the more opportunity she has for second thoughts. And, until she actually takes possession, she feels that the sale isn't complete—regardless of the legalities—and is more inclined to cancel.

Of course, thank her. Consider augmenting your verbal thanks at the time of the sale with a written note sent a few days later. Better yet, provide the customer with an unexpected bonus.

> We bought a house. Finally, all the paperwork was done and moving day arrived. We started early in the morning, and it was exhausting (190 shelf feet of books, among other things). Around noon we had just started to wonder what to do about lunch—and Juanita, our broker, arrived with a box of fried chicken.

Another important factor in follow-up is service. This is especially critical if you're selling an innovative product—first, because it may not be sufficiently debugged; and second, because the customer may not know how to use it effectively. The key point in our present discussion is that salespeople must be involved in service work.

At first they may not like it. Salespeople tend to see service work as a diversion from selling. But there are very good reasons to discourage them from washing their hands of past customers.

First, the salesperson knows the customer and her concerns. If a problem arises, a nonsales service person will have to gather all this information starting from scratch—and every minute he spends on it not only costs you money but makes the customer more irritated. Often the salesperson can solve in 30 seconds a problem that could tie up an expensive technician for hours.

Second, doing service work increases the salesperson's knowledge of the product, its strengths and weaknesses. It also teaches him a lot about his customers that he might not otherwise learn. And, unlike service technicians, the salesperson has a strong, direct personal incentive to prevent or correct QC and other problems. If your salespeople have to deal with complaints, you can be sure management will hear about problems—quickly.

Third, the customer doesn't like to be shuttled around.

There's nothing she hates more than being bounced from one anonymous telephone voice to another, each one saying, "It's not my department, but if you'll hold, I'll transfer you to . . ." From her point of view, the ideal situation is that she deals with only one person in your organization—she wants one specific, accessible, and motivated person to be responsible for keeping her happy. And she already knows the salesperson.

Fourth, past customers are your best source of new sales. Usually, you can make a new sale to an established customer with a tiny fraction of the time and effort it would require to develop a new one. What's more, your best source of new customers is referrals from your current customers.

Push follow-up. You'll be surprised what an edge it can give you over the competition. Your salespeople will become enthusiastic about it once they've seen the results—especially the reduced need for cold calls!

YOUR SALES ARMY

An oft-used analogy compares selling to fighting a war. Marketing is the general, sitting in headquarters mapping strategy. The sales managers are the field-grade officers, directing and inspiring the units in contact with the enemy. The salespeople are the grunts who actually do the fighting. The main value of this simile is that it suggests the special importance of morale in dealing with the sales force.

It is hard to find a business activity more unpleasant than making cold calls. As one sales trainer puts it, most people would find it more pleasant to stand in a cold shower and rip up ten-dollar bills. It takes real determination to make that first call, and even more fortitude to keep it up after a dozen or so rejections.

As stated earlier, every entrepreneur has to be a salesperson at least occasionally, and anyone can learn enough salesmanship to handle this need. But to sell full-time, day in and day out, is *not* for everyone. The professional salesperson, like the professional soldier, needs a special aptitude. She also needs a lot of support from above.

To nonsales types, the hoopla that surrounds selling activities can seem very childish. However, pep rallies, slogans, bonus parties, contests, awards, and so on can be valuable tools to keep your sales forces turning out to face another day of turn-downs and put-downs.

What do your salespeople need from you in order to function effectively? First, confidence in your product. Second, backup and support. Third, morale stroking. Let's take these in turn.

Salespeople, like soldiers, fight poorly for a cause they do not believe in. To convince customers that your product is good, your salespeople must believe in it themselves. So your first task is to sell your salespeople on the virtues of your product, your service, and your company. Begin with training. All salespeople should know the product thoroughly. This not only equips them to deal with customer objections, it gives them self-confidence. Your training should include a strong grounding not only in the features, operation, and applications of your product but also in your company's sales and service procedures.

The salespeople's specific duties are closing sales, maintaining customer satisfaction, and providing market intelligence. That's plenty. Don't ask them to do anything else, and help them as much as possible to make the essential tasks easy. Minimize their paperwork, and make that unavoidable minimum simple and convenient to fill out. Make sure sales administration is performed by clerical personnel—not by the salespeople. And make sure it runs smoothly; quotations, price lists, credit OKs, specification changes should be provided quickly, conveniently, and reliably. If there's any foul-up or delay on an order, inform the salesperson at once so that he can cover himself with the customer. Above all, make it clear throughout the company that sales problems have priority in the use of administrative resources. The controller's important memo about paper-clip consumption can get typed *after* the quotation requested by a new customer.

The sales clerk was just about to close a customer on an expensive camera—when the phone rang. A delivery-truck driver needed instructions in detail, and got them, while the customer fumed. No matter how shorthanded you are,

make a special effort to shield your salespeople from interruption while they're selling. The telephone is a particularly obnoxious offender. If you have a sales floor, consider
laying it out without telephones—or, if you must have
them, disabling the bells so it's impossible to call in.

Even with all this, salespeople still need to be stroked,
praised, and encouraged. Here again, it's a real advantage to
ride along with a salesperson regularly. You'll be reminded of
the difficulties and discouragements she has to face every
working day. She'll realize that top management really understands and cares about her problems.

COMPENSATION AND MOTIVATION

The compensation of sales personnel presents special problems
because of the importance of motivation. Unfortunately, one
cannot lay down exact rules in advance; each industry has its
own needs, and you'll have to be guided by the usual approach
in your industry in setting commissions, quotas, bonuses, and
other incentives. You may be tempted to try a few innovations
in this area. Be careful. It's the salesperson's bread and butter
you're tampering with. Try to work within the familiar structure if possible; if not, make the new incentives augment rather
than replace the traditional payments.

In structuring sales compensation, it is exceptionally important to tie incentives properly to objectives. A straight
commission based on sales volume may motivate neglect of
high-profit items for other products that offer easy volume. It's
common to offer bonuses for specific goals such as signing new
customers, selling some of a specific item every month, or
achieving a sales goal before a given deadline. Such objectives
may be valid, but consider possible pitfalls carefully before
imposing them. The danger is that this type of incentive may
work too well. Remember that concentrating effort in one area
almost invariably reduces it in other areas.

Consider the examples given. Salespeople, in signing new
customers, may neglect the old ones—and the new ones may
not last long if they were given one-time incentives to get that
single sale. The "sell some X every month" bonus may result in

a large order being chopped into several smaller ones, to the inconvenience and expense of Production and Administration. Contests or bonuses with a time limit may cause sales to be "borrowed" from the future. Special incentives must be structured very carefully, introduced on an experimental basis before full implementation, and constantly monitored to analyze results.

A final but by no means minor point in sales tactics is deploying your troops efficiently.

> You can observe the effects of mismanaged sales incentives by trying the following experiment. Go to any department store. Walk into the men's suits section, pick a sleeve at random, and feel the fabric. Suddenly the stillness of this deserted area will be broken as half a dozen salesmen descend on you simultaneously, like piranha attacking a lump of meat. Then, if you can break away, go over to the shoe department. You'll find the chairs filled with impatient customers, and one frantic clerk rushing back and forth trying to fit them all.

Checklist 7–2: Sales Planning

☐ Have you designated one specific person as responsible for sales?

☐ Have you made it clear to that person that sales must have top priority over other duties?

☐ Have you arranged for at least rudimentary sales training for all employees who have customer contact?

☐ Have you got a list of common—and unusual—customer objections?

☐ Have you developed a complete set of sales modules for your product, and trained your personnel in their use?

☐ Does each salesperson have the ability to use at least six different closes to sell your product?

☐ Have you made sure that each and every customer will be thanked for his purchase?

☐ Have you made every conceivable effort to get your product into the customer's hands as quickly as possible?

☐ Have you thought of a special, unexpected bonus you can add to each sale?

- [ ] Do all of your salespeople clearly understand that they are responsible for service to their customers?
- [ ] Do you have systems to ensure that each salesperson keeps track of past customers?
- [ ] Does your sales-training program ensure that every salesperson is thoroughly familiar with your product?
- [ ] Have you definitely eliminated all superfluous paperwork for your salespeople?
- [ ] Have you made it clear to all administrative people that sales jobs have priority?
- [ ] Have you taken precautions to prevent interruptions of sales?
- [ ] Have you set up a program to provide regular sales contact for each member of top management?
- [ ] Have you developed a procedure to test your sales incentives and monitor their effectiveness?
- [ ] Do you have a system to move salespeople to the areas where they are most productive?

CAUTIONARY TALE: PRINTING MONEY

After the FOTO COMP disaster, I founded another venture aimed at the publishing industry which was much more successful. At the time, typesetting was done manually, whether using the traditional Linotype or more modern machinery. One could of course do photo-offset from computer printout, but this was considered unacceptable because computer printers produced a distinctive, and ugly, typeface.

So there was a great deal of interest when a machine became available that would do true computer typesetting. Several companies bought these machines and went into the business of providing computer typesetting services to publishers. Sedgwick Printout Systems was one of them. I set up this company in partnership with the Courier Journal Louisville Times Co.

Now, we had nothing proprietary; we didn't make the machines, we bought them, and anyone else who had the money could buy one too. And we were, if anything, *less* proficient in the technology than some of our competitors. We competed and won by understanding the market and being better salespeople.

In the 1960s it was already clear that computerization was the future of the publishing industry—and publishers were scared to death. There was a lot of talk about the new methods, but nobody wanted to be first. The first high-speed typesetter was a tremendous technological advance. But it was much more expensive than the old machines, and the output was not quite as good-looking. Above all, though one could spew print out of the computer very rapidly indeed, one still had to get the material *into* the computer. So as a typesetting device, the machine was really no more than a souped-up Linotype. You still had an operator at one end keying the stuff into the machine, and type coming out the other end; only the machinery in between was different. So why should publishers pay the extra cost and take the risk involved in switching?

Our competitors' answer was: "This is hot, new, state-of-the-art technology! Look at our gleaming gadgetry! Look at the beards on our programmers! Isn't all this just too exciting for words?" This approach was not just unproductive, it was counterproductive. The more publishers heard about complex new technology, the more nervous they got.

Sedgwick Printout took an entirely different tack. I perceived the one critical advance provided by the high-speed typesetter: *while the text was in the computer it could be revised.* This was unimportant to most publishers; they set type, print the book, and throw away the type. But database publishers—those who published directories, dictionaries, encyclopedias, reference works, and so on—have to make revisions in every edition.

Consider, for instance, how a dictionary was handled in those days. Each entry was kept on a three-by-five card. For a new edition, these thousands upon thousands of cards would be spread out on long tables, and the staff would go through them by hand, putting in new cards and removing old ones. Then it was off to the warehouse, where the lead type of the previous edition was stored. For each obsolete entry, the entire plug line had to be removed. Meanwhile the new entries, hot off the Linotype, had to be inserted. Of course, this would throw off all the pagination, so they then had to go through all the type and rearrange it by hand. . . . Obviously these people, unlike the typical book publisher, had a real need for our service. We could put their whole database on the computer and store it. They could revise it easily at any time, and even pull out segments for separate printing if they wanted. So we concentrated entirely on database publishers—a key decision.

Still, we couldn't have succeeded if we hadn't used some highly effective sales tactics.

First, we had to realize that the publisher that bought our service would be changing its whole method of operation. We therefore had to focus on selling the top people in the company. It would have been a waste of time to approach the production people in the publishing house—as our competitors were doing—because they didn't have the authority to make such sweeping changes. So I made it a rule to go straight to the top. To facilitate this, we set up headquarters in Manhattan—the heart of the publishing industry.

Second, I plugged away continuously on making everyone in our company sales-oriented. Every member of the staff had to be qualified for customer contact. This included the technical people. In the nature of the business, our programmers and other technicians had to work intimately with the customers to adapt their procedures to the new technology. I made it a personal crusade to stamp out computer jargon in these communications and force our technical wizards to speak English to the customers.

Third, I realized that we were selling a rather intangible service, and that our customers—publishers—were accustomed by the nature of their business to put a lot of emphasis on appearance. I insisted that our entire operation present a class look in every way. I wanted a quality appearance to our office, our personnel, and most particularly our printed literature and brochures, which would be going into the hands of real pros.

Along with this, I worked to develop a reputation as a significant expert in this field. There was a lot of interest in the new methods in the publishing industry, and it wasn't hard to get a high profile. I gave speeches, participated in workshops, and wrote articles on high-speed typesetting. The aura of expertise thus attached to my name rubbed off on the company, which had the same name.

We had to educate our market—something that is necessary with almost any new product. You can regard this either as a terrible hassle or as an opportunity to get your company a good reputation with your customers. We took the latter tack. I got off to a good start at a major meeting of publishers and printers with a very dramatic presentation that attracted a lot of attention. (One trade journal's description: ". . . and then the microphone was given to Harry Sedgwick of Sedgwick Printout Systems, who, like a windstorm in a wheat field . . .")

But in personal sales calls I took a low-key, soft-sell approach. All of our competitors were making exaggerated claims, glossing over the problems, and offering wildly optimistic estimates of the time and money needed to convert. I, on the other hand, would spend a great deal of time explaining to a publishing-company president what the problems would be. The editors would be dealing with an entirely different medium. They would be using computer printout and editing voluminous information. Mistakes would be made in converting from manual files to computer files, and careful proof-reading would be required. It would cost far more than the initial estimates, because computer estimates in those days were always too optimistic. It would take far longer than anybody anticipated, because human factors would get in the way, and they should prepare for that and plan for it. By explaining it this way, I lowered their expectations, and they got a growing confidence that my concern was to convey to them the truth about this new technology and not to wow them with high-tech phrases. This gave us a major advantage in credibility compared to our competition.

Basically, we presented the contract as a capital expenditure, with a lot of expense and hassle up front but a big payoff once the new system was in place.

Another way we built credibility was to refrain from announcing new contracts. Our competitors blew a loud fanfare every time they landed a sale—followed by an embarrassed silence as they ran into the inevitable problems getting the system set up. We didn't say a word until we finished and everything was running smoothly. *Then* we announced that Sedgwick Printout had installed another success-ful system—and, with the satisfied customer's assistance, we put out a glossy brochure showing what we had accomplished and circu-lated it to new prospects. Since the customers had names like Standard & Poor's and The New York Times Index, these brochures developed a lot of credibility.

Although we focused primarily on the top people when making a sale, we had to take into account some of the others. The art director was usually an enemy. Our output, if one looked closely, was not quite as sharp as conventional methods could produce; one art director brought in photomicrographs to prove it. On the other hand, the marketing people freaked out when we explained the options that would now be available. For years they had dreamed of being able to, say, pull out all the names in Arizona from the database and make up a separate directory for local sales. They'd always been told that it would be impossibly expensive. Now, we pointed out, this and similar projects would become absurdly easy. In this way we developed some powerful allies in each company.

My whole approach was to jump into the buyer's head and try to see his problems and his point of view. If he didn't really need our service, I went away. Why waste his time, not to mention mine? But if he did need our service, he couldn't get me off with a barnacle remover. I would cling to him relentlessly until I got that sale. All very low-key, of course. An occasional phone call, a copy of an article, a brochure—but it just wouldn't stop until he bought. This Chinese water torture would usually bring results.

I had a brilliant idea for breaking into the market that almost backfired. We were aiming at database publishers, and I chose as our initial target one that was totally conspicuous in the publishing industry: R. R. Bowker, publishers of *Books in Print*. Of course everybody in the book business knows them, so if they signed up it would be a highly visible feather in our cap.

Well, they did sign up. But perhaps I wasn't quite low-key enough, because they were more optimistic than we were. They had appeared at the Frankfurt Book Fair for decades, and this year they wanted to show up with their latest edition done by the new computer typesetting. I told them we couldn't make it, but they brushed it off. Of course we didn't make it, which was embarrassing. If only that had been all. We also left out two whole letters of the alphabet—L and N—and it wasn't caught until the books had been bound.

What could I say? There was nothing for it but to admit it frankly and put the best face on it we could. I wrote up a press release describing the heroic efforts of Sedgwick Printout and R. R. Bowker to make the switch to this revolutionary new technology in a thrilling race against a tight deadline. Then I frankly conceded that we'd fluffed it, and explained that Bowker had set up an 800 number that people could call if they wanted to know about a book that began with L or N. They quickly got out a supplement, of course. Oddly enough, this incident seemed to work in our favor. Publishers were a bit fed up with the hype and broken promises of our competitors, so we looked refreshingly honest. Probably the fact that Bowker was also at fault (they really should have caught the omission in proofreading, though of course we carefully didn't say so) helped a bit too.

Sedgwick Printout did extremely well. After a few years I decided I was ready for something new, and I sold out my interest to the partner for a tidy sum.

It was a very valuable lesson in effective selling. Unfortunately, the sales training that most people get in this country is the full-speed-ahead, high-pressure, take-it-to-them approach. Managers don't even get that; face-to-face selling is not taught in any business school I know of. That is considered to be an activity beneath the dignity of the exalted executive-to-be. But the fact is that we must sell all the time—whether it's a piece of soap or a major financial deal. The higher you rise in business, the bigger and more critical the sales you have to make. And the need to identify with those to whom you are selling is absolutely critical to the transaction.

I think the thing to be kept in mind in selling almost anything is that your customer is ultimately your partner—the most important partner your business has. Unless you can sell your product and keep on selling it, you fail. Just as you must with a financial partner or a technical partner, you must look beyond the transaction itself to make sure that the partner is satisfied in the long term; otherwise you haven't got a business. First find out if there is a community of interest between you and the buyer. If there isn't, you might as well go away. If there is, you must build that community of interest into a permanent partnership with the customer.

HDS

8

PRODUCTION

This great increase of the quantity of work, which, in consequence of the division of labor, the same number of people are capable of performing, is owing to three different circumstances: first, to the increase of dexterity in every particular workman; secondly, to the saving of the time which is commonly lost in passing from one species of work to another; and lastly, to the invention of a great number of machines which facilitate and abridge labor, and enable one man to do the work of many.

Adam Smith
*The Wealth of Nations**

"Production" conjures up images of manufacturing—machine tools, riveters, assembly lines. But we use the word here in a much more general sense. Essentially every business has some sort of production function, because every business must create value for the customer. In a manufacturing company the production process is obvious. But in a service company, the performance of services is production. Somebody in the company has got to make, or do, something for the customer—and that process, whatever it may be, is production.

*(Chicago: Henry Regnery Co., 1953), pp. 13–14.

WHERE EXPERIENCE COUNTS MOST

In production, more than in any other aspect of business, experience is important. A marketer who's never sold a widget before can learn how without difficulty. An engineer who's never designed a widget before can develop an excellent prototype. But if you've never manufactured a widget before, you are likely to be in trouble. Successful production is highly dependent on know-how. This is true almost regardless of the industry.

> The chemical producer should know how to prevent air pollution by running certain processes under a partial vacuum to prevent leaks. This and a thousand other similar tricks make the difference between a clean, efficient chemical plant and a dangerous one.
>
> The restaurateur must know where to buy good fresh meat and vegetables and how to select them—as well as be proficient in cooking techniques that can be perfected only with practice.
>
> The warehouse manager must know not only what type of forklift to buy but also how to handle employees so as to minimize pilferage.

In each industry, there are a number of critical production skills that virtually demand hands-on experience. It's rather like training a doctor—after all the lectures, the textbook illustrations, the demonstrations, it's still necessary for an experienced doctor to take the intern into the wards, place her hands on some patients, and explain: "If it feels like this it's a tumor, but if it feels like this one it's only a cyst." We therefore strongly recommend that you have production experience in your chosen industry. If you don't, be sure you get a cofounder, or at a minimum a key employee, who does.

THE LEARNING CURVE

The importance of experience in production is expressed in the theory of the "learning curve." Simply stated, this theory asserts that among companies competing to make a certain product, the most efficient producer will be the one with the most experience—that is, the one with the highest cumulative unit output. The idea is that productivity rises with increasing experience; therefore, marketing policy should emphasize rapid acquisition of market share and sale of large volumes so as to move down the learning curve faster than competitors.

The problem with the learning-curve theory is that it is based on studies of large companies, where dozens or hundreds of individuals are involved in production management and the effects of their varied talents average out. In a small company, this statistical blur disappears. Your progress down the learning curve will depend not so much on how many units you've shipped as on how hard you've worked at learning from that experience. In reality, production expertise is not an automatic consequence of experience; it requires effort and ingenuity to learn from experience.

MANAGING PRODUCTION

The management of production has three objectives. First, the production process should be reliable—the product should be finished at the predicted time. Second, the product should be of high quality. Third, production costs should be low.

Traditionally, production management has been perceived as a matter of optimizing the trade-off between these three goals. The modern approach, imported from Japan, is to view these apparently conflicting objectives as actually complementary. Over the long run, they are. A smooth-running and reliable production process lowers costs—partly because it minimizes downtime and partly because its predictability facilitates planning and inexpensive purchasing. Attention to quality, properly handled, improves reliability, since rework interferes with production schedules—and it reduces costs, since scrap and rework are expensive. And, ironically, cost cutting can contribute to higher quality, for money saved by eliminating waste can be applied to buying improved raw materials.

Ensuring Production Reliability

The hardest task for a new business is developing a reliable production process. Nothing is more embarrassing than announcing a new product, accepting purchase orders, and then running into production problems—postponing delivery dates again and again as your salespeople phone the irritated customers with increasingly weak excuses. This kind of snafu is the bane of new companies. Your customers, who may have gone out on a limb to give your start-up a break, will hear from their friends, their colleagues—and their bosses—"See? I told you so. You should have gone with IBM." Broken delivery promises will at best inflict long-lasting damage on your reputation, and at worst sink you before you've really started.

A valuable stop-gap expedient for start-ups is jobbing out parts of the production process. Many young ventures make a mistake in trying to "cut costs" by vertical integration. "We'll smelt our own steel, roll it, draw it into wire, and wind the coils for the frammistan. Think of the money we'll save—iron ore is really cheap." This is a poor idea. By the time you master the intricacies of all those extra production steps, there will be cobwebs on your customers. Your savings on the cheap raw materials will be eaten up and more by your losses on production hang-ups. Vertical integration is for big, established companies in mature industries, and it has significant risks even for them. You should focus on the key step of production.

By "key step" we mean that step which you intend as your company's contribution. The ultimate justification for being in business is your ability to produce something better than anyone else. Somewhere along the long line between the iron ore and the completed widget there is presumably a step that you can handle better than any other company. Identify it. That is the step you should perform, and ideally it should be the only step you perform, at least at the start. Job out everything else. In this way you can get to the market quickly and minimize the difficulty of your production task. It's true that more highly finished materials and outside services will cost more—but this is really only appearance. If you do operations you're unfamiliar with in-house, it will almost always cost more than jobbing it out; the experts are usually so much more efficient than amateurs that they can cover their costs and profits and still be cheaper—that's why they're in business.

My style is to job out everything I possibly can. An example of this is what's going on right now. I am dictating into a machine; the tape will go to a typing service in the Empire State Building called QED, which will transcribe my comments and send them to Ron in Los Angeles, who will then clean up and organize my disjointed thoughts. I don't employ a secretary or own a typewriter. My job is to provide the fruits of wisdom and experience; the rest I job out.

In the case of Private Products, we jobbed out everything. The company had one employee, and we did six million a year. Not bad. On paper, we could have cut costs a lot by doing our own manufacturing, packaging, and so on. In practice, it would have meant a tremendous burden on management time. Had the 16 people working on the assembly line come in on time? Were they stealing? How was the foreman getting along with them? And so on. We would have had to rent space, worry about the ceiling leaking, buy insurance—all these costs would have eaten up our "savings" and we would have been distracted from selling the product. When the business got really large it became worthwhile to bring production in-house, but by that time we'd sold it to Coca Cola.

So my approach to this is that in the early stages of a business, you farm out everything. In fact, you don't want to own anything. In the old days, when you started a business, you bought land, built a building, put in equipment, and started up. Now, if you're smart, you spend all that money marketing. When and if you have a market, *then* you worry about whether or not it's cost-effective to integrate vertically.

One important caveat: this principle of farming out as much work as you can doesn't necessarily apply to do-it-yourself projects in setting up or improving your company's facility. Often building your own machinery or installing your own plumbing can save critical cash in your start-up phase. But don't do any more of the *production process* than you absolutely have to.

An obvious corollary is to minimize your product variety. Ideally a start-up should have only one product, and a new item should be added to the line only when production of the old one has been thoroughly debugged. This factor, however, is not really under the control of Production. The production manager can, and should, argue the point with Marketing, but if a variety of models is really demanded by the market he will have to find a way to make them. What he can do is insist that the new products be as similar as possible to the old ones in design, materials, and manufacturing process. By working closely with Marketing and R&D he should be able to come up with a reasonable if not perfect solution.

Although the two maxims just discussed can help cut the manufacturing problem down to size, they by no means eliminate it. But there are three principles that will do much to increase the reliability of your production if you apply them religiously.

First, every production problem that comes up—and they will come up—should be corrected *permanently.* Give yourself a black mark for any problem that occurs twice. Yes, this is trivial and obvious. But very few organizations actually put it into practice. Each fire is forgotten as soon as it's under control. There seems to be no reason to worry about preventing it next time—there are too many other problems to worry about. But each of those distracting problems represents a previous fire that was not quite put out, then allowed to smolder until it broke out again. If you make it a policy to concentrate on the immediate problem and don't leave it until you fix it for good, after a while you'll find there are a lot fewer problems.

Of course, it's easy to say, "Fix it permanently." The reason it's often neglected in practice is that it isn't all that easy to find lasting solutions. Quick fixes are much easier. The difficulty lies in discovering the basic cause and developing an understanding of the problem. If you don't understand how your process works and what has gone wrong, your efforts at correction will be confined to trial and error—a method notoriously slow, inefficient, and unreliable. Instead of trying changes at random—or even changes based on guesswork— conduct a systematic investigation of the source of the problem. This is painful. When you're under heavy pressure to get the line running again it's tempting to opt for trial and error, which offers at least the possibility of a quick solution. ("We're resetting the spring tension—if it works, we'll be up again tomorrow.") The systematic approach requires you to make an unavoidable investment of downtime. ("We'll disassemble

Unit 3 and test each roller at different speeds until we find the problem. It will take at least two weeks.") But this investment tends to pay off in the long run, and even in the short run.

In manufacturing a complex catalyst, a serious problem developed when an intermediate turned out to be impure. We isolated the impurity chromatographically and sent it out for analysis—which required two weeks. But from the spectrum it was immediately clear that the intermediate, contrary to its reported chemistry, had reacted with the solvent. A simple modification of the procedure quickly and permanently eliminated the problem. Since it was "known" that no such reaction could occur, we might never have hit upon the solution by trial and error.

Production will solve process problems much more quickly if there is a permanent troubleshooting team from R&D on call. The team's assistance will be greatly amplified if it is provided with adequate records. Troubleshooting boils down to an effort to connect cause and effect by making comparisons between various results.

Another chemical process gave intermittent problems over a period of years. Usually it worked, but sometimes one of the intermediates turned into a useless, sticky gum. In this case the critical information was the dates; all of the bad batches occurred during July or August. The intermediate in question was known to be sensitive to water, and summer in New Jersey is like living in a Turkish bath. We had merely to improve our precautions for protecting the material from atmospheric moisture.

Keeping complete and detailed records is a nuisance, but this is another investment in time that pays off dramatically when you get in trouble. Follow a simple principle: if you know it, record it. If you don't know it, find out, then record it. Many important things are obvious: the supplier and lot number of materials; the name of the operator; any unusual events during the production run. But the toughest production problems result from factors that nobody kept track of because they were "obviously irrelevant."

There is a story, possibly apocryphal, of an electronic

gadget that developed quality problems suddenly, for no apparent reason. After tearing their hair for weeks, the engineers working on the problem found the cause: one of the women working on the assembly line had changed her brand of lipstick. Experiments established that it was necessary for the person working at that particular position to wear a certain brand of lipstick, or the gadgets coming off the line wouldn't work properly.

Obviously you can't keep a record of details at that level; you'll have to draw the line somewhere. But draw it as low as possible, and draw it especially low around production steps with frequent problems. You'll want to design your information-gathering procedures carefully to make it as convenient as possible for your people to record the data.

Finally, a major factor in production reliability is preventive maintenance. This is where established concerns have an advantage over most start-ups. They've learned by bitter experience that the policy "If it ain't broke, don't fix it" means in practice that it will break just when you don't have time to fix it. Skipping preventive maintenance is enormously tempting in the early days of your company. When you're desperately busy with jobs that clearly *have* to be done, to waste time on "do it once a week whether it needs it or not" chores seems hopelessly illogical. The benefits of preventive maintenance are invisible—the breakdowns that *don't* occur—but nonetheless valuable.

Ensuring Product Quality

In recent years the Japanese have taught us an important lesson about quality control. American managers have usually regarded low quality as a means of lowering costs—though one might or might not choose to apply this option. Japanese managers have learned to regard low quality as a production problem. Low quality is an indication that something is wrong in the production process and should be fixed; fixing it will not necessarily raise costs and may well lower them.

Quality control is by no means restricted to manufactured goods. Whatever you sell—services, information, entertainment—quality can be defined, measured, and controlled. Much of the immense and rapidly growing literature on quality control is of limited relevance to small business, unfortunately. It deals with rather elaborate statistical methods that are hard to apply to a small operation—not so much because the procedures are too complex, but because sample sizes are too small to produce reliable conclusions. We'll give this area only a brief summary and refer you to more detailed treatment elsewhere (see the Bibliography).

The first step is to define "quality" for your product. Of course, quality is ultimately judged by your customers.

> American auto buyers traditionally judge the soundness of a car's construction literally by sound—the sound made when the door is slammed. Detroit long ago learned that a certain sound gives the optimum impression—though technically it has no connection with actual quality—and designed car doors accordingly.

Market research should tell you what your customers value. Then you must try to quantify it. This is frequently tricky, but it can usually be done. Most quality criteria boil down to four categories: performance, reliability, durability, and appearance. For manufactured goods, it is usually not difficult to devise quantitative definitions for the first three, though appearance may be tougher. For, say, a service business, such definitions may be less obvious, but they can be found. For instance, a Chinese restaurant might define performance with numbers such as the average time customers must wait for their order; reliability by the number of complaints per thousand customers; and durability by the average time until a customer gets hungry again.

Once defined, quality must be continuously and systematically measured. To the typical business, quality measurement equals "final inspection" and the big question is whether to do 100-percent testing or sample each batch. But this "one-point" measurement approach misses important opportunities. You should make quality measurement a process that operates all the way through the production cycle and beyond.

Start by breaking down your quality definitions into criteria for the various segments of your product. Then set up regular measurements all the way through the production process; check quality at each stage. This has two advantages. First, when a problem arises, you don't have to do much detective work to find out when and where the mistake was made; it's obviously at or before the stage where defects began to appear. Second, you cut waste dramatically by stopping defective units immediately instead of finishing them and then having to scrap or rework.

Even more neglected is quality follow-up after sale. Often, a quality problem will not show up until the product has been used for months or years. Such defects may be missed even by "torture testing." Use your service department to acquire data on how your product fails in use—and when—and how often. Ask market research to survey your customers also.

Finally, quality must be controlled. This is where the Japanese approach really pays off. If you define quality criteria carefully and measure quality continuously through the production process and beyond, the control will almost take care of itself. Knowing what a problem is and where it is occurring is 90 percent of the battle.

Checklist 8–1: Production Reliability and Quality Control

☐ Examine every step of the process to see if it can be jobbed out.
☐ Minimize product variety.
☐ Keep complete process records right from the start.
☐ Establish a preventive-maintenance program.
☐ Develop quality criteria, using market input.
☐ Establish a QA program in cooperation with your suppliers.
☐ Measure quality during process.
☐ Monitor quality of final product.
☐ Establish a program with customers to monitor quality in use of the product.

Controlling Production Costs

The third responsibility of Production is to make the product at low cost.

The first step in achieving lower production costs is knowing what your costs are. As soon as you pronounce this question, your office window will shatter and there, flying through a spray of broken glass, cape flowing in the wind, will land . . . your accountant. She can solve all your cost-control problems, it seems—tell you exactly how profitable each of your products is, determine where your inventory costs are worst, locate wasted materials. Of course, she'll need more complete data from you, a little more record keeping. To start with, each of your production workers should keep a log, and note what he's working on every five minutes . . .

Cost accounting has a long and honorable history. But one of the major problems of modern business management is that cost accounting is obsolete, and that there is no well-accepted replacement for it.

Cost accounting reached its zenith in the nineteenth century. Imagine a factory in 1880, making, let's say, paper clips and staples. It employs 200 people—195 production workers, 2 clerks, 2 salesmen, and the president. The owner wishes to know how profitable each of his two products is. Cost accounting is quite straightforward; the accountant simply makes up a little chart as in Figure 8–1.

Figure 8–1.   Smith & Co. Clips & Staples—Statement of annual costs.

Cost Item		Clips	Staples
Raw materials		$80,000	$40,000
Direct labor		50,000	30,000
Depreciation (mach.)		20,000	5,000
Total direct costs		150,000	75,000
		(67%)	(33%)
Office salaries	8,000		
Depreciation (G&A)	7,000		
Overhead	15,000		
allocated 67:33		10,000	5,000
Total costs		$160,000	$80,000

The 1880 company has $225,000 in direct costs, which can easily be assigned to one product or the other. Overhead, at $15,000 annually, amounts to 6.25 percent of total costs, and it can be handled quite simply by allocating it between the two products in the same proportion as the direct costs.

Consider now the modern equivalent company. It is highly automated. It employs 200 people: 15 production workers, 10 maintenance people, 65 clerks and secretaries, 50 salespeople, 15 R&D personnel, 25 line managers, 10 people in Accounting, Payroll, and Personnel, 9 vice presidents, and the president. It has a rather different cost breakdown, shown in Figure 8–2.

The 1980 company's costs are 84 percent overhead, and this is allocated based on 16 percent direct costs. Cost accounting has simply broken down; the direct-cost tail is wagging the overhead dog.

Much of modern accounting theory is devoted to methods of turning back the clock to the days when costs could be assigned to products in a simple way. Much overhead can be reassigned as direct cost if sufficiently detailed reports are obtained (Secretary X spends 34 percent of his time on correspondence relating to staples, and we therefore allocate 34

Figure 8–2. Twentieth Century Office Technology, Inc.—Statement of annual costs.

Cost Item		Clips	Staples
Raw materials		$100,000	$ 80,000
Direct labor		200,000	100,000
Depreciation (mach.)		150,000	120,000
Total direct costs		450,000	300,000
		(60%)	(40%)
Indirect labor	3,700,000		
Depreciation (G&A)	300,000		
Overhead	4,000,000		
allocated 60:40		2,400,000	1,600,000
Total Costs		$2,850,000	$1,900,000

percent of his salary . . .). But to obtain the necessary data at such a fine level of detail is difficult, inefficient, and irritating. Even in a large company, demands for cost breakdowns of this sort are so onerous that they quickly provoke a rebellion. In a small company, modern cost accounting would constitute a crushing burden.

The best way out of this dilemma is to abandon traditional cost accounting as an analytical tool (which will result in your accountant having a conniption fit, but it can't be helped). Briefly, the idea involved is this. Traditional cost accounting breaks down primarily because "direct costs" are now a small proportion of total costs in an average business, while "overhead" is the major item. It therefore makes sense to abandon the direct/indirect dichotomy, which is based on a theoretical model of the company dating to the 1800s or earlier, and instead determine where your costs actually are.

What this means is cutting yourself loose from the financial statement, which *defines* certain items as "overhead" and so on, and directly analyzing the costs of your operation. The biggest costs are identified and assigned to cost centers. Then they are used to allocate the rest of the costs. This is done without regard to traditional classifications of "direct" and "indirect" costs.

In a company doing small-scale "custom synthesis" chemical manufacturing, it turned out that the major cost was process testing and setup. Raw materials and "direct labor" were minor items. Thus the cost of a batch was calculated by costing the setup time and allocating raw materials and labor accordingly. You may ask (if you don't your accountant will), why not just use the actual values for these items rather than allocate? Because each chemist was running three to four batches at a time and could only guess at how much time he was devoting to each. Raw materials were partly dedicated and partly drawn from common stock, raising other difficulties. This particular example was a chemical company, but a similar costing problem occurs in many job-shop operations, ranging from machine-tool outfits to Chinese restaurants, and a similar solution can be applied.

Our discussion here is a brief summary of ideas developed at more length in Peter Drucker's book *Managing for Results* (see Bibliography). This approach was originally intended for dealing with the complex problems involved in the analysis of costs in large corporations. However, because of its simplicity and ease of implementation, it seems even more adapted to small business.

THE STRATEGY OF COST CUTTING

Once you have identified your costs and understand their relationship to your output, you can implement cost cutting. All companies attempt to do cost cutting, and they almost invariably fail. Successful cost cutting requires you to follow three simple rules.

First, make cost cutting a continuous activity. Most companies have cost-cutting drives at intervals of several years—generally during recessions. In between, scarcely a token effort is made to run economically. You can win big by making sure that your production manager *works on cost cutting every day.* She should be required to give a written report on her progress on cost reduction at least quarterly. This will not only reduce your problems in bad times but substantially increase your profits and cash flow during the booms. The resulting edge over the competition can be decisive. What's more, this is a much more efficient way to do cost cutting. Crash programs tend to result in process hang-ups and quality problems, because the measures taken are not well thought-out and are implemented hurriedly. Continuous cost cutting gives you the opportunity to carefully test results and avoid false economies.

Second, cut the major costs first. Traditional cost accounting tends to lead to irrational economies. Certain items are defined as being "overhead" and are automatically considered as better candidates for cutbacks than "direct" costs; overhead is allegedly "nonproductive," so naturally it should be cut first, right? But those small, seemingly useless expenditures may have a high leverage. Clear your mind of preconceived notions and examine your costs in order of size. Ask what you're getting for the money.

Third, cut costs by eliminating, not reducing, activities wherever you can. As you examine each cost center, the first question you should ask yourself is, "Can we get rid of this entirely? Is there any reason we should be doing it at all?" Don't even consider your options for reducing the cost of an activity until you have convincing proof that it is impossible to eliminate it.

There are many different ways of analyzing costs, which depend on how the company's cost structure is broken down. You can divide up costs by product, as we did above. This may result in a decision to drop the least profitable items. Alternatively, you can divide costs along the process axis: raw materials, labor, shipping, and so on. This may lead you to the conclusion that certain process steps should be jobbed out. A less common but often instructive approach is to use the product-lifetime axis: analyze costs as a function of product age. You might find from this that, for instance, older products don't yield good profits for you, and adopt a policy of licensing products after they mature. There is, of course, functional analysis: how much does it cost to run each department? You might decide, for example, to eliminate your payroll operation and have it done by a financial-service company.

Cost analyses of any of these types can be performed even before you start up, using your pro-forma financials as material. The results may not be highly accurate, of course—but that's not the important point. The real value of doing these analyses in advance is that they will result in a much clearer understanding of your cost structure. And you'll be surprised how often you'll say, "My God, I never thought of that! We'd better check into how much it's going to cost to analyze the ventricle grease."

Exercise 8–1:
Identifying Your Key Costs

Estimate your production cost, assuming your projected production rate for your first year. (If you are already in business you can use the actual figures for the year immediately past.)

A. Process axis: add up raw materials, labor, equipment depreciation and maintenance, rent and utilities, inspection, inventory and storage, packaging, shipping. Don't rely on guesswork; even if you are months away from start-up, you can get firm numbers for all these items by calling up suppliers for quotes, checking salary surveys in the trade press, and so on.

B. Product axis: if you are selling more than one product, break down your results from section A and calculate the unit cost of each.

C. You now have on paper (or on disk with your computer spreadsheet) a core model of your production costs. This will be a fundamental part of your financial projections. Using this information, you can answer a lot of key questions. For instance:

- What is the relative profitability of our various products?
- If we reduced setup time by 30 percent, what would be the effect on our costs?
- Should we buy or lease production equipment?
- If interest rates go from 14 percent to 17.5 percent, what will be the effect on inventory carrying costs?
- If we turn inventory 8.5 times per year instead of 6.2 times per year, how much money will we save?

Please note: If you find that you cannot answer questions of this type, it indicates that you do not have an adequate handle on your costs!

BREAKEVEN ANALYSIS

Of course, one of the most useful breakdowns for cost analysis, and the one most traditional for prestart-up calculation, is the distinction between fixed and variable costs. Breakeven analysis is easy to do and very instructive—more instructive, in fact, than you may realize.

To perform breakeven analysis, you begin by dividing all your costs into "fixed" and "variable" items. You must specify a production capacity. Then, given that capacity, any cost that does not depend on production rate is considered fixed. Any cost that does change with the production rate is considered variable. Certain assumptions are usually made:

- That fixed costs really are constant. In reality, some (for example, rent) are; some (maintenance costs) aren't.

- That variable costs are proportional to output. In reality, this is seldom exactly true; for instance, at high output you may get a better price on raw materials, since you're buying larger quantities—but pay more for labor, due to overtime.
- That revenues are proportional to output. In reality, your price may change as a function of output level—and you may not sell everything you produce.

Generally, it's not a serious omission to ignore these complicating factors in your prestart-up breakeven analysis; often they will more or less cancel out.

Breakeven analysis is most easily conducted using graphical methods. Let's look at some examples.

In Figure 8-3 we show a typical breakeven graph. The horizontal line represents fixed costs, which, by assumption, are the same at any capacity utilization. To this we add the variable costs to get a diagonal line representing the total cost. Another line represents revenues, which start at zero when there is no production. The intersection of the cost and revenue lines marks the breakeven point. At this level of production, the company should be breaking even. The vertical distance between the cost and revenue diagonals represents the profit (to the right of breakeven) or loss (to the left of breakeven).

The obvious value of breakeven analysis is that it allows

Figure 8–3.   Breakeven chart, commodity industry.

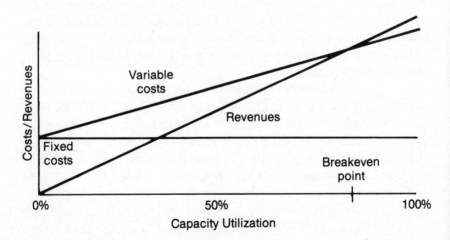

you to predict how high your sales must be for the business to break even. In addition, it provides you with an estimate of the magnitude of your profit (or loss) at any sales level. But even these very simple breakeven charts can suggest ideas about the nature of your company and your industry.

The chart shown in Figure 8-3, for instance, is typical of commodity industries such as steel, mining, or basic textiles. Fixed costs are high (plant equipment is expensive), and variable costs are also high. In such an industry, breakeven tends to occur, as is readily seen, at a high proportion of capacity. Thus a commodity producer typically is highly cyclical; in boom times, the plant runs flat out, and a small profit is made. In recessions, the company is far below breakeven, and losses are considerable. For a small company, a breakeven chart like Figure 8-3 should raise a serious question as to whether it is rational to continue in business. In fact, a number of large companies with breakeven charts of this type should be considering this question.

In Figure 8-4 we see the breakeven chart of a different sort of industry. Here the fixed costs are high, but variable costs are low. Breakeven occurs at a moderate proportion of capacity, and above breakeven profits rise quickly. This sort of situation is characteristic of oligopolistic industries—for example, the large television networks or the drug industry. The high fixed costs mean that there is a large up-front investment, which

Figure 8–4. Breakeven chart, oligopoly industry.

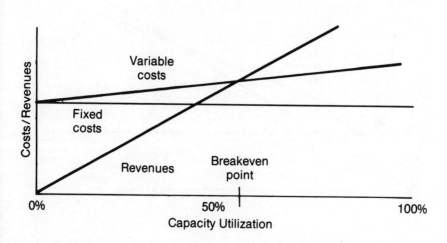

creates a barrier to entry. Thus there are only a few companies, and they are able to charge higher prices due to the reduced competition.

If your company's breakeven chart looks like Figure 8-4, it suggests that your "edge" is provided by the high entry cost. This means that in order to obtain and maintain your advantage over competitors, you must either be able to achieve lower fixed costs or be able to finance your plant on better terms. This implies that you had better be entering a new industry. If there are already established firms, their fixed costs are likely to be lower because their plants are older, were built in less inflationary times, and have already been partially or fully depreciated. (The exception, of course, is the case where existing plants are obsolete, so that the competition must also build from scratch.) Note also that established competitors—particularly if they are larger—can usually raise money at lower rates than you can obtain.

Figure 8-5 shows a breakeven chart characteristic of a dispersed industry such as retailing. In such an industry fixed costs are low, so there is little barrier to entry. As a result, there are typically a lot of players in the market. Competition between them lowers their prices and raises the costs of their raw materials, so their effective variable costs are high. Inspection of the breakeven chart shows that a company in such an industry is likely to have a moderate breakeven point and

Figure 8–5. Breakeven chart, dispersed industry.

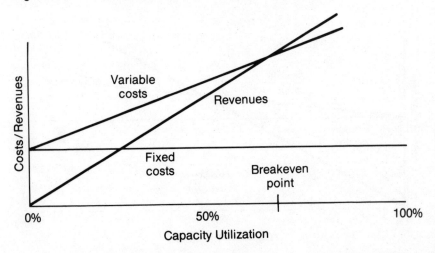

rather slim profit margins. On the other hand, when bad times come the losses are also relatively low. Thus the Mom-and-Pop retailer can survive a recession, even with low capitalization, by belt-tightening.

If you are in this sort of business you probably will have a great deal of competition. The key to success is in your variable costs and their relation to price. You can use either of two strategies. First, you may choose to concentrate on lowering variable costs. This gives you more pricing flexibility, so you can pursue a "discount store" strategy. Alternatively, you can look for a way to distinguish yourself from the competition—something that will permit you to raise prices.

The breakeven chart show in Figure 8-6 is clearly the ideal. Both fixed and variable costs are low. Breakeven is reached at a low proportion of capacity. Above breakeven the profit margins are excellent. Below breakeven the losses are small. Looks like a real winner. The question is, how do you get such a position—and once you get it, how do you keep it to yourself? Whatever it is you're doing, it's obviously so attractive that everybody else in the universe is going to want in too.

The only way you can get and retain such a breakeven chart is to possess a very high barrier to entry. The entry barrier clearly is not due to high capital costs, since the fixed costs are low. Your edge therefore must be some sort of know-how. Perhaps you have superior technology or a proprietary

Figure 8–6. Breakeven chart, high-technology industry.

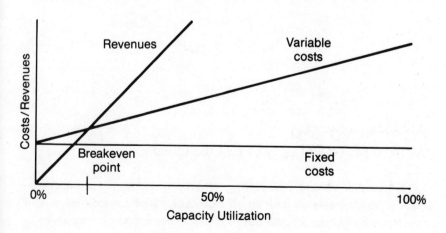

product—patented, copyrighted, or trademarked, as the case may be. Or you have a reputation built up over years, or a superb customer-service organization. Whatever it may be, you must clearly identify the barrier to entry for competition and concentrate your efforts on it. In such a case, more than any other, the barrier is the key to your business.

We've gone into breakeven analysis in this much depth not because of its intrinsic importance but because it provides a simple illustration of how to analyze your business. You cannot only produce useful numbers (such as your breakeven point) but achieve a better understanding of the characteristics of your business—how it will behave under various conditions.

A PARTING WORD ON PRODUCTION

As we stated at the beginning of this chapter, production is a hard subject to treat effectively in general terms, because the specifics vary so much from one line of business to another. We are able to give you only a few hints; you'll have to study production methods and problems in your industry carefully. Also note that we've hardly scratched the surface of the critically important subject of QC and productivity.

However, it has been more than 200 years since Adam Smith wrote the passage that we used as an epigraph for this chapter. Yet production managers are still wrestling with the same three problems he cites: training workers, reducing setup time, and automating the production process.

CAUTIONARY TALE:
MA AND PA KETTLE GET CLOBBERED

I found it very disconcerting when I developed an interest—indeed, an obsession—with small business. I had considered myself a dedicated academic type. But in my first months as an employee of

Lifesystems Company I discovered how fascinating a small venture could be. I began to read up on small business, everything I could find. When I had cleaned out the bookstores and the libraries, I turned to MIT, my *alma mater* conveniently located in Boston, and was directed to the Enterprise Forum, which was then just getting started. The more I learned, the more concerned I became about Lifesystems' future. What would I do if the company went under? (Which in fact it later did.) This was 1978, and Ph.D. chemists were not in very heavy demand; in fact, there was a serious glut. I began to toy with the idea of starting my own business.

My plans became serious when an old classmate and good friend, Dave, came to visit. He was a marketer, and his current job was using about 30 percent of his capability. He too was ripe for a challenge. The opportunity to have his marketing talent on board was too good to pass up. We decided to go ahead with what was to become Reaction Design Corporation.

Briefly, the idea was this. The chemical industry suffers from pollution restrictions, high capital costs, and high energy costs. Pollution results from inefficient chemical reactions, which produce wastes and by-products in addition to the desired products. High capital costs are due primarily to the violent conditions necessary to conduct much chemical synthesis: high temperatures, high pressure, corrosive reagents—these require costly equipment for safety. Furthermore, these violent conditions require a great deal of energy.

We believed these problems could be attacked by developing improved catalysts for chemical processes. (A catalyst is a molecule that causes other molecules to undergo a chemical reaction but is unchanged itself in the process.) A number of major advances in recent years had resulted in revolutionary new types of catalysts. Yet these improvements were not being brought out of the lab and into the plant as—in my opinion—they should have been. Using properly designed catalysts, one could run chemical processes very selectively (no waste = no pollution) and under mild conditions.

To attempt to revolutionize the entire chemical industry at once would be to bite off more than we could chew, so we decided to concentrate on a particular high-value-added sector. Some molecules are "chiral"—that is, they come in right- and left-handed forms. The two forms are identical in their chemical properties, so ordinary chemical processes produce a 50:50 mixture. However, the right- and left-hand forms differ in their biological properties. This has important consequences; the infamous drug thalidomide, for instance, was perfectly safe in its right-hand form—but the left-hand form caused birth defects.

Separating the two forms is very inconvenient and expensive—imagine sorting right-handed from left-handed gloves that are too small to see. But it is possible to design a catalyst that will work to make only one of the two forms. In fact, a number of such catalysts were already known in 1978. They were not yet commercially available, and we figured drug companies would jump at the chance to buy them.

We spent over a year developing our business plan. I studied not only general topics in small-business management but also the specialized chemical techniques needed to make the chiral catalysts. Dave conducted a market-research study. We wrote a pretty good business plan, considering that it was a maiden effort. We raised almost $120,000 in first-round capital.

Our original intention was to bring on a third cofounder to be CEO and handle administration and production. I would be VP R&D and Dave would be VP Marketing. I was painfully aware of my limited business experience, and I also wanted somebody on board who was familiar with large-scale chemical processes; I was not. We interviewed several candidates for this slot, without success. Since Dave and several of the investors wanted me to be CEO, we ended up dropping the idea of the third cofounder, in spite of my misgivings.

When we finished our business plan I asked several colleagues in the Enterprise Forum to give us an informal critique. Their major criticism was unexpected. We had planned for Dave to stay with his present job and not join the company full-time until it was running well and could support his salary. To us this seemed a sensible way to conserve cash. Our advisers, however, insisted that he should come on board right at the start. This advice we could not understand and did not take.

Dave's market study had shown that the market for chiral catalysts was currently restricted to research quantities—only about $20,000 per year—though it would expand dramatically later as customers brought new processes on stream and bought production quantities of catalysts. Obviously we needed some other products initially to provide an adequate sales level. We were considering various possibilities when our schedule was disrupted—I lost my job at Lifesystems.

It hardly seemed practical to get a new job for a few months, so we accelerated our plans for Reaction Design. We incorporated, found premises in New Jersey (home of a plurality of the big pharmaceutical companies), assembled a lab, and were in business within a few months.

It proved even more difficult than we had expected to make the chiral catalysts on a practical basis, and I threw myself into the problem of improving the technology. After a few months we began to make some pretty good progress on the production front. Fortunately—from the production point of view—the small research quantities needed could be made using ordinary lab glassware rather than the much larger "kettles" needed for plant- or even pilot-scale production. I was already familiar with the techniques involved in using these small kettles—and larger equipment tends to be much more expensive.

However, things weren't so good from a sales point of view. Dave's market research turned out to be distressingly accurate; sales of chiral catalysts leveled off at about $15,000 per year. We were getting most of the market, but it just wasn't enough.

At this point another chicken came home to roost—at the worst possible time, as they always do. Dave's company moved to another state. Reaction Design was not doing nearly well enough to pay him, so he had to find another job. He did—a demanding one that left him almost no time for Reaction Design.

The company faced a tough marketing problem, and we lacked the needed sales talent. We had to find additional products to sell that could be brought on stream quickly and that had very high value—thousands of dollars a kilogram, because we couldn't make batches larger than one kilogram.

The trouble is, there aren't many such products. Our best bet was insect pheromones (a kind of nontoxic pest-control agent), but we were never able to do much with this. It's a tricky business, dependent on the vagaries of the bugs and the EPA. Several much larger companies got bloody noses in this business, and so did we.

We took a shot at adding other research chemicals to our line of chiral catalysts. But retailing research chemicals is very different from chemical manufacturing. What's needed is not technical expertise so much as shrewd inventory control; one needs to have a large catalog and stock a complete inventory. This takes a lot of working capital—which we didn't have.

Another possibility seemed a natural: contract research. We actually did land one contract. But this, again, is a specialized business. Success depends on developing a good track record;

having some big names helps. It's not easy to get a contract-research company going quickly.

Several times sales seemed to take off and it looked like we were going to make it. But each time they petered out again. For three years, I methodically tried one approach after another, looking for the way out. There was no way out. The mistake was not a wrong turn in the maze but entering the wrong maze.

In the end, the company simply starved to death. The money ran out and we liquidated. We were able to last so long only because I was taking a salary of $1,000 per year. (How? We had no children then, and my wife was working. Reaction Design put a serious strain on our finances and our marriage, but that's another story.)

With hindsight, I can see a number of mistakes. One, of course, was not making sure, by hook or by crook, that we had full-time, professional sales skills working for us right from the start. Also worth mentioning are lack of proper planning, incomplete market research, an unfocused approach to the market, and overoptimistic estimates of R&D costs.

A minor but significant error was concentrating our sales effort on the pharmaceutical giants. Since their patented drugs are proprietary and sell at what the market will bear, these companies are not particularly cost-conscious. Our powerful cost-cutting technology would have found a much more receptive market in the viciously price-competitive generic drug industry.

But the truly critical mistake was entering a business where I lacked the necessary production know-how. More than all other problems put together, what beat Reaction Design was our inability to produce on a reasonably large scale. Our tiny "Ma-and-Pa" kettles were utterly inadequate to get us into the market on a scale where viable products existed. Of course, to have a real production capability, we would have needed someone who had the skills; we would have had to find a different location; and we would have needed a much higher capitalization. It isn't the sort of change that can be made in midstream; it would have had to be planned differently from the start.

All this is obvious—now. If I hadn't been through the experience, I wouldn't have believed that I could miss these simple conclusions every day for three-and-a-half years.

REM

9

RESEARCH
AND DEVELOPMENT

*Science is a first-rate piece of furniture for a man's upper chamber,
if he has common sense on the ground floor.*

Oliver Wendell Holmes
*The Poet at the Breakfast Table**

Who needs R&D? Not every company; the Mom-and-Pop grocery store, for instance, can usually get along without it. We
normally associate R&D with manufacturing companies, especially high-tech manufacturers. But other types of companies
may have a need for research. Software companies experiment
with new programming methods. Entertainment companies
try out new special effects—consider such films as *2001* or *Star
Wars*. The competitive position of a service company may be
vitally affected by its ability to develop improved labor-saving
machinery; as this is written, several telephone companies are
learning this lesson. Even tiny handicraft businesses often do
research; a potter, for instance, may experiment with new
coloring agents or glazes.

*As cited in *Familiar Quotations*, John Bartlett (Boston: Little, Brown and
Company, 1980).

Ironically, it is the high-tech manufacturing start-ups that are most likely to suffer from neglect of R&D. Once the first product hits the market, they often ease up in the lab, thinking their job is "done." Then they get clobbered by a competitor who brings out an even better product. Here's a rule: if you need R&D at all, your need is permanent; you can never safely stop.

THE TAX ADVANTAGES OF R&D

In the United States there is a substantial tax advantage to doing R&D. It works like this. Suppose you buy a piece of production machinery that costs $100,000 and will double your output. On your corporate tax return, you try to deduct $100,000 as a business expense. The IRS says, "No way! You've expended $100,000 in cash, but you now have $100,000 worth of machine. You'll have to depreciate it [that is, deduct it gradually] over its useful life." But suppose you spend $100,000 on research and you come up with a process improvement that doubles your output. You deduct this $100,000 on your tax return—and the IRS doesn't say a thing! It's perfectly legitimate to "expense" R&D costs as you incur them. Putting this another way, purchases of capital equipment for production come out of after-tax profits; expenditures on R&D come out of before-tax profits.

However, some companies try to "capitalize" their R&D, usually because they want to inflate their net worth on the books. The IRS is generally willing, since this will usually increase the tax bite. However, accountants tend to disapprove because of the difficulty of assessing the monetary value of R&D results.

Another possibility is stripping off the tax benefits (which sometimes are of little or no value to a lightly taxed firm) and selling them to investors. This is accomplished using the "R&D limited partnership," a complex but sometimes very valuable way of raising money.

An important consequence of the tax advantage of R&D is the principle that major equipment items needed for R&D should be leased rather than purchased whenever possible.

MANAGING R&D

No aspect of business management is so badly neglected as research management. A plethora of textbooks, audiotape courses, and seminars offer instruction in management of the marketing, financial, and production functions. Guidance and training are readily available for traffic managers and waste-disposal managers, for CEOs and for secretaries. But if your job is to manage research, the huge, complex, sophisticated management-training industry falls silent.

Part of the problem is that scientists resist being managed; indeed, they hold it as an article of faith that research is impossible to manage. "Breakthroughs," they say, "are impossible to predict. The purpose of research is to discover new and unexpected phenomena; how can it be planned?" Furthermore, in most companies scientists are systematically excluded from management. Thus nobody at the top understands research or has a clear idea of how results can be measured or objectives set. As a result, the typical R&D department is an amorphous blob that produces results—if any—on unpredictable occasions and with very low efficiency.

Yet the fact is that research *can* be managed. An R&D project can be planned; it can be scheduled; it can be budgeted; and it can be performed efficiently.

TYPES OF RESEARCH

There are two types of research: basic and applied. Almost by definition, basic research has no immediate economic payoff; though some is performed by a few very large corporations, we will ignore it except to note that even basic research can be rationally managed if desired. Applied research may be further subdivided into three categories: product research, process research, and problem research.

Product research (or "product development," "product engineering," and so on) is directed toward the design and testing of a new or significantly improved product. The objective of such a project is to know how to provide the customer with certain specified benefits. It you have successfully completed product research, you will know the nature of the product in intimate detail, and also understand exactly how and why it works.

Process research is directed toward the production process. The objective is to know how to make a new product, or how to make an old product in a new way. If you have successfully completed process research, you will know not only all the necessary details of production but also how and why each step in the process works.

Problem research (or "troubleshooting") is directed toward a much more limited goal. The objective is to know how to eliminate a specific problem either in the product or in the process. Upon successful completion of the project, you will know not only how to cure the problem but how and why it occurred in the first place.

> Troubleshooting can be very sophisticated research. Here's a not atypical case. Production of 16K DRAM chips was plagued by low yields. Careful examination of the wafers with an electron microscope indicated that 0.2-micron particles were at fault. X-ray analysis of the particles, followed by electron diffraction studies, showed that they were composed of metallic silver. The problem was then traced to a silver-plated screen that supported one of the gas-line filters.

To provide emphasis, we have repeated the key factor that all types of research have in common: the objective is to *know* something. Obvious though this may seem, one of the most common obstacles to effective R&D is the failure to focus on *acquiring new knowledge*. Management outside R&D tends to focus—understandably and correctly—on end results: a new product, a reduction in manufacturing cost, elimination of a quality-control problem. Such objectives are absolutely valid, but they are not in the correct *format* to be defined as R&D projects. The scientists themselves, however, usually do no better. They like to tinker. "Let's give this a try." "It would be interesting to look at that."

DEFINING R&D OBJECTIVES

The most fundamental task of the R&D manager is to connect the company's needs and its scientists' talents by formulating R&D objectives in a "knowledge-needed" format. The initiative may come from either side. Thus top management may assign a task: "Design a mushroom-cutting machine using the hot-wire technique which meets the following specifications . . ." Or a scientist or engineer may come up with an exciting possibility: "We could cut three steps out of the manufacturing process if we shaped the ventricles with an exponential smoother." Whatever the genesis of the project, R&D management must relate the practical results desired to the specific knowledge required to achieve them.

The rational planning of a research project begins with a set of questions. For instance, the example given above might generate questions like: (1) What is the optimum temperature to cauterize the mushroom without excessive charring? (2) To what extent does the operating life of an incandescent wire depend on its thickness? (3) What commercially available alloy oxidizes most slowly at the optimum temperature? And so on. Note how the project is broken down into a series of clearly defined tasks.

RESEARCH PLANNING

Next, each task can be further broken down into two parts: setup and experiments. The experiment is the raw material of R&D. In spite of all the nattering about "creativity" or "innovation," the success of an R&D project almost never is dependent on bright ideas. Usually it is a function of doing the right experiments and doing them properly.

> H. C. Brown discovered the hydroboration reaction—and won the Nobel Prize—not by any brilliant theoretical insight but by insisting on checking an anomalous result that appeared to be due to an impure sample.

Each of the questions that the project must answer will imply running a series of experiments. Preceding the experiments there will generally be a setup period: building, calibrating, and testing the experimental apparatus; buying materials; developing analytical or test methods. When everything is ready, the experiments are run. Preferably each experimental series should be planned for completion without interruption, over as short a time as possible, to ensure consistent procedure.

One of the greatest impediments to a productive research operation is flexible equipment. This is because setup time is almost always greater—and less predictable—than experiment run time. Time spent searching for, assembling, testing, or tinkering with research equipment is *wasted time*. Rather than buy one instrument that can be used for two types of work, you should consider buying two dedicated instruments. Calculate the savings in setup time; you'll frequently find that the payback period is less than a year.

When I was in graduate school, the department got a big grant to buy computerized instruments. The money was spent to buy the most flexible equipment possible. This turned out to be a mistake; we ended up with a room full of printed circuit boards gathering dust. It wasn't worth anyone's while to spend weeks to assemble a useful apparatus, which might at any time be disassembled to build an instrument for some other project. The equipment wasn't even useful for teaching. I have vivid memories of a course I took on computer interfacing. Every single one of the scheduled demonstrations was canceled. The instructor would get started, find it wasn't working, look into the innards, and announce, "Someone's borrowed the E-bus . . ."

In scheduling a research project, the time required to complete each task should be rationally calculated, not guessed at. If you've conducted the same type of research before, you can estimate the time requirements quite well by analyzing your previous experience. But be sure to do an explicit numerical calculation—the results may be in shocking disproportion to your intuitive impression.

In my branch of chemistry—organic synthesis—an "experiment" corresponds to running a reaction. By analyzing the lab notebooks of chemists who have worked for me, I found that the average chemist, under defined conditions, ran an average 0.5 reactions per working day and needed to run a reaction about five times to optimize the synthetic step. I could thus estimate that a synthesis of four steps would require two chemist-months to complete, in addition to setup time. Frequently I have found that the project schedule calculated by this method exceeds my off-hand estimate by an order of magnitude. The same technique can be applied to any area of research or engineering, provided you have access to good records from previous similar projects.

SCHEDULING R&D PROJECTS

At this point you are ready to schedule the project. This involves assembling the various tasks and allocating personnel and other resources. For large projects this can be extremely complicated, but effective methods are known. PERT (Program Evaluation and Review Technique) and CPM (Critical Path Method) are the most popular. References are provided in the Bibliography.

Exercise 9–1:
R&D Time Requirements

A start-up commonly faces a major R&D project right up front: developing its product. Many go under without ever making a sale, because they underestimate the time required to finish this first project and run out of money before they even have a product. Here's how you can develop a realistic estimate of the schedule for product development (or any other research project).

A. Write down a list of the things you don't know, and need to know, in order to build your product (or improve your process or whatever you wish to accomplish). *Be specific.*

B. Next, list the conjectures or hypotheses you must test in order to answer the questions you are asking.

C. Now enumerate the experiments you will have to do to test your hypotheses.

D. This is critical. Go back to experience—yours or someone else's—and find out how long it has taken to do similar experiments in the past. Be conservative.

E. Look into setup time. How long will it take to purchase materials, build test equipment, and so on?

F. Total up the technician-hours that will be required to do all the experiments and the setup work. Divide by your personnel levels, and you have the *minimum* time required to complete the project, assuming that there are *no* bottlenecks, that no critical-path problems exist, that you have analyzed the project correctly, and that no unforeseen problems occur.

HITTING SNAGS

What about unforeseen problems? Well, what about them? In research, as in marketing or production, it is sometimes necessary to go back to the drawing board when your plan is made obsolete by new knowledge. This does not invalidate planning. Follow your plan; if it fails, revise it and follow the revised plan.

The fact is, though, that when a research project gets off track, the cause is almost invariably just plain sloppy work. Even very complex projects can usually be brought in ahead of schedule and under budget if the work is done fastidiously. This means more than simply cleanliness and care. It means a policy of systematic, thorough experimentation. The unproductive scientists are usually those who habitually try to "run a quick-and-dirty experiment" to "just take a look" at a question. No matter how brilliant or creative they may be, they are not working at their full efficiency. The real winners are creative *and* also have a habit of completing projects.

Often it's higher management that is at fault. Top managers have a tendency to come to R&D with new projects whenever the need strikes them. This is commonly combined with a passionate aversion to setting priorities—or a habit of imposing a new set of priorities every week. It is the responsibility of R&D management to insist that the company's limited technical resources be allocated by explicit criteria and that every project started be taken, if not to completion, at least to a logical stopping place.

THE SEVEN DEADLY SINS

To build a productive R&D organization, concentrate on stamping out the Seven Deadly Sins of Research.

Sin #1: Reinventing the wheel. There's nothing like skimping on time in the library to get you into embarrassing situations.

> As the first employee of a tiny biochemicals start-up, I was assigned the synthesis of some prospective drug candidates designed by the founder. I started with a routine literature search and made the disconcerting discovery that several of the compounds had been patented years before by Merck.

Don't stop after checking out the major background studies. Dig into the whole subject area deeply. Compile and organize every bit of information you can find that could bear on your problem. Then set up a mechanism to keep this file up to date by monitoring the literature on a continuous basis. Be constantly on the watch for those little tid-bits of know-how that so often save weeks of work. You're more likely to find them in the older literature, before 1960 or so, when journals provided space for extensive experimental sections. These days such jewels may occasionally be discovered in footnotes, but more commonly you must get them by talking to other workers in the field. Here's a tip: don't neglect Ph.D. theses; they often contain key experimental specifications that are omitted in journal publications.

> Software engineering is a field particularly prone to reinventing the wheel. Most software makes heavy use of a few key algorithms: sorts, searches, parsing, etc. In many shops these routines are written from scratch for every new project. Experienced programmers gradually develop a library of key modules that they can plug into a program where needed. But the software development manager should arrange for a common module interface so her people can use one another's routines. She should also look ahead to future projects to maintain compatibility.

Sin #2: Unexamined assumptions. The purpose of research is to know something, and you can come to know something in just two ways: either you know because you did an experiment, or you know because someone else did an experiment and told you. You don't know something just because you think it ought to be true. Identify your assumptions and test them—test them before you begin.

Sin #3: Uncontrolled variables. A series of experiments is run in order to relate effects to causes. But the results can easily be invalidated if a single relevant variable is left uncontrolled. If you're very lucky, this neglect will cause inconsistent results in your experimental series, warning you that something is wrong; you'll merely have to do all the experiments over. If you're fairly lucky, you'll get consistently bad results, causing you to abandon a project that is actually viable. But if you're unlucky, you'll get consistently good results in the lab— and fail in the plant.

A process for an expensive adhesive additive worked beautifully in the lab, and the customer approved the sample. On scale-up, the product came out yellow and was rejected as impure. The entire batch had to be scrapped, at heavy loss. The explanation turned out to be simple: purified solvent was used in the lab experiments, ordinary drum-grade material in the plant.

Sin #4: Incomplete experimental series. You run experiments usually to get data points. When you try to get by on the cheap, you're asking for trouble. It's surprising how often the curve takes a jog just where you decided to skip a point to save time; your interpolation can be dangerously invalid. Extrapolation is even worse—often strange phenomena lurk at the edges of your data set, and in the plant, mistake or accident may move conditions into that uncharted area. Skimpy data sets are vulnerable not only to random error but to systematic error, especially if you skipped running "blanks," or controls.

Getting a complete study across the entire range of parameters is especially critical in process research. You're looking for a graph where the figure of merit shows a broad hump rather than a sharp peak. In the former case, a variation of the process parameters from the optimum will result in only a small degradation in results. If your system shows a sharp peak, however, a minor mistake in the plant—and the plant can't control process parameters as tightly as the lab—will result in serious problems.

An incomplete study can have consequences much more expensive than the cost of the skipped experiments. Ironically, though, skimping on experiments is usually motivated not by economy but by boredom.

Sin #5: Unfinished experiments. It's tempting to abandon an experiment that "isn't working right." *But an experiment that produces no information is a total waste.* The "quick-and-dirty" experiment tells you nothing if it fails, and little more if it "succeeds."

Sin #6: Incomplete records. Most scientists pride themselves on their notebooks, and most of them . . . shouldn't. This is one area in which older scientists commonly have an edge over the young whippersnappers. After you've written a dozen or so research reports, and screamed, "Why didn't I write that down?!" a couple of hundred times, you begin to write it down.

Again, programmers are notorious for carelessness in documenting their work. I found out the hard way when working on my first big program (about a thousand lines of FORTRAN) as a freshman at MIT. Nobody had told me that there was such a thing as documentation, so I did none. By the time I was done with the first version, I'd forgotten how the early parts of the program worked and was completely incapable of debugging it. Though most programmers are more sophisticated (so am I, now) they may still fail to document thoroughly enough to trace the effects of program changes during debugging.

Sin #7: Unorganized data. This requires little comment. What good are data if you can't find them?

The unifying theme again in this discussion is knowledge—information. We can rephrase the seven points as follows: (1) Don't pay for information that's available free. (2) Don't mistake a hypothesis for information. (3) Information is valid only in a defined context. (4) Interpolation and extrapolation do *not* produce information. (5) Don't stop an experiment until it finishes producing information. (6) Don't throw away information. (7) Don't lose information.

ENCOURAGING INNOVATION

Most companies, in spite of good intentions, do very poorly at nurturing innovation—and this includes small as well as large companies. The proper approach is to treat an idea rather like a child. When it first appears, it should be handled like an infant—very protectively. Killer phrases like "We tried that once" or "Would it be cost-effective?" should be banned at this stage. The creator should not be expected to "justify" or "defend" her idea. Instead, she should be encouraged to expand it, amplify it, explore it, elaborate it. In a strong R&D organization it is very easy to get approval to start a new project. The major criterion is simply the inventor's commitment to her own idea. Is she willing to work on it, study it thoroughly? If she is, she should be given the go-ahead.

But as the innovation matures it should, like a growing child, be exposed to increasing challenge. The swaddling appropriate to an infant will "spoil" an adolescent. Similarly, as a research project progresses it should be required to meet increasingly strict criteria—technical, financial, and marketing—to qualify for continued funding.

Most organizations do it backward. They come down on infant ideas like Herod slaughtering the Innocents. Every suggestion must run the gantlet just to get a chance at initial funding. The more original an innovation, the less chance it has of passing the intimidating checklist of requirements.

But once a project gets started, it tends to be overprotected. The older it gets, the less it is challenged. Large companies often pour millions into such projects, years after it has become clear that the idea isn't ever going to work in the lab, let alone in the marketplace. Partly this is due to reluctance to write off a bad investment: "We've spent so much on this we can't afford to quit now." But usually the major factor is managerial ego. Too many important people have signed on and now refuse to lose face by admitting they were wrong.

And don't kid yourself that this sort of thing happens only in big, bureaucratic companies. It happens all the time in small companies too, including some "highly innovative" high-tech start-ups. If you don't watch out, it will happen in *your* company.

The Stop-Loss Technique

A small company cannot afford an unfocused or undisciplined research operation, but neither can it afford to stifle the creativity of its innovators. The correct balance is not easy to achieve. Probably the most effective approach is to attach a "stop-loss" flag to every project.

At each stage, when a project is initiated, continued, or expanded, the investigator should be asked to set objectives for the coming phase. He is, of course, likely to be overoptimistic. There's no need to curb his enthusiasm, but he should be required to suggest a stop-loss flag for the project. Ask: "What results—or failure—would convince *you* that this project should be abandoned?" You may need to negotiate the exact terms, but get it in writing right from the start and hold him to it. This will prevent those drawn-out disasters where the advocates of a hopeless project keep clinging to your knees, pleading for "just one more chance." Incidentally, the same trick in reverse can be used to pry a new product loose from a perfectionist designer. Make her agree in writing in advance on the product specs; then use the agreement when she tries to delay introduction to add a few "important improvements."

PROTECTING YOUR INNOVATION

To patent or not to patent—that is a question which has been heavily debated. There is no single answer. However, it cannot be emphasized too strongly that a patent is a hunting license and nothing more. It gives you the privilege of suing infringers, but there's a big difference between suing and winning. Since judges know nothing about science or engineering, and juries less, the odds of getting justice in a patent suit are lower than for any other kind of case except product liability. And if the infringer of your patent is a large corporation, your "hunting license" is about as valuable as a license to hunt elephants with a pea-shooter. Keep in mind also that the U.S. government has been known to rip off patent holders, and that many foreign countries refuse to recognize or enforce patents of certain types.

There is a wide variation in the effectiveness of various types of patent. A "composition of matter" patent is relatively easy to obtain and easy to defend. (However, most foreign governments do not recognize this form of patent.) Device patents are less reliable. A process patent may be almost unenforceable, even for a large company.

Before you apply for a patent, consider several questions. What are the alternatives? Trade secret, of course, but what about a design patent, copyright, or even trademark protection? If you do patent, who is likely to infringe? How much would it cost to sue them? How long would it take? Be sure you consider these questions *before* you apply for the patent.

There's one reason you may want to apply for a patent even if you have no realistic hope of enforcing it: investors like patents. This should be taken into account.

Perhaps the most significant factor is your objective in applying for a patent. Specifically, do you want to maintain complete exclusivity in using your invention, or are you willing to license? If you really want to maintain exclusivity, a patent is risky at best. You're telling the world how to do it by getting the patent, and enforcement is very difficult. If, however, you're willing to license, a patent becomes much more attractive. Even the more brutal behemoths will usually pay royalties rather than infringe *if* you give them the option. Infringement tends to occur when a license is unavailable or unaffordable.

Whatever approach you take to protect your inventions, you must institute policies to define and control your proprietary information. There are well-known guidelines for laboratory record-keeping to establish patentability (if they're not well-known to you, see the references in the Bibliography). It is not sufficiently appreciated that maintaining a trade secret also imposes certain legal requirements. Indeed, since the law doesn't really approve of trade secrets—the government would prefer to have you get a patent, that's why patents exist—you have to be especially careful. Without going into the details here, we will simply point out that to enforce secrecy, you must define what you consider to be proprietary information, take reasonable precautions to protect it, and be prepared to prove that your employees and anyone else with access to it knew it was a trade secret.

THE CONSULTING TRAP

It is common for high-technology businesses to start as consulting or contract-engineering firms and later make a transition into manufacturing. This has a number of obvious advantages; in particular, the fees received often effectively finance the initial product development.

However, the technical types who typically found such companies frequently fail to realize how very difficult it is to move from custom services to proprietary manufacturing. These two types of business are pretty close to being completely orthogonal, and many high-tech outfits have crashed and burned in the attempt to switch from one to the other.

If you plan to go this route you should be especially careful. First, you and your cofounders had better give unusually thorough consideration to your personal career objectives. If you really enjoy contract research, you probably will detest running a manufacturing operation. Of course, the latter is much more likely to make you rich. Is that enough incentive? If you decide to go ahead, don't underestimate the changes it will force you to make. Seriously consider setting up a brand-new company to do the manufacturing—instead of, or better, in addition to, the contract R&D firm. Make an intentional break in continuity to rid yourself of policies that are inappropriate to the new business. And be sure that you bring on someone with manufacturing experience.

WORKING WITH OTHER MANAGEMENT

The R&D director must establish a productive relationship with both Marketing and Production. The success of a technology-based company is dependent on cooperative effort among the three branches. No one can be allowed to dominate. If Production is in control, the company will devote too much energy to cash cows and lose the future; within a few years, you'll have a beautiful plant optimized to make an obsolete product. If Marketing dominates, you'll play it safe; then one day, a more innovative competitor will come out with a breakthrough product and jerk the rug right out from under you. But a company where R&D has unrestricted power may never get its brilliant innovations to market. A system of checks and balances is needed.

You can do much to forge such a system by establishing a simple policy. Nobody should be promoted into R&D management until he has worked in Quality Control or handled some troubleshooting assignments in the plant—*and* put in some time doing market research in a customer-contact capacity. In short, get at least your managers out of the lab. In your early days, everybody will be intimate with Production anyway; but you'll have to make a special effort to keep your research people in contact with customers.

You will have to force upon the various branches of management the fundamental choice of innovation. *A company can be on the leading edge of technology. Or it can produce a reliable product. One or the other—but not both.* This is a message that your cofounders probably will not want to hear. It is a message that the R&D team will find particularly repugnant, especially in view of its natural fear that the marketing people will choose reliability over technological leadership. But it simply is a fact that innovative products require a prolonged shakedown period and that early models will be debugged by the customers. Instead of trying to deny this reality, condition your team to accept it and plan how to deal with it.

THE LOSS-LEADER TRAP

One of the most insidious traps for young companies is the R&D loss leader. One day your struggling start-up is approached by a really big potential customer. They are very interested in buying large quantities, and buying it from you— only, it's a product that you haven't developed. Here are the specs; would you be interested in looking into it and giving us a quote on developmental quantities? Sure you would—this is your big chance. So all of your talent, not to mention your meager cash reserves, goes into R&D on this project. Naturally you gave Mr. Big a very low bid, because this is your big chance and you don't want him to take it elsewhere. And of course you can't expect him to pay you until you actually get into production and start shipping. So you turn in a proposal, and it's accepted, and you work day and night, and you turn in progress reports, and one day Mr. Big sends you a letter which very apologetically tells you that the project's been canceled, or postponed, or they've decided to do it in-house. . . . And as your attorney explains to you the provisions of Chapter Seven, you realize that you gave Mr. Big thousands of dollars worth of R&D work and didn't charge him a cent for it.

The marketing guys are frequently going to be on your case trying to get you to do free R&D for your customers. If you're in a technology business, that's to be expected, and it's often a very good thing to do. But insist on approaching these projects in the rational manner that you use to evaluate in-house ideas. Make the marketing wallahs specify what the payback is to be and how it can be justified and how it fits in with the company's priorities. Ask them to specify a stop-loss flag.

A small company has very limited R&D resources. It is the responsibility of the R&D manager to see that they are allocated effectively. It is inexcusable to run a project just because he has a whim to look into the question. It is equally inexcusable to run a project because his fellow managers have a gut feeling that they can sell a million of 'em.

CAUTIONARY TALE: BLOOD WILL TELL

A couple of years ago Dr. Alan Johnson, a hematologist of considerable note, developed an improved process to prepare a product essential for the treatment of hemophilia. This material, "Factor VIII," is isolated from normal blood and used to prevent severe and potentially fatal bleeding in hemophiliacs. Dr. Johnson is a faculty member at NYU and a distinguished, not to say renowned, scientist in the area of blood diseases, blood treatments, and blood products. He developed the original process to extract Factor VIII from plasma 15 years ago. This process was a miracle of medical science at the time and has saved the lives of a lot of people, but there was plenty of room for improvement. The existing isolation method is inefficient—it has only 18 percent yield—and the product is impure, so that patients run the risk of getting infectious hepatitis or even AIDS. Dr. Johnson had developed a new process that raised the yield to 30 percent and increased the purity a hundredfold. He proposed to base a new business on this innovation.

Having developed the process in the lab, he began work on scaling it up for production and also tried to find financing. He became involved with several promoters who really didn't understand what the business was about and who probably weren't all that competent at raising money anyway. Among them were a couple of Florida real-estate developers who weren't, shall we say, ideally suited to building a high-tech business. Then he talked to a number of small brokerage firms that had claimed that they would be able to raise money for him. Unfortunately, not understanding how that business worked, he gave the assignment to several of them simultaneously. Of course they learned about each other, and all of them got mad at him because they didn't have exclusives. In short, he just didn't understand the rules.

I met him by happenstance because his daughter was engaged to my nephew. She brought along Dr. Johnson's business plan to a family weekend—he'd asked her to help edit it—and she asked me to take a look at it.

As it then stood the plan was, I'm sorry to have to say, a total disaster. At the beginning, the doctor listed all of his credentials—a list very imposing but rather tedious—and his bibliography. Then those of his team members. Then a history of hemophilia. On and on and on, until finally, at the end of the plan, he began to say something about what he intended to actually do and why it was worth doing. This plan had no chance of getting funding, because no investor would waste his valuable time wading through it to find out what it was about.

Shortly thereafter Dr. Johnson and I met. We liked each other, and I was invited to help out in getting his company, Hemotech, financed and operating. We were fortunate to secure the participation of Nelson Thun, who came from the medical industry, as the company's CEO.

The first step was to clean up the business plan. I started with a paragraph stating the *need*. There are some 450,000 hemophiliacs worldwide, most of whom need Factor VIII to control their bleeding.

Currently, the worldwide market is $250 million a year. The cost to the hemophiliac runs about $5,000 to $10,000 per year. You'll note that these numbers don't match up; that's because a large number of hemophiliacs don't get any Factor VIII, either because they can't afford it or because not enough is available. Generally these unfortunate people die, and it would be nice to do something about it, like making Factor VIII easier to make. That is what Dr. Johnson had accomplished—in the lab.

We then went on to point out that Dr. Johnson was the recognized leader in this field, who had developed the previous technology and now had developed something better. Obviously the financial world should beat a path to his door and finance the venture. Of course we had the usual description of the market, the company, the details on the people and their credentials, the competition. All this, however, was now concise, so that the prospective investors would not have to fight their way through a lengthy and not particularly readable narrative to find out what the thing was about.

Our plan was to develop the process, install it at the plants of all Factor VIII manufacturers, and be paid a royalty. Our capital requirements were to come in two stages. First, $400,000 was needed to get the new method into the marketplace. This would develop a stream of royalties from licensing of the process to the various blood fractionators. In the second stage, we would need $1.7 million to continue research to purify and identify the actual active molecule. You see, Factor VIII, even with the new process, is still a *melange* of molecules, most of which are useless. The right compound is in there somewhere, we know, because the stuff works, but nobody knows exactly what it is. If it could be isolated completely pure, we could turn it over to the genetic-engineering people, and they could presumably clone it instead of deriving it from plasma.

It certainly looked like the kind of deal that venture capitalists should salivate over. They're always talking about the importance of the management team, how they want to see first-rate people even if they have only a second-rate product. The Hemotech team could hardly be called anything less than first-rate: a CEO who'd been in the blood-products business for years, with a sound operating record; the scientist himself, a highly respected, enormously accomplished man, world-renowned as the leader in the field; a board that included a lot of people from the blood-fractionation industry; and, of course, your humble servant.

Furthermore, here was a process that was six months from being market-ready, because a lot of the R&D and scale-up had already been accomplished. There was a large, visible, identifiable market that was crying out for a new process because of the tremendous media attention focused on the risk of AIDS for hemophiliacs. There was tremendous pressure from various groups such as the National Hemophiliac Society and the International Hemophiliac Society to get an improved product.

We were willing to give up 50 percent of the company for the $2.1 million we wanted. That's a pretty good deal, considering the credentials of the founders, the urgency of the market, and the limited risk. Basically the idea was to finish the product, license the patent, and rake in a very nice royalty stream—about $100 million over the next 15 years. That wasn't pie in the sky, either; remember, this process improvement would increase the gross margins of the blood fractionators by 70 percent. We knew they'd pay a royalty, and how much it would be, because they are already paying a royalty on the old process.

I'm forced to say that I was stunned when the venture capitalists turned us down. Part of the problem was that they had a little knowledge of biotechnology—just a little. While we were trying to raise capital, Genentech made a splashy announcement that it had cloned the AHF molecule, from which Factor VIII is derived. Of course, if the people at Genentech could just clone as much of the stuff as they wanted, who needed our process? What wasn't understood by the amateur tekkies in the venture-capital firms was that Genentech had cloned the whole humongous protein, of which Factor VIII is a small, short strip. It didn't, and still doesn't, and for a long time won't, know how to chop out the Factor VIII, which the human body somehow mysteriously does. In fact, Genentech doesn't know which strip to chop out, even if it had a way to do it. As a matter of fact, the Genentech people have told Dr. Johnson that his work is a much more important breakthrough than theirs, and that they'd like to collaborate with him on a joint venture.

The other problem we faced resulted from the fact that venture capitalists nowadays aren't really independent investors. For all practical purposes, they are just scouts for the investment bankers of Wall Street. In order to sell out their successful investments—if any—they must take them public eventually. That means that they are enslaved to the prejudices, foibles, and irrationality of the stock market. And as it happens, one of the ridiculous rules of thumb of stock investors is that a royalty stream is to be valued at only half the same revenues derived from manufacturing. Personally, I figure cash flow is cash flow, except that cash flow for which you have only to stamp the checks and mail them to the bank is better than cash flow for which you have to endure the hassles of running a factory. But there's no arguing with the market.

When our deal had been bagged by half a dozen venture-capital firms, I decided we'd better rethink our approach. The obvious answer was to try some sort of investor who didn't care about how the stock market values earnings streams. And, more important, the problems we'd had with the Genentech announcement reminded me that I'd failed to apply my important principle: find investors who already understand the technology.

We ended up with two investors. One is a pretty smart company called Eli Lilly. Its management knew the work of Dr. Johnson, knew what could and couldn't be done by gene splicing, and wanted to get into the business. It is providing half the financing. The other half is coming from a very wealthy friend of mine. He's a medical-products/health-care analyst on Wall Street who instantly understood what we were doing. And he had no problem at all investing in a company that's going to draw a modest $8 million in royalties in year 4 if we meet projections.

Meanwhile, the manufacturers of Factor VIII, of which there happen to be eight, have gotten word of what we're doing and they're beating down our door. However, as this is written we're having a devil of a time getting through the paperwork due to hassles at NYU. Since the research was done on NYU's campus, it has a thumb in the pie. It'll pull out a very nice financial plum when the deal goes through, but unfortunately, that doesn't seem to motivate the university bureaucracy.

This case illustrates a number of issues that are typical of high-tech start-ups. First, it's critical to develop a complete team, especially when the technical type lacks key communication and management skills. Second, be sure you approach investors who understand the technology and the industry—which is not the same thing as investors who *think* they understand it. A "strategic partnership"—an alliance with a large company—can be a very good approach in such cases. Third, never underestimate the difficulty of dealing with intellectual property rights. If the early stages of your R&D were sponsored by a university, the government, or your previous employer, you may have significant problems getting unhindered control of the technology.

HDS

10

FINANCIAL PLANNING

Happiness is positive cash flow.

Fred Adler*

An indispensable ingredient of any business plan is a set of *pro forma* financial statements. Nothing gives the entrepreneur more trouble than developing financial projections; nothing seems more unrealistic and useless. What's more, although investors insist on seeing a complete set of projections, nothing will satisfy them. If you make your projections conservative, you'll be told, "This company clearly isn't going to have enough growth and profitability to justify the risk of the investment." If you avoid this complaint, your plan will be rejected because "Your sales and profit estimates are wildly unrealistic."

THE VALUE OF PROJECTIONS

So let's forget about satisfying investors for the moment and consider why *you* need financial projections. Does anyone really believe that you can predict the future results of your company quantitatively?

*Used by permission of Fred Adler.

234

No. Not at all. The purpose of financial projections, however, is *not* prediction but preparation.

Each type of business is unique and has distinct financial characteristics. By doing *pro forma* financial statements, you will begin to get a feel for the peculiar nature of your company's financial structure. In doing so, you may learn some things that will surprise you.

Just what is involved in constructing financial projections? First, you must identify your *assumptions* about the financial and operating characteristics of your start-up. Second, you must develop *sales and budget projections.* Third, you must assemble these into a *P&L projection.* Fourth, you must then translate this into a *cash-flow projection.* Fifth, you must check your results by projecting your *balance sheet.* And finally, you should do *ratio analysis* to compare your company's projected behavior with that of similar companies.

As you do this, you will become aware of certain considerations that had previously escaped you. You will begin to see how your decisions regarding marketing, production, R&D, and so on affect the profitability and liquidity of your company.

In order to show you how projections are done, and illustrate some of the issues involved, we are going to walk through the process, using our hypothetical start-up, Incandescent Fungoid Cutters, Inc., as an example. Now, at this point we must make certain apologies. In the nature of things, this chapter is bound to be the most tedious in the book. In order to make it slightly less soporific, we have greatly simplified the process for this example. In doing so, *we have left out a number of factors that most certainly would have to be considered in doing a real set of projections.* We will warn you of some of the major omissions in a series of notes.

Please keep in mind that this example is extremely oversimplified. We had to oversimplify it to keep this chapter from turning into a book itself.

In the sample projections shown here, we show figures on a monthly basis, for the first year of the company's operations. For a start-up's business plan it is common to project monthly figures for the first two years, quarterly figures for the next two years, and yearly figures after that, out to five to ten years.

SPECIFYING ASSUMPTIONS

The basic assumptions for Incandescent Fungoid Cutters are as follows:

1. Unit price is $10,000.
2. Direct production cost is $6,000 per unit—that is, gross margin is 40 percent.[1]
3. We sell through reps, who get a 10 percent commission (payable when product is shipped), and there are no other marketing expenses.[2]
4. Taxes are 46 percent of profits.[3]
5. We use straight-line depreciation for this example.[4]
6. We assume the following sales cycle: shipment one month after order; payment within 60 days of shipment; manufacturing time one month.[5]
7. Initial capitalization is $500,000, of which $100,000 is used to buy plant and equipment and the rest is used as working capital.[6]
8. We get 12 percent interest on our cash.

Projected Revenues and Budgets

The sales projections should be based on our market research. For purposes of this example, we assume that sales begin immediately. This is not too realistic—we've left out the entire development period during which the product is designed and debugged. We've also assumed that sales will grow at about 10 percent a month.[7] This is a bit optimistic—it's equivalent to about 150 percent per year—but it's the sort of growth venture capitalists say they want to see (though when you project it they'll say it's unrealistic).

Then you have to budget your costs. This is not a matter of plugging in some more or less arbitrary numbers. You should be able to estimate your costs *as a function of sales.* Of course, our cost of goods is based on our manufacturing-cost estimates. There will also be selling costs. We have simply assumed they are 10 percent of sales for this example.[8] R&D expense we will treat as a constant, but in reality, it too should be tied to sales projections; thus, if we project starting sales of the Mark II cutter in year 3, we should budget an amount for the R&D that will be necessary to develop the Mark II. Administrative expense we again assume here to be constant; in reality, much administrative cost is proportional to sales, and this really should be taken into account.

The Income-Statement Projection

In Figure 10–1 we show the *pro forma* income statement (or "P&L") for the first year of Incandescent Fungoid Cutters. We constructed this as follows:

The "sales" line comes from our sales projections. Note that for purposes of the P&L, sales are recognized when the product is shipped and the invoice is sent out. (If your company is well run, these two events will occur on the same day.) Thus we show no sales for the first month, since the orders taken in January are not filled until February.

"Cost of goods sold" is, by our assumptions, 60 percent of sales. Note that for the P&L, this is recognized as of the time of sale.

"Gross profit" is simply the difference between sales and cost of goods sold.

"Marketing and sales expense" we have assumed to be 10 percent of sales, and we recognize it at the time of shipment.[9]

"Research and development expense" we have simply set at $5,000 per month.

"Depreciation" is calculated assuming that we depreciate our $100,000 of capital equipment on a straight-line basis over five years. (Accountants insist that depreciation of manufacturing equipment should be put into cost of goods sold. This is indeed the logical way to do things, but because fudging depreciation is so common, many investors prefer to see it broken out so they can keep an eye on the chicanery more conveniently.)

"General and administrative expense" is assumed constant for the first year at $5,000 per month.

Summing up the expense rows and subtracting the total from the gross profit gives us the "operating profit." We then take into account other items—in this case, just the interest we

Figure 10-1. Incandescent Fungoid Cutters, Inc.—Projected income statement ($000).

	Jan	Feb	Mar	Apr	May	June	July	Aug	Sep	Oct	Nov	Dec
Sales	0	100	110	120	130	150	170	190	210	230	250	280
Cost of goods sold	0	60	66	72	78	90	102	114	126	138	150	168
Gross profit	0	40	44	48	52	60	68	76	84	92	100	112
Marketing expense	0	10	11	12	13	15	17	19	21	23	25	28
R&D expense	5	5	5	5	5	5	5	5	5	5	5	5
Depreciation	2	2	2	2	2	2	2	2	2	2	2	2
G&A expense	5	5	5	5	5	5	5	5	5	5	5	5
Total expense	12	22	23	24	25	27	29	31	33	35	37	40
Operating profit	-12	18	21	24	27	33	39	45	51	57	63	72
Other	4	3	2	1	1	1	1	1	0	0	0	0
Net profit (pretax)	-8	22	24	26	29	34	40	46	52	58	63	72
Net profit (after tax)	-4	12	13	14	15	19	22	25	28	31	34	39

Note: Some columns do not add up precisely. This is due to rounding.

receive on our cash—and the result is "net profit" (before taxes).

As you can see, our assumptions have resulted in a very nice projection. We are in the black by our second month of operations, and thereafter, we make a substantial and continually increasing profit.

The Cash-Flow Projection

Now we can return to our assumptions and build the cash-flow projection, which is shown in Figure 10–2.

In the first line we show the cash on hand at the start of each month. Recall that our initial capitalization was $500,000, of which we spent $100,000 on capital equipment, so we have $400,000 left as working capital to start with.

We then take into account the sources of cash. The second row shows revenues from sales. Since this is a cash-flow analysis, we don't recognize this revenue until it turns into cash—which is two months after the sale is made, by our assumptions.

Our only other source of revenue is interest on the cash we have on hand, which is shown in the third row. Summing this with the sales revenue we get, of course, the total revenue in cash.

We then must account for expenditures of cash. Our assumption is that manufacturing takes one month; so, in order to ship a unit in March, we must receive materials in January. During February we manufacture the unit, and in this month we must pay for the materials (on 30 days) and pay our laborers. So, given our simplified assumptions, we will be paying out the cash for materials and labor one month ahead of shipment.

Our other expenses, we assume, are paid in the month they are incurred. We omit depreciation, which has no immediate effect on cash flow. (Of course, if we were to buy any capital equipment during the year, the cost would have to be taken into account.)

Income tax must be allowed for. We've chosen a very simplified model for tax payments here.

Subtracting the total cash out from the cash revenues, we

Figure 10-2. Incandescent Fungoid Cutters, Inc.—Projected cash flow ($000).

	Jan	Feb	Mar	Apr	May	June	July	Aug	Sep	Oct	Nov	Dec
Cash at start	400	338	245	143	133	118	97	68	43	20	1	−21
Sales revenue	0	0	0	100	110	120	130	150	170	190	210	230
Interest revenue	4	3	2	1	1	1	1	1	0	0	0	0
Total revenue	4	3	2	101	111	121	131	151	170	190	210	230
Materials & labor	60	66	72	78	90	102	114	126	138	150	168	186
Other expenses	10	20	21	22	23	25	27	29	31	33	35	38
Taxes	−4	10	11	12	13	16	19	21	24	26	29	33
Total outflow	66	96	104	112	126	143	160	176	193	209	232	257
Cash flow	−62	−93	−101	−10	−15	−22	−29	−25	−22	−19	−22	−27
Cash at end	338	245	143	133	118	97	68	43	20	1	−21	−49

Note: Some columns do not add up precisely. This is due to rounding.

get net cash flow, and using this we can determine the cash balance at the end of the month.

You should realize that this kind of cash-flow statement is rather foreign to the way accountants like to do it. They prefer a "Statement of Sources and Uses of Funds," which is obtained by analysis of balance-sheet changes. Roughly speaking, they take profits and compute cash flow by adding depreciation back in. (Hence their mysterious talk about how a change in depreciation methods will change cash flow.) Flow-of-funds analysis can be very informative, however, if you have enough expertise in accounting.

Look at Figure 10–2 for a moment. Believe it or not, this is the same company as in Figure 10–1! Although Incandescent Fungoids is projecting terrific sales and excellent profits, by the end of its first year, it will be broke.

THE PARADOX OF GROWTH

How can this be? How can a successful, growing, profitable company go bankrupt? It's very easy.

Incandescent Fungoids, in our projection, is like many manufacturing companies in that money—cash—must be paid out well in advance of shipping the product on which it is expended, and money—cash—is not received in payment for the product very promptly. The first delay results in a significant cost for *carrying inventory* (in this case mostly work in process); the second results in the need to *finance receivables*. The money needed to perform these two functions is called "working capital."

Every type of business has its own, distinct working-capital needs.

> The working capital of a grocery store goes almost entirely for inventory, because sales are made for cash.
>
> The manufacturing business with a long production cycle also uses working capital primarily for inventory, though in this case it is work-in-process inventory rather than finished goods.
>
> Some direct-marketing companies are able to get along with almost no working capital. They get their goods on consignment and are paid by their customers in cash. Nice work if you can get it.

If a company is doing about the same volume of sales every year, it will need a roughly constant amount of working capital. One need only make sure, in planning such a business, that an adequate amount is allowed for. But a high-growth company presents a different problem; as we've seen, it needs increasing amounts of working capital to finance the growth. Now, you might think it would be possible to get around this problem by improving sales. Perhaps, if sales grow fast enough, the revenue coming in will eventually increase to the point where it can be used to make growth self-financing. You can test this approach, if you like, by reworking Incandescent Fungoid Cutters' projections using, say, a 20-percent monthly growth rate instead of a 10-percent rate. What you'll find is that *the faster growth will make the cash flow worse, not better.*

This discovery comes as quite a shock to many entrepreneurs. But it is a fact that *high-growth businesses tend to have a tremendous appetite for cash.* It is mature, stable businesses that throw off cash.

THE CRITICAL POINTS

Now, if we view financial projections strictly from the point of view of satisfying investors, it is possible to conceal any problems that may appear by fudging the assumptions used. Sophisticated investors are of course hard to fool in this way, but it can be done. It is, however, a more rational policy to try to eliminate the problems in reality. Financial projections are extremely valuable as a tool for exposing and analyzing defects in your planning—in fact, that's what they are for. The invention of the spreadsheet computer program has made the development and testing of financial projections much easier. In the old days, when we had to do it with paper and pencil, it was a hellish task to test the effect of a change in assumptions. Now it's just a matter of a few keystrokes.

The biggest value of financial projections is the ability to isolate the key factors in your business. Keep in mind that you as the CEO of a small business cannot keep track of everything. You are going to have to monitor and analyze the operation of your company using a very limited amount of information— far, far less than is used by the management of a big company. There are two reasons for this. First, to gather and organize information is costly—someone has to do it, and that someone must be paid for it. Second, even if you could get plentiful information, you will lack time to analyze all of it because you have too many other responsibilities. Harold Geneen could afford to spend almost his entire workday analyzing "the numbers" of ITT—you can't. Now, what this means is that you must discover what the key numbers are—the truly critical factors that make the difference between success and failure—and watch them carefully. What are those key numbers in *your* business? You can find out by looking at your financial projections.

In working with Vanguard Ventures, I recently set out to finance a group of three retirement centers developed by a group in Alabama. The group sent us a set of financial projections indicating that it would require $1 million in equity funding to execute its marketing program and cover its working-capital needs. This assumed that it would take a year to fill up the units (to 95 percent, which is full occupancy in this business).

I looked at this assumption and felt extremely skeptical. So we put the numbers on our computer model and began to play various "what if" scenarios. What if it took a year and a half to fill up the units? Two years? Three years? What if the group never got 95 percent and had to settle for 90 percent or 80 percent? This is commonly referred to as "sensitivity analysis." Thank God for computers, because with computers you can do it in minutes; manually you could take weeks to run through these numbers.

It turned out that the capital requirements changed dramatically, depending on the length of time required to get up to full occupancy. That was really the key factor in the business plan, and I just didn't believe that management could be that certain of getting there in a single year. And if it didn't, $1 million wouldn't be anywhere near enough. We finally settled on $3.25 million, and I still feel just a bit nervous.

It is absolutely critical to make conservative assumptions and go out and raise all the money that you'll need to get to positive cash flow. If you fudge it and try to get by with a financing that's too small, you can get in real trouble. It is very difficult indeed, if not impossible, to go back to the financial market and say, "Well, we were wrong. We're still wonderful, we're destined to be a big success, but it turns out that we need some more money." At that point your credibility is gone.

The example of Incandescent Fungoid Cutters is an instructive one. Suppose we start up this company without doing projections. Around May or so, the rapid evaporation of our bank account is likely to result in some alarm. If we still do not analyze our financials, we may take the intuitive, obvious corrective action: try to increase sales. But, as we've seen, if this strategy succeeds, it fails. Higher sales growth will actually make the cash-flow situation worse.

By financial analysis we learn that the really critical factor is the length of the sales cycle. What's really killing us is putting out all that cash three months before we get paid for the product. Knowing this, we can start thinking about taking corrective action. Can we find a way to shorten the manufacturing process? Can we job out part or all of production? Can we reduce our raw-materials inventory? Can we get our suppliers to give us more generous credit terms? Can we get our customers to pay us faster? Can we finance our receivables?

If we play with the numbers a little more, another factor becomes apparent: a lot of the problem lies in the gross margin. That 40 percent is really not very impressive. Can we cut our costs? Can we raise our price?

All these questions relate to reducing our need for working capital. But we may also wish to consider increasing our working capital. We could, of course, try to raise more money. Another possibility is to look again at that $100,000 worth of capital equipment. Do we really need it? Could we get it cheaper? Could we finance it with debt instead of equity? Or lease it? That would free up that $100,000 for use as working capital.

CHECKING YOUR WORK

Before you finish with your projections, you should do another one to provide you with some additional information and serve as a means of checking your results. The balance-sheet projection for Incandescent Fungoid Cutters is shown in Figure 10-3. Developing the balance-sheet projection serves as a valuable check of your arithmetic; thanks to the miracle of double-entry bookkeeping, if you make a mistake in your calculations (or in your input to the computer) the balance sheet will not balance.

The balance sheet also gives you a picture of your future business from a different perspective, and this may help you spot problem areas that are not obvious from the P&L or even

Figure 10–3. Incandescent Fungoid Cutters, Inc.—Balance-sheet projection ($000).

	Jan	Feb	Mar	Apr	May	June	July	Aug	Sep	Oct	Nov	Dec
Cash	338	245	143	133	118	97	68	43	20	1	−21	−49
Acc. receivable	0	100	210	230	250	280	320	360	400	440	480	530
Inventory	60	66	72	78	90	102	114	126	138	150	168	186
Fixed assets	100	100	100	100	100	100	100	100	100	100	100	100
less depreciation	2	3	5	7	8	10	12	14	15	17	19	20
Total assets	496	508	520	534	550	568	590	615	643	674	708	747
Common stock	500	500	500	500	500	500	500	500	500	500	500	500
Retained earnings	−4	8	20	34	50	68	90	115	143	174	208	247
Total liabilities	496	508	520	534	550	568	590	615	643	674	708	747

Note: Some columns do not add up precisely. This is due to rounding.

the cash-flow projections. In our example, for instance, the cash-flow projection tells us that Incandescent Fungoid Cutters has a problem; the balance-sheet projection gives us some very useful suggestions as to the nature and source of the problem. Examining the balance sheet, we observe the inexorable decline of cash; we also see the steady climb of receivables and inventory. With a little thought, we can see that the latter explains the former. (What we're doing here, in fact, is a primitive form of flow-of-funds analysis.)

DOUBLE-CHECKING YOUR RESULTS

So far, we have done the following: (1) Identified the assumptions we have made about our start-up and its economics. (2) Calculated the consequences of our assumptions. (3) Checked to make sure that our calculations were correctly done. There is one more task yet to do: we should use our projections to test whether our assumptions are reasonable.

This is accomplished using "ratio analysis." The idea behind ratio analysis is that if there are a number of companies, all engaged in the same line of business, and all about the same size, their financial characteristics should be similar. Therefore, the ratios of various items in their financial statements should be similar.

What sort of ratios? Well, an obvious example is the ratio of profits to sales—"net margin." This ratio is razor-thin for some types of businesses, such as supermarkets, and very high for others. If you are proposing to open a supermarket and you project profits of 10 percent of sales, your investors are going to question it. You will have to explain why and how you are going to do so much better than everyone else in the industry. If you project a margin lower than the industry average, that too is likely to lower your credibility with investors.

There are literally dozens of ratios that can be calculated, some of them rather esoteric, some (like net margin) very fundamental indeed. Any sophisticated investor is going to look at your financial projections and do a few calculations to see how your ratios stack up against the averages for your industry. (These average or "standard" ratios are available from a book called *Annual Statement Studies*—see the Bibliography.) Then the investor is going to ask you to explain any discrepancies. So you'd better check out your ratios first.

Does this mean you should diddle your assumptions until the ratios come out right? Not necessarily. The important thing is that *you* must understand *why* your ratios deviate from the average. For instance, suppose your ratio of inventory to sales comes out much lower than the industry average. This is a signal to go back and look at your assumptions in that area. Have you been overoptimistic? If so, correct your assumptions. Have you, on the other hand, developed a revolutionary new inventory-control system? Fine—just be ready to explain it to a skeptical investor.

Checklist 10–1: Some Useful Financial Ratios

- ☐ Current assets/current liabilities ("current ratio")
- ☐ Cash & receivables/current liabilities ("acid-test ratio")
- ☐ Current liabilities/tangible net worth
- ☐ Net profit/net sales ("net margin")
- ☐ Net sales/working capital ("turnover of working capital")
- ☐ Net profits/tangible net worth ("return on investment")
- ☐ Accounts receivable/daily credit sales ("collection period")
- ☐ Net sales/inventory ("inventory turnover")
- ☐ Total debt/tangible net worth ("debt-equity ratio")

SCENARIOS

A few years ago, there was a vogue for putting three sets of projections in a business plan: optimistic, worst-case, and median. This seems to be going out of style, and we approve the trend. It's best to put one good, conservative, reasonable set of numbers in your plan. But there's much to be said for doing the calculations to test the effect of variations in your assumptions. This is no longer difficult, given a personal computer and spreadsheet software, and it can give you a better feel for your business and the hazards it will face.

Best-case or worst-case scenarios are usually defined in terms of sales growth. They probe the effects of better- or worse-than-expected sales. Such projections are worth doing but should not be overemphasized.

The point of checking out scenario projections is to be prepared for contingencies—to avoid being taken by surprise. Now, the kind of contingency that tends to arise in real life is not the kind that is normally assumed in business-school calculations. "Sales growth equals 10 percent instead of 15 percent" just doesn't correspond to the way things happen in real businesses. Realistic contingencies tend to be sharp jerks, not a change in the growth rate of a smooth variable, and the variable in question is often something other than sales.

> A company with about half a dozen employees manufactured a gadget that monitored vending machines. Suddenly PepsiCo handed the company a major order, and it had to expand production fast. Where would *you* stand if a big new customer handed you a purchase order for a year's production?

> Our biggest customer suddenly and without warning—disappeared. Letters were returned, phone calls connected to a phone-company recording stating that the phones had been removed, the principal could not be found. Another company lost its biggest customer when a competitor threatened to sue over a patent-infringement issue. Where would *you* stand if your sales were cut in half overnight?

In many industries, particularly electronics, the price of a newly introduced product tends to drop dramatically with time (think of calculators, disk drives, RAM chips). Start-ups frequently die because their financial projections fail to take this into account or underestimate how precipitous the price drop will be.

Checklist 10–2: Contingencies for Planning

- ☐ Sudden loss of a major customer
- ☐ Sudden acquisition of a major customer
- ☐ Serious QC problem in major product
- ☐ Fire, earthquake, tornado, or the like destroys plant
- ☐ Your product is found to be carcinogenic
- ☐ Government regulations change
- ☐ The area containing your facility is rezoned
- ☐ A key employee leaves suddenly—and goes to a competitor

☐ Interest rates double and stay there
☐ Inflation goes to 100 percent
☐ Key raw material becomes unavailable
☐ Competition forces you to cut prices

THE BOTTOM LINE

Financial projections are tedious, but they are *important*. They will constitute the heart of your business plan—only your market research will get more attention from investors. But still more important, financial projections give you the means to perform trial runs of your business. You can play the game on paper, without having to pay if you lose. It is not possible, of course, to guarantee success from doing financial projections, any more than from playing the stock market on paper. But you can learn much about your business quickly and cheaply. Not everything—but the more you learn in advance, the less you will have to learn later when you have to pay for your mistakes.

NOTES

1. Costs for materials may actually vary with production level, since you can usually get a better price on larger lots. Labor costs are also oversimplified. Even for a very large business, labor costs do not vary smoothly with production levels—it's just not that easy to lay people off when production declines, or to hire and train them when it increases suddenly. For a small business, labor often is effectively a fixed cost.

2. In real life, farm equipment is much more likely to be sold through distributors than through reps. Also, a 10 percent commission is rather optimistic. Even if reps are used, there will still be costs for advertising, brochures, sales training, travel, and so on. We assume here that the commission is paid when the product is shipped.

3. Our income-tax model is grossly oversimplified (that cash refund in January would have them rolling on the floor at the IRS), and of course state and local taxes, real-estate taxes, payroll taxes, sales taxes, and so on must be taken into account when real projections are done.

4. The strange and mystical variations of depreciation methods, like the distinction between Homoousian and Homoiousian, are not to be appreciated by mere laymen. Suffice it to say that there are several ways of depreciating capital costs; that the method chosen can drastically affect a company's profits and therefore its taxes; that it does not at all affect the company's cash flow; and that fiddling with depreciation can be a very effective way to frustrate the IRS, bamboozle investors, and get yourself so confused that you don't have the vaguest idea whether you're actually making money or not. See your accountant.

5. If you think that assuming receivables are collected in 60 days is pessimistic, you probably never tried to collect from a sales rep. Another tricky point: our assumption that we're paying for materials on 30 days. A start-up may well have to pay C.O.D., or even pay in advance; it may take months or even years to develop credit. We are also assuming that we can project sales perfectly so as to order exactly the right amount of materials for next month's production; this is easy to do on a projection *but by no means trivial in reality.*

6. We have ignored all sorts of minor start-up expenses. Also, we have not provided any reserve for contingencies.

7. Again, the sales projections are not very realistic. For one thing, the market for farm equipment is quite seasonal, and this will affect sales. Please note that many other products have highly seasonal markets *and it may not be obvious that it is so.* Another unrealistic aspect of our sales projections is the assumption we start making sales smoothly in the first month. Finally, 10 percent growth per month is really very high growth. In the rare cases when this kind of rate is actually achieved, it never comes as a steady, month-by-month increase but as big, irregular jumps, and these sudden surges hit your cash flow like a karate chop in the kidneys.

8. Selling costs can be estimated from your market research. How many sales calls will it take, on the average, to make a sale? How many sales calls can a salesperson make per day? From these numbers you can calculate how many salespeople you will need to employ to achieve a given level of monthly sales.

9. Even if you don't actually pay the commission until shipment, your accountant may make you recognize it at the time the sale is closed.

CAUTIONARY TALE:
MONEY GROWS ONLY ON FEMALE TREES

I encountered Jim Brown in 1981 when he made a presentation to the Enterprise Forum in New York City. (Ron, who was a panelist for the session, met him at the same time.) His venture interested me, and I worked with him for a couple of years in locating R&D financing.

Jim was, and is, a real kingpin in the jojoba-bean business. The jojoba plant is a tree—more of a large bush, actually—which has long grown wild in the Great American Desert. It produces "beans"—actually nuts—about the size of filberts, which can be crushed to give jojoba oil. For years, Indian and Mexican kids have gone out into the desert and picked beans and sold them, but there was little demand for the oil until the 1970s. What happened was that the maritime nations finally got serious about protecting whales from extinction and cracked down on trade in whale products. Sperm-whale oil, which was more or less essential for certain specialized lubricants and such, became unavailable. It turns out that jojoba oil is chemically similar to sperm-whale oil. It is, in fact, absolutely unique among vegetable oils and has many useful properties.

But what really made the jojoba industry was the idiosyncracies of American tax law. The jojoba plant comes in two sexes, and only the female bush produces beans. What's more, you have to wait about five years after you plant it before it starts to bear—*if* it's female, and you don't know in advance. This made farming jojoba a very enticing tax shelter. You could write off expense for several years before the farm actually started producing. So a lot of farms got started, a lot of jojoba trees got planted, and a lot of tax deductions got taken.

Jim Brown was an MIT graduate in chemistry with a good background in management. He was working for International Flavor & Fragrance when, around 1978, he started brokering jojoba oil as a part-time business. This grew into Jojoba Growers & Processors.

Jim was not interested in farming jojoba. He saw an opportunity for someone to actually produce the oil rather than tax deductions. So he set out to squeeze the beans, purify the oil, and market it.

He began to look into applications of jojoba oil. For instance, it had potential as a noncaloric cooking oil. Because of its unusual chemical structure, jojoba oil cannot be metabolized by the human body. There were of course the specialty-lubricant possibilities. For instance, IBM experimented with the stuff as a disk-drive lubricant. But the biggest potential market was the cosmetics industry. Initially, it used jojoba purely for hype. Cosmetics companies would put half a drop of jojoba oil in a ton of face cream and then advertise the hell out of it. Gradually, however, their R&D people got interested and, on investigation, found that the stuff really did have some uniquely valuable properties for cosmetics formulations.

Jim began, as I've said, by brokering the oil; most of it, in the early days of course, came from wild beans. But quality was a problem, because the crushing of the beans to get the oil was being conducted on pretty much of an amateur basis. So Jim built a processing plant in Apache Junction, near Phoenix. He leased some equipment and soon was turning out an excellent product.

The next step was to do some effective marketing. Here he ran into two fundamental problems (and this is where I came in, incidentally). First, he needed to demonstrate the usefulness of the oil. This meant doing applications research, to produce results he could show to prospective customers in various industries. Second, to market the oil in volume he had to give customers some assurance about future prices. In the early 1980s, the oil was going for about $20/lb. Presumably, when all those tax-shelter farms started producing, the price would plummet.

Jim was a good chemist himself, and he had some talented assistants, so the first task was not too difficult. By the time he made his Enterprise Forum presentation he was able to show us some of his jojoba derivatives. For instance, he had a sulfonated form that had detergent properties, and a hydrogenated "jojoba butter."

The relation between viable applications and price was much more difficult to analyze. After putting in a great deal of work, Jim was able to predict that various applications would come on stream when the price of the oil declined to certain levels. The big question therefore was: just exactly how fast would the price of the oil drop? The sales projections depended very strongly on the assumptions made about future oil prices.

So Jim couldn't stop at projecting the plans of his business. He also had to project the results of the jojoba farmers. How many trees would be planted? How many of those would be female? What would be the average annual yield of beans per female tree? How would these supply factors affect the price?

As a result of all these complexities, the generation of financial projections for Jojoba G&P was an unusually difficult exercise. I was involved in it because Jim asked me for help in raising funds. The projections we produced were unusually sophisticated in that they took into account future changes in the price of the product. Many, many start-ups ought to do this, but few do. Of course, the case of Jojoba G&P was unusual because a drop in the price of the product was *desirable;* the elasticity we projected for the market was such that sales and profits would increase as the price dropped.

This case is a good example of the principle that money has tastes. It was the kind of deal that has little appeal to typical funding sources, as Jim had discovered. I located two possibilities, however, that were very interested.

One was Jack Hesse, a Boston venture capitalist. He specializes in agriculture and related industries. The other was a British food company owned by an Indian family. They were interested in growing jojoba in Africa and Asia and thus were favorable to the idea of getting a position in a processing operation. Unfortunately, neither of these prospects worked out; the interest was there, but they could not agree with Jim on the company's value. Another powerful negative was that Jojoba G&P depended for raw materials on all those tax-shelter farmers, who included a lot of pretty flaky specimens.

In the end, the potential investors were quite right to be skeptical. Everybody had assumed that domesticating the jojoba would be a cinch. Hell, it grew wild, didn't it? It's practically a weed; it should grow like kudzu if you cultivate it. The farmers found, however, that jojoba is a wild, untamed creature and not very cooperative when grown on a plantation. So jojoba-oil prices remain high, relegating it to fairly narrow applications, largely cosmetics still.

However, Jojoba G&P remains a fairly successful company. Jim lives quite happily with his family outside Phoenix, operating his processing plant, purchasing beans from brokers, who buy them from Indian kids, who pick them off the bushes in the wilds. He hasn't gotten rich quick, but he's having a good time. And who knows—maybe someday jojoba plants will be domesticated successfully, the price of beans will drop, and Jojoba G&P will belatedly hit the big time.

HDS

11

MANAGEMENT SYSTEMS

The best ruler, the people hardly notice; the next best, they love and admire; the next best, they fear; and the worst, they hate.

Lao-Tzu

One famous gangster, when invited to take that short walk from his cell to the electric chair, responded, "The thought is repugnant to me." Most entrepreneurs react in the same way to the idea of setting up management control systems. "After all, the reason I quit Monolithic Mushroom Machinery and started my own company was to get away from all that bureaucratic nonsense."

We hope to convince you that management systems are not synonymous with bureaucracy or red tape. In fact, their purpose is not to take up your time but to free up your time.

THE CLASSICAL GROWTH MODEL

In the conventional wisdom, a new company starts out with essentially no management controls. The freewheeling entrepreneur manages by instinct, running the company out of her own head. As the company becomes larger and more complex, the founder is no longer able to handle management in this manner. In delegating tasks, she is forced to set up some control systems, since she cannot rely on her subordinates to make decisions without guidance. Furthermore, the "family feeling" of the original tiny group dissipates with growth, and it becomes necessary to police those who handle money rather than trusting them as before. Thus the growing company gradually accumulates rules, which grow into a rigid structure. Eventually the structure becomes an elaborate maze of red tape, and the company subsides into a safe but stultifying bureaucracy.

Now, there is nothing wrong with this model from the point of view of accuracy. This is exactly the way most companies evolve. The problem is that many theorists of business structure approve of this process, or think that it is natural and unavoidable even if not completely desirable. The standard view is that it is impossible to run a small company with formal management controls—and that it is impossible to run a large company without a bureaucracy.

More recent work has challenged these conclusions. Books such as *In Search of Excellence* (see Bibliography) and *Theory Z** have described large companies that have become successful precisely by avoiding the development of bureaucracy. As a corollary, we would like to suggest that the success of a small company can be immeasurably assisted if well-designed management systems are set up right from the start.

PURPOSE OF CONTROLS

Only a very small company can afford to be amorphous. To look like an amoeba is fine if you're microscopic in size, but if you're going to grow very large, you need a skeleton. And, to continue the metaphor, to start out with a skeleton and let it grow along with you is a better strategy than to try to install it surgically in a shapeless blob that's grown too big to move.

As we pointed out in Chapter 3, your company's employees will resist almost any major change in the rules. The older and bigger the company becomes, the stronger this resistance will

*William Ouchi (Reading, Mass.: Addison-Wesley, 1981).

be. If you wait to install controls, your people may evade them or even sabotage them.

Management controls are an advantage even to—or especially to—the small company, because they save time. A good control system will allow you and the other members of your team to spend your time productively. Your company will be more efficient and able to move more quickly.

Finally, a good control system unifies your company and supports your company culture. It focuses all your people—from top to bottom—on your objectives and encourages them to pull together to achieve common goals.

We therefore strongly recommend that you set up a simple but effective management system before you even start up. As your company grows, you should gradually add additional controls—but if you've done it right at the beginning, you'll find that you'll never need to establish a bureaucracy. Red tape is characteristic not of planned systems but of those which "just grew."

Most management control systems, however, do "just grow," and consequently they are real junk. It is this sort of random mess that most of us are familiar with from experience and want to avoid in our new companies. A truly effective management control system should accomplish the following things for you.

First it should *make the operations of your company conform to the company objectives.* Obvious though this may seem, it is very difficult to put into practice. It isn't all that hard to make rules that will result in the accomplishment of the company objectives—the hard part is defining the company objectives. Now, if you have a really good top-management team, it will of course clearly define and enforce these objectives—until it becomes too busy with operating responsibilities. Then the company's objectives will gradually drift out of focus. How is this to be avoided?

Some theorists rely on exhortation; top management, they say, should simply avoid being caught up in operating work and concentrate on strategy. However, few executives have the ability to hold themselves aloof in this way—and even if they could, should they? Others recommend that a separate "strategic planning" staff be set up. Unfortunately, a small company can seldom afford this—and is it really desirable for strategy to be separated from operating responsibilities? We advocate a more modern approach: set up management systems that involve considering and setting objectives as an inherent part of the process.

A small manufacturing company was run completely by the seat of the pants. There was no marketing strategy; whenever a customer asked for something new, the company attempted to make it, so that in a few years its product line was a real hodgepodge. The founder, as is so often the case, thought of his company as "market-driven," when in fact it was sales-driven—a very different and much less desirable approach. The plant was expanded in a similar, opportunistic manner, ignoring financial and tax considerations and disregarding the rather important question of site limitation. The company has seemingly prospered, doubling sales every year, due to a series of brilliant improvisations by a founder of unusual ability. But every month he adds a few more balls to the large number he is already juggling, and the future looks ominous.

Second, good management control systems should *motivate all employees to accomplish the company objectives.* Perhaps the major fallacy of the bureaucratic organization is the belief that people will do something simply because they are ordered to do so. Human beings just do not behave that way. Thus in the typical organization the rules end up being rather ineffectual. The people working there will do what the system motivates them to do, which seldom has much to do with company's objectives. In order for your management control systems to work effectively, you must set things up so that your people are rewarded for doing what needs to be done, and punished for doing things that hinder achieving the company's goals.

Many of us have seen in person the classic example of poorly designed controls: end-of-year budget bulge. A department is given a certain budget for the year. If an unexpected contingency comes up and the budget is exceeded, the department manager will be punished. So he "pads" his budget to establish a protective reserve. But then if no emergency comes up, he'll have excess funds at the end of the fiscal year, which will result in a big cut in his budget for the next period. So just before the end of the year he spends money like mad on anything remotely justifiable.

All this is very bad for the company. Valuable capital is tied up unnecessarily, then spent wastefully. Even worse, the department manager and his subordinates become cynical and resentful. And having once lied in order to get along in the system, they become more vulnerable to serious dishonesty.

Note that all this results from the contradiction between what the company says and what it does. Managers who run their operations efficiently and cut costs, as they were told to do, get punished by having their budgets cut. Managers who inflate their costs and corrupt the system are rewarded.

Third, you should set up a system that *runs without continual attention*. All the procedures involved should be as simple as possible and virtually self-enforcing. A system that requires constant top-management attention to make it work is a bad system. Not only does it waste the valuable time of executives, but its obtrusiveness irritates their subordinates and damages morale. What's more, it tends to subjective operation and to accusations—usually correct—of favoritism and unfairness. A well-designed system is, as they say in the computer business, "transparent to the user." You hardly notice the working of the system until an "error message" appears to demand top-management intervention. Such a system lets your top people devote their time to their real work, and their subordinates are guided almost without feeling the reins.

THE STRUCTURE OF A MANAGEMENT CONTROL SYSTEM

Just what does a management control system consist of? It is, of course, a set of rules and procedures, with several components. First, there must be procedures for setting company goals. No doubt you will set goals at the start-up, but you need an ongoing procedure to redefine your goals as the company grows and the situation changes. Second, there must be provision for assigning the company's people the necessary tasks and objectives to accomplish the company's goals. Third, there must be a structure of rewards and punishments so that employees will be motivated to accomplish their tasks and do them well. Fourth, there must be a reporting structure; top management must be able to monitor progress. Fifth, there must be some sort of enforcement to ensure that all this actually gets done.

It is not particularly difficult to set up systems that will perform these functions. What is hard is to integrate the various functions so that they work together. Usually, the rules have little or nothing to do with the company goals, the rewards and punishments are tied to arbitrary factors rather than performance, and the reporting structure produces stacks of computer printouts that tell nothing of importance.

Goal Setting

We already discussed in an earlier chapter the necessity of setting objectives for your company. Presumably, you have by now developed a set of goals for your start-up. But you must recognize that your company's objectives will inevitably change with time. Your company, your market, and the society in which you are embedded are all going to evolve over the years, and your original objectives will become at least partly obsolete. You must realize that (assuming you have not yet started your company) you are in an unusually favorable position. You have the opportunity to think about your company's objectives and set them at leisure, undistracted by operating responsibilities. In an ongoing company, it is not nearly so easy. There always seems to be some task more urgent than thinking out new objectives.

It seems almost impossible to convey to someone who hasn't yet been there how *distracting* it is to be an entrepreneur. A few months after I had started Reaction Design, the evidence began coming in that we were completely off the track. It was critical to rethink our entire approach and make major changes in our objectives and operations. Why couldn't I see this? Was I just stupid? Not really. There was just too much going on—too many important decisions to make, too many urgent problems to solve. The last batch of naphthylalanine has hung up; what is poisoning the catalyst? That big check we've been waiting for has arrived—and bounced; how to meet payroll? Aldrich is considering distributing some of our products, but wants them at a devastating discount; if we accept, will it make us—or break us? The HPLC is down, and that order *has* to ship next week . . . the last lot only 96 percent purity—if we recrystallize, we'll lose at least a fifth of it and we'll have to run another batch to make up the order . . . Martin wants a quote on grandlure right away . . .

In short, it's not as easy as it may seem to maintain an objective view of the business and revise your strategy as needed. I remember a scene from an old Western in which a cowboy is tied to a horse's tail and the horse ridden off at a fast trot. The victim would run like mad for a few yards, then fall and be dragged along, then get back on his feet briefly. . . . That's what it's like being an entrepreneur.

This is why it is desirable to set up a *system* for continued goal setting. Almost all big companies, and many small ones, pretend to have such a system—five-year plans, annual "strategy sessions," and so on. In reality, such procedures rapidly degrade into ratification of the previous course with only cosmetic changes. To prevent your company strategy from degrading in this way, you should use the following techniques.

First, attach your company's objectives to its operations. Most company "strategies" or "objectives" or "goals" or "principles" are actually nothing of the sort; they are merely words in the annual statement or the personnel manual. The top management may sincerely believe in them, but no action is taken to implement them, because they are detached from the management structure.

Second, set specific, measurable goals. A goal is of use only if you can determine whether or not you've met it! This doesn't necessarily mean that all objectives have to be numerical in form. But for every objective you set, develop a measurement for your success.

Third, avoid long-term goals. A big business cannot effectively plan more than five years ahead; a small business, no more than three years. It is impossible to set a rational objective for a decade or more; it's too difficult to predict the environment you will be operating in. Such goals are actually just dreams. Dreams are good—in fact, they are indispensable—but they should not be confused with objectives. Besides, if you set goals a year at a time, you'll be forced to reexamine them frequently.

Setting Standards

Once you have set goals, you must then translate them into standards in order to make them effective. For example, suppose you have set the goal: "We will manufacture the highest-quality widget in the industry." To turn this into a standard, you would survey your competitor's results and set your requirements accordingly: "We will have fewer than 0.2 percent returns, fewer than 0.5 percent complaints, MTBF over 5.5 years." Similar standards can be set for any type of goal: sales ("$1 million next year"), profits ("20 percent before-tax ROI"), technological leadership ("Megabit RAM chips in production quantities within 18 months"), workplace quality ("Less than 10 percent turnover in programmers"). If it's a real objective, you will always be able to transform it into a measurable standard. If you can't, maybe it's just a dream.

It is crucial to set the *right* standards. When I worked for AlCan, the head of the sales department set up standards for the performance of our salespeople. Each district was judged on the basis of how many sales calls were made, as measured by the number of "call reports." But sales statistics showed that the best sales figures came from districts that produced the lowest numbers of call reports. Taking time to close the sale produced much better results than rushing off to try to maximize the number of sales calls.

Using Motivators

Now we come to the key part. No goal, however noble, no standard, however ambitious, is of any use at all unless your system is set up to *motivate* your people to meet the standard and accomplish the goal. Your most difficult and most rewarding task is to build a process that will tie rewards and punishments to your company's objectives.

You have basically three types of reward that you can use to motivate your employees: money, status, and recognition.

Money is simple and objective, relatively easy to handle. At the beginning of each year, when you set objectives and define standards, develop a bonus schedule for each of your employees. Decide (in consultation with the person in question, if at all possible) what the employee's contribution to the company should be during the coming year; set up a compensation schedule of the type we discussed in Chapter 3. This is the backbone of your motivational system.

Note how this approach ties in your management system and makes it effective: quite simply, you are now *paying* your people to do what needs to be done, and that will have an amazing effect on how much actually gets done. What's more, the fact that you have this system in place *forces* you to set objectives and standards, and it also forces you to revise them as conditions change—if you don't, some people will get absurd bonuses.

Most of us tend to set goals with just sales and profits in mind; if we're very bright, we consider productivity. But if you wish to build a growth company, attracting, keeping, and above all developing good people are crucial. This is where status rewards—promotions—come in. If you promote haphazardly, your personnel development will be randomized. Promotion policies should be part of your management system. This means deciding what talents your company needs and will need in the future, and offering promotion to your employees in return for developing those talents.

Recognition . . . all of us know this is a powerful motivating factor, but almost all of us use praise on an occasional and random basis rather than systematically. Cold-blooded though it may sound, recognition can be made a regular, controlled part of your motivational management system.

> One of the major factors in the early rise of IBM was Thomas Watson Sr.'s shrewd use of systematic recognition, particularly for salespeople. The Hundred Percent Club, the Golden Circle, awards banquets—all were put on a standardized, formal basis. The company *made sure* that the employee who performed was rewarded with recognition, by making it policy.

Establishing a Reporting Structure

The fourth element of your management control system is a reporting structure. You must have some sort of feedback to let you know how you are doing and whether your people are performing. The nice thing about setting up a motivational payments system is that it automatically requires you to develop a reporting structure so that you will know how to distribute the rewards.

It obviously is important to avoid burdening your company with a complex structure of reports. The question is: what is the minimum amount of information I need to control the company? What are the key numbers that define the really important information?

At Sedgwick Printout I received a report every morning from my secretary. It included: pages produced; page rates; dollar volume; new orders; accounts receivable; and the location of our sales and system people for that day. This briefing took her only a few minutes to prepare the previous evening and kept me on top of all our key parameters at all times.

You'll find that your accountant is both your best assistant and your biggest obstacle in setting up an effective reporting structure. The accounting system for your company is its basic information-gathering mechanism, and if it is structured properly, it can be used to carry not only the standard financial data but most of the other information you need.

For a very tiny company, it proved quite satisfactory to handle the entire accounting system by hand, using the traditional handwritten journals and ledgers. I set up the bookkeeping so that the original records contained extra information. For instance, the sales journal contained, in addition to the normal entries, the customer's purchase-order number, our invoice number, and notations of all transactions related to the sale. This centralized the information and made it very convenient to deal with inquiries or overdue receivables.

The whole science of accounting consists of the development of reporting structures, so your accountant will be very pleased indeed to be invited to perform this task for your company. Unfortunately, you will probably have to fight some major battles with her to get a usable system.

A number of factors make accountants much less useful than they should be to small businesses. For one thing, accounting is organized as a profession with the aim of preventing or at least exposing any hanky-panky in the books of the client companies. To facilitate this objective, strict rules are set down which inhibit innovation. (Note that "creative accounting" is a synonym for suspicious, if not improper, reporting.) As a result, small companies and innovative companies often find that the rules prevent development of an accurate model of the business. (One can't blame the accountants alone for this; IRS and FASB (Financial Accounting Standards Board) regulations mandate a great many ridiculous procedures.)

An aggravating circumstance is the heavy reliance of modern accountants on "canned" computer programs, which are incapable of any significant flexibility. The computer also has made it easy—too easy—to perform complicated calculations such as elaborate overhead allocations, which obscure rather than illuminate the essential characteristics of your business.

Finally, many accountants suffer from a chronic inability to understand that there is a cost associated with gathering information, and that management would prefer receiving only an approximate account of the source of its profit to getting the exact information at such cost as to result in a loss.

There is a tendency to neglect the details of your accounting system when you start your business; it seems like a necessary but dry and rather unimportant task. In fact, though, it can be critical, and you would do well to sit down with your accountant for a couple of days and thrash it out thoroughly. Also, budget some time for revisions during the first year, for you will find that a considerable shakedown period will be needed before the system operates efficiently.

Unless your company is large enough to have a full-time CFO right from the start, I would recommend that you do your own bookkeeping for the first year or so. It is a terrible drain on your time; and if the ancient Greeks had known of double-entry accounting they would have made Sisyphus balance a ledger instead of rolling a stone. But there is no better way to delve into the bowels of your business and truly understand its fundamentals.

A very valuable technique for building useful control systems is the "problem flag."

As your business grows, you and the other members of your team will find your time increasingly tied up in overseeing critical tasks to make sure they get done properly. You really do need to keep track of an expanding number of key processes—but the trouble is that soon you have no time to think about strategy, objectives, or innovation. To avoid becoming bogged down in this important but routine activity, you can set up a flag system.

Simply define key factors in your operations and "flag" exceptions. For instance, your production people might be instructed, "Notify me at once if the yield on step 4 drops below 90 percent." This might be a long-term flag; one can also set up temporary flags: "Notify me at once if the big order for IBM falls behind schedule." It's important to realize that flag conditions should never be defined as a disaster—your people will presumably notify you without being told if something really catastrophic happens. The good flag condition is the small cloud no bigger than a man's hand that presages disaster in advance; that way you get told in time to take action.

The key to making a flag system operate is twofold. First, make it clear that you mean it and that heads will roll if a flag doesn't go up. Second, once you've set it up, forget about it until a flag does go up. The whole point of this system is to free up your time. If you constantly look over your people's shoulders to make sure they're keeping you posted, they won't take the system seriously. Make it clear that you're relying on them and they'll generally live up to it.

KEEPING 'EM HONEST

If entrepreneurs have a universal failing, it may well be that they are too trusting. Fortunately, a good management control system can do much to make up for this deficiency. Double-entry bookkeeping contains, as an integral part of its design, safeguards that make it difficult, complicated, and perilous to falsify records. The use of regular, or better yet irregular, audits augments these controls substantially. But people's ingenuity can find a way around even the best of bureaucratic controls. Your company's real protection from internal fraud results from your people.

Your motivational reward system is a source of temptation, but also a means of control. You will obviously need to take precautions to ensure that those whose rewards depend on a certain indicator are not in a position to manipulate its readings. On the other hand, it will usually be the case that an attempt to inflate one indicator will result in the depression of others, and those whose bonuses would thereby be decreased will act as your police force to prevent such fraud.

But ultimately there is no substitute for a company culture that is based on strict honesty. Employees who are encouraged, or even permitted, to enhance their company's profits by sharp practice with customers will invariably feel free to cheat their employer if they think they can get away with it.

> Few entrepreneurs need to be told that they should not tolerate dishonesty in themselves or their company. But many need warning against excessive charity in dealing with the dishonesty of others. Often an honest person, on being cheated, will refuse to "make a fuss," out of a paradoxical embarrassment. But this toleration sets a bad example, encourages further offenses—and may even be misinterpreted as evidence of complicity by onlookers who do not know all the facts. One need not pursue a vendetta against dishonest associates, but it is wise to make one's position clear even if one chooses to turn the other cheek.

Exercise 11–1:
Outlining a Management Control System

1. Define the key objectives of your company, if you haven't already done so. There should be no more than five, and preferably no more than three, on the list.

2. Translate your objectives into standards. Each objective should result in *measurable* standards of some sort—accomplish some specific thing during or by the end of some specific period of time.

3. For each standard, decide who will be responsible for meeting it. Then decide how you will reward them for achieving it, and possibly punish them for failure to achieve it.

4. Ask yourself what you need to know to be sure your standards are being met. Then design reports that will provide that information to top management. Include a flag system.

5. Go over the system you have constructed and look for contradictions. For everyone subject to it, ask yourself what will happen if he complies or if he doesn't. Are you sure he will be rewarded in the former case and punished in the latter? Then ask yourself who has the opportunity to rip you off. What checks will you set up to police these persons?

6. Schedule a top-management "retreat" on a regular basis to review from the ground up, and if necessary revise, your company's control systems. We'd recommend doing this quarterly for your first year, semiannually until you're five years old, and annually thereafter. Don't let this degenerate into a routine endorsement of the status quo. The trick is to ask, "How are our systems working? What is failing?" Missed objectives should not be shrugged off—dig into them until you understand what went wrong, and then *change the system.* Peter Drucker suggests an approach that is terrific for this kind of session: If we weren't already (in this market) (making this product) (running this project) would we start it now? No. Then let's *cancel it instantly.*

COMPUTERIZATION

It used to be—not very long ago—that no company would consider computerizing until it could afford to buy a mainframe computer and hire a data-processing department. Since the advent of the microcomputer, it seems only a matter of time until your daughter's lemonade stand does its accounting by computer.

This may be a good thing, because one of the first principles of effective company computerization is *do it early* if you're going to do it. There is a tremendous amount of hassle, inconvenience, and confusion associated with putting your company's procedures on the computer. The larger and more complicated your management and accounting systems, the longer it will take and the more it will cost to adapt them to the computer. Thus it's better to computerize when you are small and simple, and to expand the system gradually.

The president of a very successful mail-order operation with which I dealt for a while once confided to me that computerization had given him some scary moments. His company developed an integrated system that combined sales and order entry with automatic inventory control. It proved immensely valuable once it was running. However, the cost of setting it up vastly exceeded estimates—and, much worse, the firm experienced devastating foul-ups during the transition period, when neither the manual nor the computer systems were operating properly.

Another good reason for early computerization is that all your written data will at some point have to be put into the computer. Somebody will have to sit down at the keyboard and type in all those records. The older you are, and the bigger you are, the more time it will take.

The second principle of computerization is related: *allow for expansion.* Switching from one type of computer system to another is almost as difficult as switching from manual to computer. Select your computer vendor very carefully. Try to get someone you can stick with for many years. When you first computerize, sit down and generate a rough plan for expansion. If you're going to buy a microcomputer, plan for when you buy two or three more; how you will eventually tie them into a network; and beyond that, how you might make the transition to a mini. You can't make really detailed plans far into the future because computer technology changes so fast. But think about such issues as standard equipment and procedures, compatibility, and so on.

The third principle of computerization is: *put it all on the machine.* There's a tendency—especially when you see how complicated computerization is—to limit your use of the computer to keeping financial records and generating standard accounting statements. This is a mistake. The big value of the computer is in its ability to quickly find, collate, and analyze information.

Try the following experiment. Keep track of your clerical workers' time use for a few days. You'll find that an absolutely astounding proportion of their time is devoted to locating information in the files. The average secretary can type four letters in the time it takes to find a letter you wrote a year ago. A word processor's real value is not that it reduces the letter-typing time by 30 percent but that it reduces the letter-finding time by 95 percent.

Try to get as much information as possible off paper and onto disk. Try to integrate systems as much as possible—for instance, tie your inventory records into the accounting system directly. And try to computerize even simple tasks that can easily be done by hand, if it looks like they will grow in the future.

Finally, a word should be said about getting expert help. Use your accountant heavily as a computerization consultant. (The big firms are usually more helpful in this area than the small ones.) The other source of helpful information is your vendor—whether it's the manufacturer of the equipment or a distributor or a value-added reseller. Especially if you're naive about computers, you should stick to dealing with relatively big and reputable firms with long track records. It's too easy to be intimidated by some jargon-talking expert and get ripped off. Before you start paying, make sure you have it in writing what the system will do and *when*, and try very hard for a penalty clause.

CAUTIONARY TALE: SUNKEN TIMBERS

Some years ago I became involved with a company called Inter-Allied Resources. This was a small public company, but the securities didn't trade. It was what is referred to as a nonreporting public company, with a couple of hundred shareholders and one operating subsidiary.

To understand why this company was interesting, you need to realize that for a company to "go public" is a very difficult and expensive proposition. For most young companies it is possible only during exceptionally good bull markets, and the SEC requirements and other regulatory hassles make going public a very complicated process. But being public has some very substantial advantages, particularly in the ability to raise new capital by selling stock. So just being a public company is an asset with a tangible value, and even if the company has no other assets and no ongoing business, it may be kept in existence as a "public shell" that can usefully be merged with a real, operating company. You can see ads for these shells in *The Wall Street Journal* sometimes.

My partners, who were very active in another business but were very deal-oriented people, saw this as an opportunity to pick up a public shell, turn around its operating subsidiary, refinance it, and then enter or acquire other businesses. If a history of success could be established, a larger public offering could take place further down the road.

The operating subsidiary was a distributor of industrial fasteners—nuts and bolts, in other words. It bought fasteners in Japan and other parts of the Far East and sold them to manufacturers up and down the East Coast through direct solicitation, telephone salesmen, and a string of reps. I took over the operation as CEO and went to work on turning it around.

We had a sixth-floor walk-up loft in a building on Leonard Street in Lower Manhattan, where we paid some modest rent to the previous owner of the company. The personnel had a rather vague idea of where the products were. There were thousands and thousands of nuts and bolts of many sizes and head shapes and threads and so on. But there was no clear inventory-control system, so the place was a real mess. The first thing I did was to bring in a major accounting firm to set up a control system. It was a manual system, but even without a computer, within six months we had a handle on the system. We now knew what our inventory was, what we had, what we needed to buy, and—very important—how long it took to buy. When you order material from Japan, you've got to plan on a four- or five-month delivery cycle. To run this new system, we hired a person who had worked with Abraham & Strauss as a systems control manager, and we really got the nuts-and-bolts company running like a well-oiled clock.

My partners and I went out and got some long-term contracts from major industrial concerns for some new products. We brought the products in; there were significant margins; and we began to really make money. Within a year we were doing $4 million or $5 million in sales. The Chase Manhattan Bank was the company's major lender; it had been very nervous before we came in and now was very pleased because we had developed a substantial net worth. We raised more capital. We had a going business; we were meeting our debt service; and there was general satisfaction all around. I'm happy to say that I was blamed for all this success, although, needless to say, a lot of other people played important roles.

By this time we felt ready and mature enough to go into another business. There was inadequate room for expansion in fasteners. We had demonstrated our ability to function well in the trading business, so we wanted to set up another distributor of some sort. I looked throughout the economy and came up with the idea of becoming a distributor of railroad ties and other forest products—grade lumber, specialty logs, and so on. My partners were active in the railroad industry, and this seemed a logical approach. At that time the larger American railroads were upgrading their road beds—which hadn't been done in a major way since the Korean War—so it looked like an excellent time to enter the market.

The concept was this. There were a number of small sawmills in the concentrated hardwoods area of the Southeast—Tennessee, Kentucky, and Alabama mostly—that needed help with distribution. They were too small to generate enough wood to justify the cost of direct marketing. So we planned to establish so-called concentration yards at various key points. We would buy from the small mills, and sell in quantity—ties to the railroads, grade lumber to furniture manufacturers, high-quality logs to German interests who made veneer out of them.

We started out by getting a very substantial order from the Chessie System for railroad ties, and that was the backbone of the whole operation. Against that order, the Chase lent us a significant amount of money. We got another order from Burlington Northern, we ran the financing up to a couple of million dollars, and we started buying railroad ties like they were going out of style.

I was flushed with my recent success in fasteners, the board of directors was totally supportive, the banks were enthusiastic—and I became more interested in building volume than in the quality of the results. Of course, I fully intended to put in management controls. But

I had no idea of the various quality differences of railroad ties or lumber; I didn't understand the lumber business and failed to hire people who could make up for my deficiencies in this area.

The disaster really began when we decided we could get an edge on the competition by going around to the small mills, buying ties on the spot, and paying cash. As a means of maximizing the flow of lumber into our concentration yards, this was a truly brilliant innovation. Every mill operator in the Southeast was tripping over his own feet in his haste to get to us before we changed our minds. From the point of view of financial controls, we were calling in artillery strikes on our own position. Our agents, of course, were equipped with checkbooks to make these payments, and we didn't know how much they'd spent till they got back from a trip and turned in the stubs. It was like the problems of a husband-wife joint checking account but a thousand times worse. We never knew how much we had in the bank and our accountants were going bonkers.

All this while we were accumulating a *lot* of railroad ties. Now our agents, in going around to the various mills, were buying stacks of ties. They could see what the ties looked like on the outside, but the quality of the ties in the interior of the stack was anybody's guess until we sent them to the railroads and they got inspected. The idea was that this was no problem because our agents knew the various mills and their reputations and would buy only from people who could be trusted. But could our agents be trusted? We had no *system* to monitor and enforce the rules, so they tended to follow the line of least resistance.

Pretty soon we had $2 million worth of railroad ties—correction: ties for which we had paid $2 million, in cash. Chessie and Burlington then inspected them and let us know what they actually were worth, and it turned out to be much less than $2 million. As the quality reports came in, I suddenly realized that water was pouring over the gunwales. In just five months we had gone from success story to disaster.

I scrambled to keep us from sinking. The first priority was to plug the leak; I instantly stopped the purchasing program. Then I located a fellow who had run a huge concentration yard for IT&T's forest-products subsidiary and who really did know the business. He straightened things out quickly, changing the operation so that ties were delivered to our yards, where they were inspected individually by qualified people, using a monstrous moving table.

Unfortunately, this turnaround came too late. We had shipped too much water, and even the buoyancy of the nuts and bolts couldn't keep us afloat. Some of the people who a few months before had been chanting, "There is no god but Mammon and Sedgwick is his Prophet," now looked upon me, shall we say, somewhat less favorably. I stepped aside as CEO, though I remained on the board. There was nothing for it but to take our bath, so we liquidated the company. However, we maintained the public shell. About a year ago we merged it into a successful West Coast company that supplies plastic parts to high-tech companies in Silicon Valley. We as investors were of course heavily diluted in this operation, but the stock is up, and if the company continues to do well we may yet come out fairly well.

Not one of my greatest accomplishments. The nuts-and-bolts operation succeeded because it was right under my eye and I made sure that management control systems were operating. But when we went into lumber, the operation was spread out over half the country. I couldn't personally watch over it, so it was crucial to set up a *system* to monitor our employees and our suppliers. We needed rules to control our disbursements, rewards to ensure the rules were followed, and reports so we'd immediately know what was happening. Failure to properly attend to these boring details was sufficient to destroy a thriving business in a matter of months.

HDS

12

THE BUSINESS PLAN

The planning is more important than the plan.

General Eisenhower

In recent years, entrepreneurs have become increasingly sophisticated. As recently as 1978, when the MIT Enterprise Forum started, our request for a business plan sometimes brought the response, "What's a 'business plan'?" A couple of years later, we generally heard, "Yes, well, I know we should have a business plan, but we've never gotten around to writing one." Today, our presenters almost invariably have business plans and are worried about their quality. But still, they tend to see a business plan as a sort of tedious and useless excrescence—necessary to satisfy investors but otherwise of no value.

Investor attitudes toward the business plan have also changed. A decade ago, investors generally demanded massive tomes loaded with information, graphs, tables, and above all financial projections. Perhaps venture capitalists became tired of all this prolixity as their deal flow increased, for now they prefer short business plans—twenty pages or so, and double-spaced too. In fact, some of the more macho gunslingers brag of deals based on plans scribbled on a napkin at a Santa Clara restaurant. No doubt by the time you read this, fashion will have changed again. But they will certainly be demanding business plans, and a good plan will still have the same basic characteristics.

One of my hobbies is watching Japanese soap operas, which are shown on one of the Los Angeles TV channels. The plot of one show concerned a woman who divorced her abusive husband and, to support herself, started a telephone message service. As she went through the start-up process, I found the scenes amazingly familiar. Our Japanese heroine went through all the typical stages: getting advice from some experienced entrepreneurs, finding partners, scrounging around for capital—and writing a business plan. Even in Japan, where customs are frequently so different from ours as to seem more extraterrestrial than simply foreign, the process of starting a business follows the same path.

Now the fact is that a business plan has, or should have, a great deal of value quite aside from its utility in raising money. It should organize your strategy for the business, identify and test your assumptions, simulate your results, and provide you with a convenient summary of essential data. However, the standard definition of a good business plan is that it is one that assists you materially in getting your hands on a lot of capital, and who are we to argue with tradition?

So, how can you write a plan that will appeal to investors?

THE STRUCTURE OF A SUCCESSFUL BUSINESS PLAN

To you, your plan describes a business, a start-up, a new venture. To an investor, it is simply another "deal," part of his "deal flow." And he has a lot of deal flow. He is not going to waste time on a plan that does not get to the point very quickly and tell him what it's all about.

There are all sorts of models, guides, and outlines for business plans available. But you won't go far wrong if you imagine that you are faced with a skeptical investor who asks you the following questions:

- What need do you propose to satisfy, and how big is that need?
- How do you propose to satisfy it, and make money doing so?
- What are the prospects for success—what have you got that will make you successful?
- What do you need to do it?
- What's in it for me, the investor?

A good business plan, very simply, answers these five questions; answers them in a satisfactory way; backs up those answers, where necessary, with strong evidence; and does all this in a simple and lucid manner so that the investor can see it almost at a glance.

The Executive Summary

This has become a standard part of almost every business plan. The trouble is that most Executive Summaries are just awful. Partly, this is due to the fact that writing something short is much harder than writing with unrestricted length. But the big problem is that entrepreneurs look at the Executive Summary as a short sales pitch, a teaser. This approach generally does not work. The investor wants an Executive Summary that gives him the key information quickly, not a collection of vague generalities about the tremendous opportunity open to him.

The recipe for a good Executive Summary is simple. To each of the five questions given earlier, write a two-sentence answer. That's your Executive Summary.

The Need

Most first-time entrepreneurs (especially those of us from a technological background) tend to construct a business plan in a very logical form, starting with what we propose to do, that is, the product. This is a poor idea. Instead, the first thing the reader encounters should be a succinct explanation of the *need* for the product. Every successful business is born of human frustration. People want something, and they can't get it, and the entrepreneur finds a way to make it available to them—at a price.

By beginning your pitch with a description of the need you propose to fill, you avoid one of the major perils of financing: being stigmatized as "a solution looking for a problem."

What you are really doing in this section of your plan, of course, is defining your market. In your Executive Summary, this takes only a paragraph, or perhaps only a few words ("mushroom farmers"). Later on you'll have to get down to specifics. Who is your market? (Specifically, medium- to large-scale mushroom farmers who need mechanized mushroom cutters.) How big is the market? (1,500 mushroom farmers in the U.S. alone, and they spend $9 million on cutters.) And from there into all the other questions we talked about in Chapter 4 when we discussed market research.

The Business

Once the investor has been satisfied that there is a need, the next question is: how do you propose to satisfy that need? Most entrepreneurs try to answer this question by giving a detailed . . . very detailed . . . very, very detailed description of their product. This is a turn-off. Let's rephrase the question a bit: Just exactly what are you going to do to satisfy the customer? A description of your product is not enough. You must also explain—just as you would to a customer—how the features of your product translate into benefits for the customer. You should do this much in your Executive Summary. Later, in the body of the plan, you must also specify how and where you are going to sell the product, how you will service or follow up, how much you are going to charge for it, and a host of other factors. Does all this sound familiar? You're quite right; this section of your plan is really devoted to market strategy, and must deal with the various considerations we discussed in Chapter 5 and 6.

I recently had occasion to study the business plan of a start-up that plans to make certain imaging chemicals for use with CAT scanners and other medical devices. Page after page is devoted to the superior qualities and features of the product. But the whole focus is on the *technological* superiority of the product. What the founders who wrote the plan have consistently omitted is: what's in it for the *customer*? Somehow it just didn't occur to them that the customer should have any say in whether this product is going to sell.

Another business plan I examined dealt with a novelty product that was to be sold by direct marketing. The inventor had been ripped off by the company that had initially distributed the product and now resolved to do it herself. I advised her to get, by hook or by crook, the sales figures of the outfit that had cheated her. Those figures would provide tangible proof that this product would sell.

The Qualifications

Our third investor question is: what are the prospects for success? By this time you have, you hope, convinced the investor that there is a need in the marketplace of sufficient magnitude to support your company, and that you have a viable approach to satisfying this need. The next step is to convince him that you, your team, and your company can handle the job, can actually accomplish your objectives. In other words, this part of your plan is concerned with *qualifications*.

Four of the traditional business-plan chapters come under this heading. First, *the team*. You should demonstrate that your people are highly qualified in business management as well as in their own fields. Second, *production plans*. You should demonstrate the feasibility of manufacturing your product, or providing your service, with low cost and high quality and reliability. Third, *the competition*. It's not enough to be good—you've got to be better than the other guys. You should objectively analyze the strengths and weaknesses of your competitors and demonstrate that you can defeat them. Fourth, if appropriate, your *R&D plans* come under this heading—especially if your product is not yet fully developed. You need to demonstrate that it is actually possible to make your widget, and that it will work once made.

Financial Plans

Now we come to the fourth question: what are the capital requirements of your business? This obviously is to be answered by your financial projections, which should show in detail the financial characteristics and operations of your company. In addition, you should write a section devoted explicitly to "use of funds"—that is, when you get the money, exactly what are you going to spend it on, and why?

The use-of-funds section is very important. Don't skip it! The investor really is a little bit curious about what you are going to do with her money. So tell her exactly: "I'm going to spend this much on buying machinery, that much on a national advertising campaign." Be sure that in this section, or elsewhere, you explain *why* you are going to spend the money in this particular way. It's got to hang together with the rest of the plan. Why are you buying this machinery rather than leasing or jobbing out the production? Justify each piece of spending.

The Deal

Finally, you must deal with the fifth investor question: what's in it for me? In other words, you must specify the deal you are offering. How much do you want the investor to put up? In what form? What will he get for it? How is ownership in the company currently distributed, and how will it be distributed after the deal? What are your plans for future financings, assuming you complete this one?

It is neither necessary nor desirable to put any "boiler plate" into your business plan. Don't insert disclaimers or legal language. The business plan is *not* an offering memorandum—unless you make the mistake of converting it into one. If you must have an offering memorandum (many states require them for private placements, and your lawyer can tell you all about it) make it a separate document. Give it to the investor *after* he's committed. Remember that many blue-sky laws restrict the number of prospective investors you can even *approach*—and generally, when you give an investor an offering memorandum, you've "approached" him. Don't use up these opportunities pointlessly.

HOW ABOUT A SAMPLE?

Nowhere in this book do we provide a sample business plan to guide you in writing yours. In fact, we're not even going to give you a detailed outline. That's intentional.

We could show you very, very good plans, plans that easily raised millions of dollars from venture capitalists. The reason we don't is that your plan is going to have to compete for attention with a lot of other plans. Many of them are going to be careful copies of those spectacular successes of the past, and they are going to look monotonously similar.

Your plan has no chance of success unless it is read by the investor and chosen over competing plans. It cannot be too strongly emphasized that *freshness* is critical. Your plan should not be flashy or showy or in poor taste. It should be complete and well organized, and use formats and terminology that the reader will understand. But it should also stand out. The appearance, the style, the approach should be as unique as you can manage. Concentrate on conveying the unique value of your company, and you can write a superb business plan the first time, without copying anyone else's format. When you're funded, you'll find other companies will want to imitate *your* plan.

An understated style is a real asset to a business plan. A project I'm working on now is devoted to providing highly effective medical illustrations of injuries for use in malpractice suits. The founder's original version of the business plan started with an extremely portentous explanation of the threat to Western Civilization posed by the medical malpractice insurance crisis. Needless to say, toning down this purple prose was one of my first tasks in rewriting the plan.

THE PITFALLS

There are certain clichés of the business-plan *genre* you should be careful to avoid. These bromides are almost universal among writers of business plans; if you avoid using them in yours, it will really stand out. Here are some of the worst:

Chinese-Glove Theory. We heard this one from Barry Unger of the MIT Enterprise Forum in Cambridge. "There are 800 million Chinese, that's 1.6 billion hands. Now, assuming we got 1 percent of the market . . ." This, of course, is the standard top-down market-research approach, and venture capitalists react to it as to fingernails scraping a blackboard. If you do real market research—even though it may be a bit sloppy—you'll get a substantial edge right at the start.

Humongous-Market Theory. Even if you've done good, bottom-up market research, avoid the "1 percent of a trillion-dollar market" approach. Define your market more tightly. Investors would much rather see you project 60 percent of a $100-million market than 6 percent of a $1-billion market.

"Up Like a Rocket . . ." Entering a strong growth market can make up for a multitude of management sins, but its efficacy must not be overestimated. A forecast of 50 percent annual market growth out of Predicasts is not a panacea. The fact is, if you're entering a market that is starting to experience that kind of growth, you're probably getting in too late. Remember, everyone else is looking in *Predicasts* too, so you're going to have a *lot* of competition.

> A couple of years ago, it was obvious that demand for floppy-disk drives for microcomputers was going to grow like mad. So dozens of entrepreneurs decided to fill the need—and dozens of venture-capital firms backed them. Each group saw itself as the only entry, or one of only a few. Now the market is saying clearly that it doesn't need a couple of hundred disk-drive manufacturers. A lot of venture capitalists are feeling very queasy in their stomachs, and aren't much in the mood to gobble up new companies in high-growth markets.

Hockey-Stick Theory. You generally see this one in the plan of the company that's been around a year or two and hasn't shown much for sales. But its projections show a sudden dramatic jump in sales to appear soon—when a new product goes to the market, or that big customer is landed, or something. These "hockey-stick" sales charts have been peddled so often that they are a joke among investors.

Hundred-Year Theory. "Management has over 100 years of combined experience in the electrical fuzzmagoo business . . ." This generally translates as, "My partners and I have been not-too-successful middle managers at big companies. We're getting on in years, and we figured it would be nice to start a company and get rich before we retire."

What? Me Take a Risk? Look, anyone who will consider

financing a new venture knows it's going to be risky. Don't try to snow him into thinking otherwise. You'll lose credibility. Instead, identify the risks, estimate how serious they are, and tell him how you'll minimize them.

Speedy Gonzales. How is your tiny little start-up going to compete successfully with much larger established companies? Well, because you're smaller, you can move much faster, right? You're going to zip into the market, slurp up the cream, and move on before IBM even notices your existence. Yup. Any professional investor has heard this one more often than why the chicken crossed the road. It may be true, but it isn't *automatically* true. What *evidence* do you have that IBM will be slow to respond? Assuming that you *are* first, what evidence do you have that you'll really gain all that much advantage from it? What *specifically* are you going to do to get the jump on the big guys?

The Headless Horseman. This is sort of a reverse cliché— not something that's seen all the time, but something that's almost never seen: a real board of directors. Every business plan on the venture capitalist's desk has a very nice, neat organization chart (which, incidentally, he doesn't believe in for a minute) with the board at the top. But that box is almost always empty in reality, if not on paper. Recruit two or three strong outside directors and put their résumés in your plan. When Ms. VC sees that, it will jolt her like a thunderbolt.

Business Utopia Theory. Most entrepreneurs have strong ideals and see their businesses as vehicles for implementing them. We all want to demonstrate how one really *should* treat employees or customers or the local community. But beware of inserting a statement of your business philosophy in your plan. A list of lofty ideals is a turn-off—*unless* it is accompanied by some very specific discussion of how you are going to implement those ideals in practice, and how those ideals are going to result in greater profits for your investors.

COSMETIC FACTORS

Investors do judge your book—your business plan—by its cover. If your plan is reproduced with a cheap photocopier on low-grade newsprint and held together with a rusty paperclip, it doesn't give your company the image of a class act. If you take so little care with your business plan, you must not have much regard for its value; why should the investor be interested in your business?

On the other hand, an ostentatiously luxurious binding and material will arouse suspicion. Are you trying to impress the investor? If you'll spend your money recklessly just to make your business plan a triumph of rococo, will you waste the investor's money on a luxurious office and a company Porsche?

The best policy is to reproduce your plan cleanly using good-quality paper and binder. Use a typewriter with clean keys, or a letter-quality printer. Have every member of your team proofread it; a typo or misspelling can ruin your image. Check the grammar too; the investor who reads it may be one of those eccentric characters who know that "presently" does not mean "at present" and understand the distinction between "disinterested" and "uninterested."

Merrill's Law of Proofreading: The average number of typos per double-spaced page equals the reciprocal of the number of *different* people who have proofread the manuscript.

We've several times mentioned the Executive Summary. Every business plan should have one; many investors will not bother to read a plan if they have to search through the whole thing to get the key points. They also use it as a screening device, on the basis that if you can't sum up the major factors of your plan in two pages, you don't have a clear idea of your business.

Finally, show respect for your plan by restricting its circulation. If you run off a hundred copies and float them all over town—or if you even appear to be doing so—it will turn off almost any investor. You shouldn't be paranoid about secrecy, but exhibit some discretion. Every copy of your plan should be numbered and tracked. Send low-numbered copies to prospective investors. If an investor is reading copy number 17, she's going to wonder which competing venture firms have copies 1 through 16.

REVISIONS

The most valuable thing about getting second- or third-round financing—more valuable usually than the money—is that it forces you to update your business plan. If you're lucky, conditions will force you to rewrite your plan almost from scratch and thus reexamine the foundations of your business.

The value of a business plan is threefold: It helps you raise money. It gives you a handy reference document. But above all, writing it forces you to *think* about your business.

Checklist 12–1: Common Business-Plan Deficiencies

- [ ] Hype of any sort
- [ ] No Table of Contents
- [ ] No Executive Summary
- [ ] Executive Summary doesn't summarize
- [ ] Executive Summary too long (more than 10 sentences or two pages is too long)
- [ ] Business plan too short (less than 10 double-spaced pages is too short)
- [ ] Business plan too long (more than 30 double-spaced pages is too long—currently)
- [ ] Plan doesn't say what's in it for the customer
- [ ] Plan doesn't say what's in it for the investor
- [ ] No market research
- [ ] No description of specific market strategy
- [ ] Excessive fixation on product
- [ ] No consideration of production costs
- [ ] Founding team not adequately described
- [ ] (If company not a start-up) No historical financials
- [ ] No financial projections
- [ ] Financial projections too skimpy (for example, broken down only by year, or lacking detailed expense breakdown)
- [ ] Sales projections drawn from thin air
- [ ] No cash-flow projection
- [ ] No balance-sheet projection
- [ ] No consideration of possible problems
- [ ] Projections incompatible with standard ratios of the industry, and no explanation given for the deviation

- [ ] Plan does not present proposed deal specifically (what do you want from the investor, for what?)
- [ ] No discussion of proposed use of funds
- [ ] Use of Funds section is vague
- [ ] Company is grossly overvalued
- [ ] No consideration of when and how investor can cash in
- [ ] Present stock distribution and debt situation of company not described
- [ ] Plan has too many typos or sloppy grammar
- [ ] Plan is shoddy in appearance—or excessively luxurious
- [ ] Plan is out of date

CAUTIONARY TALE: A BILLION DOLLARS WORTH OF SQUID?

Several years ago, I was involved in financing a fish-processing vessel. In doing so I happened to meet Ray Gerson, who at that time owned a Dutch-registered processing boat of his own. Some time later he approached me about a new project, and in March 1982 we began working together on what became Fisheries Development.

Ray's idea was to build a large squid fishing and processing vessel for use in Atlantic coastal waters. For reasons I'll discuss shortly, this was a very shrewdly conceived business venture. However, he had a quite justifiable suspicion that persuading investors to put up $10 million for a fishing project, let alone a squid fishing project, would be somewhat of a challenge. The general view of the fishing business is that it is a declining industry due to disappearing fisheries, foreign competition, and so on. My task was to write an effective business plan and get us funded.

The idea of intentionally fishing for squid sounds almost perverse to Americans, but squid is an esteemed delicacy in much of the world, particularly the Far East and certain parts of Europe. The worldwide market for squid turns out to be about $1 billion a year; about 60 percent of it is consumed in Japan.

The particular opportunity that interested Ray resulted from the

Magnussen Act. Passed in the 1970s, this law restricted foreign fishermen in the United States coastal waters. The U.S. "economic zone," out to 200 miles from the coast, was limited, with certain exceptions, to vessels that were U.S.-built and U.S.-owned. As a result, foreign squid fishers (mostly Italian) had been more or less expelled from certain rich areas in the Atlantic. This created an opening for an American vessel to go in and take over much of the production.

Now, modern commercial fishing is a complicated business, and the squid sector is especially tricky. Squid *must* be frozen almost immediately after they are caught—not because they spoil but because the flesh becomes rubbery. This means you can't just catch them, throw them in the hold, and bring them back to port for processing, as with many other types of fish. You have got to process them out at sea, and this requires a big, complicated, and expensive vessel.

Ray's plans called for a 217-foot boat with a complete on-board processing capability, built in the United States to comply with the Magnussen Act. This would cost about $6 million. In addition, the venture would need $4 million more for other expenses and working capital.

The cost could have been reduced by buying an older boat (U.S.-built, of course) and modifying it for our purposes. Ray had some pretty convincing arguments against this approach. However, at my prompting he agreed to make the design a little more versatile. We modified the plans so that, if necessitated by a failure of the squid catch, we could move the vessel to the West Coast and use it for cod and pollock.

With our concept worked out, the next step was to develop a strong business plan. I put together a 20-page plan—short, but very clearly written. We had to deal with a number of serious questions that could be raised by investors.

In this particular case, proving the existence of a market was relatively simple. The market for squid is mature and well established. We could easily show that plenty of squid was being bought, name prospective buyers for our catch, and demonstrate that market prices would be sufficient to provide us with a tidy margin.

On the production side, however, we faced an inherently unanswerable question: would we be able to catch enough squid? No fisherman can guarantee a good catch, of course. We could cite massive data, available from the U.S. government, that certain areas in the Atlantic were just swarming (schooling?) with squid eager to be caught and converted to *sashimi*. And, of course, we had our fallback position in cod and pollock.

We developed a thorough study of production economics, based on the past experience of four Italian squid boats. Before approaching investors we had our homework done and could display, if needed, a complete analysis of the effects of catch rate, prices, fuel costs, labor, and other variables.

A special effort was necessary in some areas. Maintenance of ocean-going vessels is a very specialized subject, and marine insurance is also very complex.

The credibility of our personnel was even more critical than usual in this venture. Ray Gerson, the founder, was an MIT Ph.D. in chemistry, not the best preparation for a fishing tycoon. He had worked for New York City under the Lindsay administration, then for a nonprofit technology-transfer organization, before getting into the fishing business. However, his previous maritime venture, though not very successful, gave him a lot of relevant experience. We backed him up with an extremely competent shore agent and an experienced, mostly Italian crew.

We also had to assure investors of our knowledge of, and compliance with, an immense number of complicated regulations, ranging from the Magnussen-Act restrictions on foreign participation to sanitary requirements on fish processing laid out by various customer countries.

With the business plan in hand, we were ready to tackle the investment community. Ray had asked how long it would take to get funded. When I told him six months to a year, he was almost speechless—but the estimate turned out to be accurate.

This venture was a tough sale, but we succeeded by using a principle I have found to be critical in funding unusual businesses: approach investors who are already familiar with the unique product, technology, or market. We made a point of dealing with people who already knew something about the fishing industry and ocean-going vessels, so that we didn't have to educate them from scratch.

Without going through the whole war story, the deal was eventually structured in two parts. We put together a $3.9-million limited partnership and financed the remaining $6 million with bank debt. The key to getting the banks to go along was the insurance company that covered the vessel. It was an experienced marine insurer, and knowing the value of the vessel, it guaranteed the banks that it would buy it for $6 million if we defaulted on the loan. (To get this we had to pay the insurance company a $350,000 fee up front.)

As of this writing, the vessel has been built and is out on the ocean. The fishing for squid hasn't been great so far, so we're pleased to have the fallback option for cod and pollock.

This was a start-up where the business plan was absolutely critical. It was an unusual venture with some unfamiliar risks. We could never have obtained funding had we not demonstrated very clearly that we knew exactly what we were doing and that we had all our ducks (if not squid) in a row.

                                                                          HDS

13
FINDING CAPITAL

"Your insight is clear and unbiased," said the Sovereign. "But however entrancing it may be to wander unchecked through a garden of bright images, are we not enticing your mind from another subject of almost equal importance? . . . in the trivial matter of mere earthly enrichment—"

"Truly," agreed the other. "There is, then, a whisper in the province that the floor of the Imperial Treasury is almost visible."

"The rumour, as usual, exaggerates the facts grossly," replied the Greatest. "The floor of the Imperial Treasury is quite visible."

Ernest Bramah
*Kai Lung's Golden Hours**

Young and growing companies have an absolutely astounding appetite for cash, and unless you are very wealthy or very lucky the floor of your company's treasury will be alarmingly visible throughout its early years. Until you go public, you can expect to spend between 20 percent and 80 percent of your time raising money. (After you go public, you will spend a similar proportion of your time explaining your company's situation to investment analysts.) You will therefore need to master the elements of raising capital. This is a distinct professional skill. Large companies often do not attempt to maintain

*(New York: Ballantine Books, 1972), p. 200.

such skills in-house; they hire investment bankers or under-writers to raise money for them. This option will probably not be open to you.

From your financial projections you should be able to determine how much money you need. The total financing your company requires is the sum of three items: fixed capital, working capital, and reserve for contingencies. The fixed-capital component can range from almost nothing (for, say, a brokerage sales organization) to many millions of dollars (for some manufacturing operations). It is basically a measure of how much physical facility you need in order to produce. Working capital similarly can range from nothing to millions of dollars; the amount needed depends primarily on how much inventory you have to carry and how fast your customers pay you.

In any case, you will need a substantial reserve. We recommend that you provide for a reserve equal to 50 percent of your calculated needs—and this assumes that your estimates are very conservative. There is a trade-off, as always. Some experts recommend that you seek the minimum you can get by with in your initial financing. The reasoning is that as your company matures and grows, it will be worth more; you will thus give up less of your company over the long run by financing as little and as late as possible. If you can get enough capital for 40 percent of your company, why surrender 60 percent in order to get that reserve? This is certainly the most effective strategy—if nothing goes wrong. But if you run into a snag, what will happen?

You'll have to go out into the capital markets at a time not of your choosing and try to make a deal when your company is not looking good and you're under pressure to make your next payroll. You may not be able to raise money at all under such conditions, and if you do you can bet the investors will impose terms very unfavorable to you. Unless you are very confident that reality will not deviate from your projections, it's well to have something extra in your pocket. Of course, many investors will resist letting you get a reserve, precisely in order to maintain the upper hand. If you expect this problem, you can "hide" a lot of reserve simply by being more conservative in your assumptions.

FINANCING STAGES

Always remember that your initial financing probably will not be your last safari into the financial jungle. The more successful you are, the more money you will need to raise. A typical growth business will go through about five financings in its early years. It begins with "seed money," which pays for developing the product prototype, market research, and other preliminary work. Usually this is provided by the founders. Then comes the "first-round" financing. This provides the money needed to actually get the business started. After the company has established a track record and shown good growth potential, it will usually look for "second-round" financing. This money is used to get on a high-growth track, by leapfrogging the need to accumulate working capital and funds for expansion out of retained earnings. The next step might be "third-round" or "mezzanine" financing. Usually this is aimed at expanding and consolidating the company's position. Assuming the company continues to be wildly successful, it will need really large amounts of capital to become a big business—the kind of money available only by going public.

CONTROL: 51 PERCENT VERSUS REALITY

The entrepreneur's objective through all this is to get the money he needs while giving up a minimum of equity in his company. There are two reasons you want to retain equity. First, it's worth money. Other things being equal, the more equity in your company you retain, the richer you will get. The operative phrase here is, "other things being equal." It's a truism that "it's better to own 10 percent of a billion-dollar company than 100 percent of a million-dollar company." As far as strictly financial motives are concerned, it's in your interest to sell equity if the funds received for it will increase the value of your company by more than the proportion you gave up. But of course very few entrepreneurs are motivated strictly by financial considerations. The other value of equity is that it contributes to control. Most of us are in business primarily in order to get our destiny into our own hands; getting rich is a secondary objective. But what is control? It is not simply a matter of holding 51 percent of the common stock.

> Three engineers fresh out of MIT started their own com-
> pany and developed an extraordinarily successful elec-
> tronic testing gadget. Soon they were doing a million a
> year in sales. They wanted to maintain complete control,
> so they adamantly refused to sell any equity at all; they
> kept 100 percent of the stock among themselves and fi-
> nanced expansion with bank loans. Then they blew it; they
> spent too much money on R&D and found themselves in a
> cash-flow crisis. Because they were technically in default
> on their bank loan, they had a choice: do as the bank said,
> or be pushed into bankruptcy. They still held 100 percent
> of the stock, but they had to raise a hand and ask permis-
> sion from the bank before going to the bathroom. Did they
> have control?

Control of a company is a subtle phenomenon. There is no such thing as absolute control; if nothing else, you are subject to the "control" of the market. Your customers are your bosses—and they can fire you by not buying your product. So the ultimate source of control is success in the marketplace. With it, you need little else to maintain control of your com-pany. Without it, no amount of stock, no majority on the board, no agreements, bylaws, or influence will do you any good. If you concentrate on making the company successful, control will almost take care of itself.

Almost. And most of us would still like to maintain con-trol, or as much control as possible, even if things don't go perfectly. Operating control of a small business resides in several factors.

First of all, there is indispensability. Especially in the early days of your start-up, you will have control simply because there would be no company without you. As the key founder, you are more or less essential to the enterprise, and all you need to maintain control is the threat to walk away from it all if you don't get your way. Of course, it won't be effective unless you have the guts to face the financial losses, the stigma of failure, and possibly some nasty lawsuits. As the company matures and develops a full management team, this source of power will become much less effective.

Another factor, of course, is voting stock. If you hold a majority, or if you can muster a majority with the help of your cofounders or sympathetic investors, you're obviously in a strong, though not invulnerable, position. Another point to keep in mind is that a majority of the stock need not necessarily translate into a majority of the board of directors. Corporation law can be quite peculiar, especially in states like Delaware, and there are such things as preferred stock. Finally, if your company continues to grow, the chances are that you will come to the point where your equity holding has been diluted by the various financings to the point where it has little influence. But even so, you can hold control the way management does in big companies: by contract. If you are shrewd enough to look ahead and negotiate terms early, you can end up with a tiny minority of the stock but an employment contract that gives you a virtually impregnable position.

All these specific techniques should be applied. But if you're doing well, it's unlikely that your investors will want to remove you. On the other hand, if the company is flaming out, they'll either find a way to eject you in spite of all your precautions or arrange to bail out and leave you spinning down alone, in full "control" of the burning wreckage.

DEBT VERSUS EQUITY

The fundamental question in raising money is the balance between debt and equity. The distinction between the two is not as sharp as you might think. Simple common stock is certainly equity, and a loan from the bank is certainly debt, but there are all sorts of hybrid instruments—warrants, options, convertible bonds, preferred stock—which are not purely equity or debt. Deciding on the proper format for your offering may be very complicated. The correct approach depends on many factors—the financial characteristics of your business or industry, your growth expectations, the state of the markets, tax considerations, and the current investment fads.

Entrepreneurs often prefer debt financing to selling equity because they believe it maintains control. As we've seen, this may not be the case. A bank loan, for instance, invariably comes with "restrictive covenants"—acres of fine print specifying what you may or may not do and providing that you are automatically in default and must repay the loan on demand if anything whatsoever goes wrong. In practice, the bank will be reluctant to try to take over and run your business unless the situation becomes desperate indeed—but it probably won't hesitate to give you some gentle hints with an unspoken "or else." Always remember that debt is "leverage" not only in terms of control, but in terms of finance. When things go well, it allows you to multiply your profits. When things go badly, debt will often fatally complicate your problems.

The key point is the way the pie is divided up when a failed company is liquidated. Except for Uncle Sam, the secured creditors—that is, your bank—are at the head of the line. Then come employees, then unsecured creditors, and last of all the wretched stockholders. Suppose the day comes (and it may very well come—many ultimately successful companies have been there) when you're in big trouble and just barely hanging on. This is the time when your stockholders will rally around. They'll almost certainly lose their whole investment if you go under, so they have a strong incentive to help out; they may even dip into their pockets and throw some good money after bad. The bank, on the other hand, may turn into an enemy. Its situation: if you go under now, it gets first cut at your remaining assets and should come out whole or nearly so. But if it waits, you may expend everything trying to save yourself and leave the bank with nothing to foreclose on. So it has an incentive to stomp on your fingers and watch you go over the edge, planning to be first vulture on the corpse. Does this mean that bankers are nasty, vicious characters who are eager to destroy young companies? Not at all. Most are very nice people. But in a situation where they have such a strong financial incentive to foreclose, they may succumb to the temptation.

With these preliminaries out of the way, let's consider the specific problems involved in raising capital. We'll concentrate on the first-round financing, which is really the crucial one, because it usually defines the structure of your company. So assume you've provided the seed money out of your own pocket, you have a working prototype, a market study, and a business plan. Now you're ready to go out for funding.

TIMING

It's nice if your start-up can raise money and enter the market with perfect timing—at an ideal point in the business cycle. This is difficult, because you can't predict the business cycle at all accurately. (If you can, forget about starting a business— you can easily get rich in the stock market.) Still, if you choose, you can do surprisingly well. The key is objectivity.

Every month the government releases, and *The Wall Street Journal* publishes, indexes of leading, coincident, and lagging indicators. The ratio of the last two is a sort of "superleading" indicator that gives you an early warning several months ahead of the leading index. These figures are prominently displayed for all to see, but most businesspeople derive very little advantage from them. The secret that gives you the edge is simple: watch these indicators, and be *willing* to believe them.

As a business expansion matures, the coincident/lagging ratio will eventually wobble, then begin a clear decline. This is your signal to get hopping and finish your business plan. You're now entering the ideal time to raise money. Many investors have cashed in their gains from the rising stock market and are looking for new worlds to conquer. At this time, the height of the boom, optimism is king. Recession is inconceivable. The only worry is inflation—and to beat inflation, investors naturally think of venture capital. Normally staid gray-suit types are in a feeding frenzy, buying stock in anything that claims to be a "growth company."

A few months later, leading indicators will start to fall. The rule of thumb is that three declines in a row signal a recession. By now you should have lined up your money and have the checks safely deposited. If not, you still have some time, because most people are still saying, as they ram their heads deeper into the sand, that the good times aren't over yet. Watch the business press. After the first monthly decline, you'll read: "It's just a statistical blip. The economy is basically sound." After the second decline: "Two months don't mean anything." The third consecutive decline will invariably bring articles pointing out that "after all, leading indicators have predicted nine out of the last five recessions." Around the fifth month, you'll see grudging admissions that maybe a recession is coming, but only a very mild one, because *this* time businesses haven't engaged in excessive inventory buildup or committed the various sins that made previous recessions so bad . . .

And what are you doing as the economy crashes and crumbles? Waiting, mostly. Tidying up the incorporation and other legal work, and putting the finishing touches on your product development and market research. You should wait—wait until the economy touches bottom. You are now in that ideal situation where great fortunes are founded: at the bottom of a recession, with cash and a cool head.

Now the business press will be full of articles demonstrating that the country has entered another Great Depression. And now, with gloom everywhere, is when you start operations.

Why? Because before you start selling, you'll have to buy. You need to lease premises for your business. In a recession, there's plenty of office and factory space to choose from, and you can get terrific rates. You need to buy equipment and furniture. Go around to auctions and bankruptcy sales, and you'll find some astounding bargains. You need to line up vendors for raw materials. Now, during the recession, they'll give you a good price—and that's not all. You won't have to worry about shortages or long lead times; service will be excellent; and vendors will be surprisingly liberal about credit terms. You need to hire workers; in a recession, plenty of good people are available, and they'll be reasonable about salaries too. We guarantee you'll be pleasantly surprised what cash in the bank can accomplish in a recession if you use it shrewdly.

But what about sales? Well, chances are your first few months, maybe your first year, will be lousy no matter how you time it. Your production process will take longer to get running than you think. Your product will be full of bugs, and you'll have to deal with all sorts of unforeseen QC problems. Your advertising will be misdirected. Your sales presentations will be ineffective. Your instruction manual will have to be rewritten from scratch. A million things will go wrong that you did not and could not predict. (This is the way it will be if you've done your homework very carefully. If you haven't, it will be a hundred times worse!) If you start in a recession, you'll have time to iron out all these problems before business picks up. Meanwhile, you won't be missing much. If you start during a boom, you'll probably get your act together just about the time the next recession begins.

The big timing problem comes when you're successful. Sales are taking off; you've just gone deep into debt at high interest rates to expand production; you've just promised your investors that you'll double sales next year again—and you find yourself saying, "Oh, a one-month decline in leading indicators doesn't mean anything. . . ."

Now, we don't for a moment wish to imply that the only factor in timing your start-up is the business cycle. But—with only one exception—it is the only *external* factor of any importance. The essential factor in timing is simply your readiness. Don't go out for capital until you are prepared. Of course you shouldn't dawdle during your planning phase, but never skip essential tasks—like market research—because you're in a hurry and fear an investor or a market will get away from you. The exception is the fad item; if you plan to sell a hula-hoop or a pet rock or a book about dead cats, you must obviously move instantly before the market window closes, and take your chances. But nonfad businesses should never be forced into premature birth; urgent though an opportunity may seem, there's always enough time to do it right.

I like to remind myself of the story of the surgeon who told his students that a certain suture must be completed within 30 seconds or the patient would die. "But don't worry," he would say. "You can do it in 30 seconds easily—if you don't hurry."

The one other outside factor that you should be concerned with is the state of the financial markets—specifically, the stock market response to initial public offerings (IPOs). A good market for IPOs is a phenomenon that occurs only for a brief period, at intervals of several years. These periods (called "windows" in the trade) have an electrifying effect on the availability of venture capital. This is of course totally illogical; except for mezzanine financings, a venture capital investment can't possibly be brought to maturity and cashed in during the few months an IPO window lasts. But you will still find that second-round, and even first-round, financing is easier to obtain when the IPO market is hot.

COMPANY STRUCTURE

There are five simple ways to structure a company: sole proprietorship, partnership, limited partnership, corporation, and Subchapter S corporation. Then there are a variety of more complicated structures.

Sole Proprietorship

The sole proprietorship is the oldest and simplest form of business organization. You simply run the business out of your own pocket. You are the sole owner; at any time you can transfer funds freely into or out of the business from your personal assets. Setting up legally is very simple; usually, it's a matter of getting a "DBA" ("doing business as") or similar form from the state government. Its simplicity and convenience make this the usual form for the microbusiness. But if you're planning anything much more ambitious than a push-cart, the sole proprietorship can lead to problems. Because there is no solid distinction between the assets of the business and your personal assets, liabilities of the business are your personal liabilities and creditors can attach your house, car, or bank account if the company's funds are inadequate to pay them. Since you, as the owner, are personally subject to unlimited liability for the company's obligations, a sole proprietorship should be used only if you intend to run very conservatively, with little or no debt.

Partnerships

The ordinary partnership simply combines the assets of two or more individuals in the business. You and your partner(s) can define your relationship pretty much any way you wish; simply write the partnership agreement to specify how much capital is contributed by each partner, what his duties are, and what his cut of the profits is. Note, however, that the partnership is similar to the proprietorship in that each partner has unlimited liability for the company's obligations, and worse in that each partner remains liable even if debts are incurred by another partner without authorization. Because of the high risk that results from this rule, partnerships, which were very common a century ago, now are limited mostly to legal, accounting, and other professional firms that have certain specialized needs for this type of organization.

The Limited Partnership

The limited partnership is used mostly for tax shelters. It resembles the ordinary partnership except that some of the partners are "limited"—that is, their liability for the company's obligations is limited to the amount they invested. There must be at least one "general" partner, however, who is fully as exposed as a sole proprietor or an ordinary partner. The limited partners, moreover, are forbidden to participate in the company's management and thus lose control over their investment.

The Corporation

The simple corporation should be regarded as the default value for company organization; this is the form you should use unless there is a good reason to do otherwise. A corporation, as the word implies (it is derived from the Latin for "body"), is an artificial person with a separate existence for legal, tax, and economic purposes. Thus the investors can lose no more than they have invested; they have limited liability. (This is why British corporations have "Ltd."—"Limited"— after their names.)

A corporation is quite easy to set up; there are even kits that will help you do it yourself very cheaply, but it's usually advisable to spend a few hundred bucks and have a lawyer take care of it. There are some formalities—you generally must have a board of directors, even if it consists only of yourself, and hold meetings for the record—but the corporation is almost as convenient and simple as a sole proprietorship. Partnerships, and especially limited partnerships, are much more complicated.

There is one important point that is not as commonly understood as it should be. The limited liability conferred on investors by the corporate form applies only to conventional business debts. If the corporation goes bankrupt, the creditors cannot take their pound of flesh out of the personal assets of the stockholders. But the limited liability does *not* cover criminal or improper actions. The corporate form does not automatically protect the management of the company from lawsuits directed against them personally, and in certain circumstances even stockholders may be sued successfully.

The Subchapter S Corporation

Finally, there is the Subchapter S variant of the corporate form. Because a corporation has the privileges of a separate existence, it also has the responsibilities—in particular, it must pay taxes on its income, that is, its profits. This means that the return of the investors is taxed twice—once as profits of the corporation, and once as dividends to them. Subchapter S allows small businesses, under certain circumstances, to avoid this double taxation. The corporate form remains, with its limited liability, but the profits are treated directly as income to the stockholders for tax purposes and are free of the corporate income tax. There are certain restrictions, which occasionally change. As this is written, a Subchapter S corporation may have no more than 35 stockholders, all of them must be U.S. citizens, and so on. Generally Subchapter S is of no value to growth companies; it is useful primarily in the case of the small but established and steadily profitable company—a cash cow.

Keep It Simple

Before deciding on a form for your business you should go over your plans carefully with your lawyer. Usually one of the five simple forms will be appropriate, and it's well to keep things as simple as possible; the paperwork, meetings, and negotiations required by more complex organizations can be a serious drain on your time, and the legal and accounting fees a serious drain on your money. Be wary of advice that a more complicated approach will offer big tax advantages.

> One company was organized as a limited partnership, of which the general partner was a corporation, the stock in which was held by the founders and also by another corporation, the stock in which was sold to employees! It's not clear that the alleged tax benefits of this structure were worthwhile, and setting it up and maintaining it used up a lot of management time.
>
> Another Enterprise Forum presenter, with less than $1 million in sales, had issued common stock, warrants, and three classes of preferred—in addition to setting up an R&D partnership. This mess was a serious handicap in raising new capital.

DESIGNING THE DEAL

Once you've decided on a structure for your company, the next question is the deal. What kind of offering will you make? There are hundreds of ways to structure an offering, most of them legal, and most of them unnecessarily complicated. Try to keep your deal as simple as possible. The more complex it is, the more chance for error; for misunderstanding that can cause friction; and for inadvertent violation of federal, state, or local laws. *Please note carefully that whenever you offer an investor something that is, or could be construed to be, a "security," you make yourself subject to federal security laws, and also to state "blue sky" laws.* Get a complete briefing from your lawyer before you start talking to investors. This includes any investor, even (or especially) your brother-in-law.

The Equity Deal

The simplest deal is straight equity: you sell stock to the investors. This involves putting a value on the company. If you and the investors can agree that the company as it currently stands is worth $500,000 on the hoof, and if they are to invest $200,000, then obviously they should get 40 percent of the company. There's really nothing to it—except for getting an agreement as to how much the company is worth.

Let's go into this in a bit more detail, because it is a frequent source of confusion and conflict when entrepreneurs go out for financing. Any financing, and most particularly an equity financing, is equivalent to selling part of your company—it is a *marketing* task. As in any sale, the prospective purchaser is likely to be concerned with getting value for his money. So any professional investor will ask the question, "How much is this company worth?" This is an embarrassing question for many entrepreneurs, who prefer to focus on how much it will be worth, after their dreams come true. But when a little company with half-a-million in sales and six employees asks a venture capitalist for $1 million for 20 percent of the company—a not uncommon proposal—it may simply be laughed out of the office. Here's a simple rule: ask yourself whether you could sell your entire company at the proposed valuation; if not, you're not likely to sell part of it for the same price.

There are a few complications even in the simplest stock sale. The investors will want some control over future issues of stock. They can't allow you to just issue more stock whenever you please, thus diluting their holdings. On the other hand, you'll probably need to do more financings in the future. The usual solution is a restriction on how much stock may be issued in later financings, and a minimum price for it. There is also likely to be a "preemptive rights" clause, which gives the original stockholders first crack at any later issues if they choose.

A seemingly trivial decision can have surprising consequences: how many shares should you issue? Many founders like to issue a large number, giving each share a very small value. This makes it convenient to distribute small percentages to key employees, for example, without getting into fractional shares. But there's much to be said for having a smaller number, say a couple of thousand shares, with each having a high value. For one thing, it gives your company a blue-chip image; a company whose shares are valued at $500 apiece obviously must be pretty substantial, right? Limiting the number of shares also simplifies your stockholder relations by limiting the number of stockholders. If you have a million shares and 500 stockholders, you're going to be spending a lot of time and money just keeping track of them all, recording transactions when they sell shares to one another, and so on.

When Reaction Design Corporation was set up, I found to my astonishment that New Jersey actually had a tax on the formation of new corporations, which was based on the number of shares issued. Fortunately it did not apply if 2,500 or fewer shares were issued.

Speaking of selling shares, keep in mind that until you go public your shares are "unregistered" and subject to special restrictions, some of which may astound you. Check with your lawyer on this too—in advance.

One thing you should probably always do is issue your stock under Section 1244 of the IRS code. This makes it "small business" stock. As such it limits the downside risk of your investors, because losses on 1244 stock can be deducted on their tax returns against ordinary income. Normally investment losses can be deducted only against capital gains. Be sure to make your own stock 1244 too. The requirements are not particularly onerous; the major restriction is that there can be only one class of stock in the company—you can't issue preferred or other types of stock with different voting rights, for instance.

A tricky problem can arise with founder stock and incentive stock. Many founders—and investors—want to motivate key people by rewarding them with stock when milestones are met. Thus, there might be a provision to give the Marketing VP 1,000 shares if the first-year sales projections are met. The problem is that the company's stock has value—increasing value, one hopes. When the VP gets her stock reward, she'll have to report it to the IRS at market value, and the tax on it may crush her. Furthermore, the frequent stock issues required to implement this method may cause problems with voting control, 1244 stock requirements, and so on.

The best solution may be to have each cofounder buy his stock at incorporation. During the planning phase, pay each cofounder a "consulting fee" for his contribution. The larger his contribution and the better his performance, the higher the fee. Each cofounder buys stock at the same low price—formally—but the superior performers can afford more in reality because of the offsetting payments. (Those who are unsatisfactory can simply not be allowed to buy stock; they have no basis for complaint, since they were paid for their work.) Of course, taxes must be paid on the "fees," but these can be minimized by the use of offsetting deductions. The purchase of stock is of course a tax-free transaction. In this way you are able to evaluate the quality of your team members before committing stock to them, yet issue the stock cleanly without tax complications. However, you still face the problem of motivation after the start-up; cash bonuses or stock options may be effective.

Borrowing The Money

Debt financing may be classified along two axes: long-term vs. short-term (one year is a good dividing line), and secured vs. unsecured. The first thing you must realize is that it is very difficult to get any sort of debt financing for a start-up. Instruments used by large companies, such as bonds or commercial paper, are generally not available to you. Whereas equity investors are motivated by the hope of substantial gains, debt investors are dominated by the fear of loss. The critical question from the lender's point of view is: will you pay it back? With an unsecured loan, the evidence that it will be repaid is based of necessity on the company's record. A start-up has no record, so few lenders will consider it at all. That leaves secured loans. Long-term loans are usually used to provide fixed capital, and are secured by real estate or plant equipment. Short-term loans provide working capital, and may be secured by receivables or inventory.

From your point of view, the critical factor is the interest rate. You can expect to pay much higher rates than a big company would. Also, you will almost certainly be subjected to the infamous "compensating balance." This is a requirement that a certain portion of the loan be left in your account unused. Thus a $100,000 loan at 16 percent nominal interest may require a $15,000 compensating balance—bringing the true interest rate to 18.8 percent.

You must be aware of the true interest rate that you are paying, because *it is irrational to borrow money unless you can invest it to get a higher return than your cost of funds.* This obvious rule is frequently violated, and not just by small businesses.

Deals To Avoid

Straight equity and straight debt deals are the most common ways in which companies are financed. There are a wide variety of other options, most of which are essentially tax gimmicks. Generally it is a poor idea to try to package your company as a tax shelter unless you are advised by a real expert in the field—not a self-described expert, but someone with measurable experience in the tax-shelter game.

Another unattractive deal involves convertible bonds (warrants are sometimes used to accomplish similar objectives). In this deal, the investors buy bonds from your company—or perhaps we should say "bonds," since these securities are unregistered and illiquid; in effect, the investors are giving you a loan. The bonds are convertible to stock at the owners' option. Thus, if your company is successful, the investors will of course convert the bonds, and become owners of substantial equity in your company. If, on the other hand, you get into trouble, they'll collect on the bonds. In short, heads they win, tails you lose. It's not a total disaster if you accept such a deal, but it certainly cannot be regarded as favorable to the entrepreneur. If you can't get anything better, perhaps you should go back to the drawing board.

Really ridiculous is the buyback deal. This occurs when the value of the company is so low that the entrepreneur cannot raise enough money by a stock sale unless she gives up control. The investors may offer to let her buy back the controlling stock later if the company is successful, perhaps at a "favorable" price. If you're naive enough to think you're going to save your pennies and purchase control of your company in the future, you're probably not ready to be CEO of anything larger than a lemonade stand. Ironically, it's not even a good deal for the investors. Their "control" does them no good during the company's early growth, because the founder has "indispensability" power. Their "controlling" interest in the stock does nothing more than reduce the entrepreneur's motivation during a critical phase. If in spite of this the company does well, they end up with the entrepreneur trying to get control of the company at just the wrong time. When the company has been successfully launched, is growing well, and is starting to need big-company management—that is usually the time when the founder should be encouraged to step aside and start something new.

The Leasing Option

If your business needs a major piece of capital equipment, how should you finance it? Buying it out of equity is conservative but not a very efficient use of funds in most cases. Especially if you plan fast growth, your limited equity should be jealously conserved. Debt financing is possible, but you usually cannot raise the full price of the equipment this way; also, the debt load on your balance sheet may interfere with other financing options. Leasing may be the best approach. From your point of view, you in effect buy the equipment on the installment plan, at a somewhat inflated price. What's happening is that the tax benefits of owning the equipment—particularly the investment-tax credit and depreciation—are stripped off and handed to the investor. You get a good deal; the tax deductions are worth much more to the investor, who is in a high bracket, than to you (your start-up won't be making a profit at first and has little use for tax benefits).

The intelligent use of leverage can reduce your capital requirements amazingly.

A beautiful example of leverage was provided by a presenter at the New York Enterprise Forum. His idea was to develop a regional beer aimed specifically at the New York City upper-class market. He had a very solid market study and a well-written business plan. Still, he was shown the door by every venture capitalist in the city. So he re-thought his financing needs.

Instead of building or buying a brewery, as he'd initially planned, he arranged with Schlitz to use some of its excess capacity. Then he abandoned his innovative—and expensive—advertising campaign. Instead, he went around to bars personally, carrying a few cases in his car and pushing bartenders to try it and recommend it. When word of mouth began to take effect, he used the same sales technique to penetrate delicatessens and grocery stores. The company consisted essentially of only two people: the CEO and his master brewer. This highly successful company, by shrewd leverage, required very little capital investment.

Exercise 13–1:
Outlining Your Deal

Use of Funds:
Capital equipment　　　　　　　　　　＿＿＿＿＿
Working capital　　　　　　　　　　　＿＿＿＿＿
Reserve for contingencies　　　　　　＿＿＿＿＿

Total needed　　　　　　　　　　　　＿＿＿＿＿

Source of Funds:
Sale of equity　　　　　　　　　　　＿＿＿＿＿
Long-term debt　　　　　　　　　　　＿＿＿＿＿
Short-term debt　　　　　　　　　　　＿＿＿＿＿
Leasing　　　　　　　　　　　　　　＿＿＿＿＿

Total to be raised　　　　　　　　　　＿＿＿＿＿

SELECTING THE INVESTOR

Once you have decided what sort of deal you would like to offer, you must decide what kind of investors to approach and how to find them. You may want to offer several types of deals—sell some stock, get a loan, and lease some equipment, for instance. This would mean approaching three different kinds of investors. You should also consider carefully how many investors you want to have. It's not totally up to you; securities regulations may restrict how many stockholders you may have, and even how many prospects you may approach. If you have one or two big investors, they may wield too much power. On the other hand, if you have many investors, you'll be kept very busy indeed with paperwork and hand holding.

Among other important questions you'll want to consider are these: What do you want from investors besides money? Don't just settle for a check. You should get more—access to financial expertise, advice, connections, introductions to prospective customers, prestige. What sort of people can you live with for the long term? You will probably be stuck with your initial investors for a long time. What can they contribute in the future? You're going to have to raise money again someday—perhaps sooner than you expect. Will your first-round investors be able and willing to ante up in the second round? Are they willing to make a commitment to do so? Even if they are able to contribute only a small portion of what you expect to need, it will help immensely—it's that first commitment that's hard to get. Beware of the first-round investor who not only won't contribute to the next financing but will try to stop you from getting the money elsewhere. This sometimes occurs with investors who fear dilution of their holdings, or who wish to influence or control management.

THE APPROACH

Let's suppose you have decided how much money you need; what you plan to use it for; how you are going to structure your company; and what kind of deal or deals you want to make. At this point, you are ready to start seriously searching for investors. There are many different sources of capital you can approach, and we'll consider some of the more important types shortly. But there are four rules you should follow in dealing with *any* sort of investor.

First, approach the right sort of investor for the deal.

Money has tastes. A deal may be very appealing to a venture capitalist but horrify a banker—and vice-versa. Each general type of investor specializes in certain sorts of deals, and within investor types, individual investors may further specialize. A deal that one bank would jump at might be unacceptable to another bank. Before you approach an investor, find out what sorts of deals he does.

Second, understand the investor's objectives. A surprising number of entrepreneurs regard investors simply as passive moneybags, whose function in life is to hand out money. Fact is, most investors have a terribly crass attitude and a distressing tendency to ask, "What's in it for me?" It is essential to understand not only that the investor wants a return on his investment but also that he will have very specific ideas about what sort of return is acceptable, how long-term the commitment of funds should be, how much risk is acceptable, and how much oversight he will exercise. If you make it a point to determine what his objectives are and structure the deal to satisfy them, you have good odds of getting a check. If you rush blindly ahead without bothering to find out what he wants, you don't.

Third, approach the investor properly. Most people who have money to invest have a lot of applicants and find it necessary to set up procedures, formal or informal, to screen them. You may find his rules arbitrary, but it's his football and if you want to play with him . . .

Fourth, evaluate the investor carefully. There's a tendency to assume that anyone who has money is the answer to your prayers. But your relationship doesn't end when you pick up the check. You're going to be living with this person a long time, and a nervous or hostile investor is like a rusty nail in your knee. Not everyone who has a lot of money is nice. Check him out thoroughly before you even approach him—and this applies whether you're approaching an individual investor, a bank, or a venture-capital firm. What is the investor's history? Look especially at his previous investments. How did he behave? Was he constantly interfering with management? Did he act as a gadfly? Did he welsh on commitments for additional funding? Was he a nervous type, always calling up the CEO to demand reassurance? If you're expecting him to sit on your board or give advice or provide contacts with customers, how did he perform for previous investees?

INVESTOR TYPES

Sources of capital are everywhere, limited only by your imagination. We'll consider in detail nine of the most commonly approached investor types: (1) family and friends; (2) other amateur investors; (3) venture capitalists; (4) SBICs; (5) banks; (6) leasing firms; (7) the SBA and other government sources; (8) vendors; and (9) customers. Some other alternatives are listed in Checklist 13–1.

Family and Friends

This is the most common source of seed money, except for the founder himself. It is probably the easiest way to raise money, and the way most likely to cause problems. It is not uncommon for such investments to result in broken friendships, or in vicious family feuds that last for generations. The mixing of business considerations with family or social bonds at best creates an area of tension in the relationship. Differing opinions as to how the business should be conducted can cause strain even if things are going well. If the business fails, the financial troubles of the parties involved may be dwarfed by the emotional consequences.

Nonetheless, many of America's most successful companies would never have been created if it had not been for this sort of financing. If you're going to use it, you can avoid many pitfalls by treating it just as you would any other investment. Tailor the deal to the investor, for instance. Uncle John is approaching retirement; he needs a relatively safe investment that gives him a tax benefit now and a steady income stream later. He may be an ideal candidate for a leasing deal. On the other hand, your reckless brother-in-law who's always putting money into wild schemes may want to buy equity. Presumably you know your relatives and friends well, so there's no excuse for failing to evaluate their characteristics in advance.

Private Placement

To call individual investors "amateurs" is perhaps a bit unfair. The word implies that they are in it for fun, which most of them would deny. However, they are not professional investors in the sense of being paid to manage other people's money, and this has important consequences for your dealing with them. If a professional makes a bad investment and takes a total loss on it, he'll usually take his licking like a man (even if it's a woman). The "amateur" may do the same—or may not. She's playing with her own money, and she may get very upset indeed if she loses it. The professional is associated with an organization, and that organization—usually—has a track record. The individual investor may be very hard to investigate. On the other hand, the individual investor is the backbone of innovation capital. These are the people who take the big risks and thus play an important part in developing major innovations. With any individual investor (including family and friends) it's well to offer a fairly conservative, low-risk deal, and above all *make sure the individual in question can afford to lose her whole investment.*

Sticking with Tradition: Venture Capitalists

Of course, the capital source that comes to mind first when considering start-up financing is venture capital. Because venture capital is so important, and so commonly misunderstood, we'll consider it in detail.

As a rough rule of thumb, of one hundred business plans submitted to a venture capital firm, ten will be read, and perhaps one will result in an investment. How can you make yours that one? You'll have a substantial head start over competing business plans if you understand the basics of the venture-capital business.

A venture-capital fund may be defined as one that makes *equity investments in small, high-growth companies.* Although there may be some ambiguity about the meaning of "equity" and the other terms in this definition, most venture capitalists would agree that it sums up their business pretty accurately.

So the basic principle of dealing with venture capital is: don't even approach them unless you have this kind of deal. This means specifically an offer to sell stock in a small company that has realistic prospects of doubling sales every year or so for the next five to ten years.

Venture-capital funds come in a wide range of sizes; the smallest have a capital pool of several million dollars; the largest have several hundred million dollars. The nature of their business imposes several other restrictions that affect your dealings with them. One requirement is that you must ask for an investment in the right size range for the specific fund you approach. No venture capitalist is going to put all her spondulics into one company. A $5-million fund will not make a $5-million investment in your company. A $100-million fund might. However, each fund will have not only a maximum but a minimum investment limit. The reason is contained in two legal phrases. Venture capitalists earn their living by investing other people's money (mostly), so they have "fiduciary responsibility." Consequently, they are bound, not just ethically but legally, to exercise "due diligence" in investigating potential investments. In other words, each deal must be thoroughly checked out; otherwise, if it goes wrong, the people who put up the money for the venture fund—and the SEC—will get very nasty in court. Now, it takes just as much time, effort, and money to do "due diligence" on a $50,000 deal as it does for a $500,000 deal. So each fund will have a lower limit on investment size; it won't consider a smaller deal, no matter how attractive it might otherwise be. These days, most funds aim at deals around $1 million to $2 million, to be split between two or three venture firms. However, there are funds that do bigger deals and funds that do smaller deals; you can search out such funds if you need them.

Another requirement is that you must match the venture capitalist to your area of business. None but the very largest venture funds have enough personnel to investigate and monitor a wide variety of businesses. So most funds specialize: some make investments only in computer-hardware companies, others in biotechnology, others in retail services, and so on. If your firm sells educational software, it's a waste of time to approach a fund that specializes in aerospace-instrumentation companies. They won't even look at you. It should also be noted that many funds prefer strongly to invest in local companies rather than distant ones. There is also specialization in the age of the enterprises that are considered for investments. As of this writing, most funds prefer to make second-round financings in companies a few years old. But some specialize in first-round deals, others in third-round or "mezzanine" fundings.

A final requirement is that *the venture capitalist must be able to exit from her investment in your company.* Normally a venture fund has a turnover cycle of five to ten years. Its objective is to buy stock in a company, help the company grow very rapidly, then sell out. Your plan must provide for making your stock liquid at some point, and there are really only two practical possibilities. One is to go public—fulfill the necessary legal requirements to have your stock listed in the over-the-counter market or, if you're spectacularly successful, on one of the national exchanges. The other possibility is to be acquired by a larger company. If neither of these options appeals to you—if your objective is to remain a privately held, independent company indefinitely—forget about venture capital. The venture capitalist has no intention of holding your company's stock forever—at least not if she can help it. She must, of course, risk the possibility that your company will neither take off nor fail—that it will become one of the "walking dead" and she'll be stuck with your stock. But she won't go into such a situation intentionally.

To sum up, if you wish to access venture capital as a source of funds, you must: (1) offer an equity investment; (2) have good prospects for extremely rapid growth; (3) request an investment that is neither too large nor too small for the fund approached; (4) approach a fund that specializes in investments in your industry; (5) have a convincing plan for making your stock liquid within a decade if not sooner.

You should also be prepared for the venture capitalist to take a pretty active posture in working with you. He'll almost certainly put an associate on your board of directors, and expect you to call on him for advice and assistance, especially in the area of financial management. Venture capitalists are the antithesis of the passive investor.

There are venture-capital directories that list funds with their addresses, preferred investment size, industry preference, and geographical location requirements. Or you can get recommendations from business associates. Once you've located a venture fund that looks like a good prospect, there are certain points of etiquette you should keep in mind.

You must have an introduction. The venture capitalist is bombarded with business plans in every day's mail. At social occasions he is relentlessly pestered by would-be investees, the vast majority of them utterly hopeless. Thus it is neither courteous nor productive to tackle him cold. Do not mail your business plan to him. His secretary will mail it back to you unread. Do not call him up for an appointment. It will be regretfully declined. The proper approach is an introduction by a mutual acquaintance. If you have a reasonable business-contact network, this should not pose an insuperable problem. Try your lawyer, your accountant, your banker. All these people make it a point to spread their nets as widely as possible; chances are one of them knows, or knows someone who knows, the person you want. You're looking for someone who knows a principal at the venture firm, who can call him up and say, "I have a deal here I think will interest you." The venture capitalist will ask to see your business plan, and this way it will get read, or at least glanced at. If it's good, he'll ask you to come in and make a presentation. You've passed the first hurdle.

It's well to give the venture capitalist some time to absorb the idea of your company, particularly if you are being very innovative technologically or otherwise. One technique that I've found very useful in presenting companies to investors is the descriptive letter. The CEO simply writes me, Harry Sedgwick, a letter describing the essential points of his company in three pages or so, and asking my advice about funding or other matters. I then pass this on to the investor with the usual, "You might find this interesting." He thus gets an advance preview without any pressure at all.

You must be presentable. Venture capitalists see themselves—quite sincerely—as bold, innovative, and open-minded. However, most of them come from an investment-banking background, and in spite of their honest efforts are a great deal more conservative than they think. They tend to be prejudiced against entrepreneurs who look, sound, or act "un-businesslike." Those of us who come from the lab, the plant, the computer terminal, or other informal milieus may need to, shall we say, temporarily suspend our sartorial individuality. In other words, show up for your little chat with the venture capitalist in a three-piece suit, not in denim shorts and a T-shirt.

Don't shop the deal. Or rather, don't shop it too flagrantly. This is another point of etiquette. Venture capitalists are clubby and gossip among themselves quite a bit. If you're peddling your wares at every fund in town, word will get around quickly, and you'll find nobody wants to deal with you—first, because your actions indicate a lack of confidence in your company, and second, because you are a bounder and a cad. Jolly bad show, Old Chap, just isn't done, you know? Of course, nobody really expects you to be totally faithful to your first prospect, especially if you're not making progress, but don't flaunt your alternatives. No pressure, no threats, no bidding wars—such tactics won't do at all, unless very subtly handled. But it's okay to discreetly pursue a limited number of carefully selected possibilities.

SBIC Loans

An SBIC or "Small Business Investment Company" is an institution that receives a license from the SBA and may qualify to receive long-term loans from the SBA. In return, the SBIC must invest only in small businesses (although by the government's definition almost anything smaller than a *Fortune* 500 company qualifies as a small business) and must make either equity investments or long-term (five years or more) loans. In effect, the SBIC is a hybrid of the venture-capital firm and the bank, and that's the way it behaves.

Your Friendly Banker

The bank is an institution that most of us feel familiar with. But if your dealings with banks have been confined to your personal transactions, you may be in for a shock when you go in as an entrepreneur. As an individual, you probably found it easy to borrow money from the bank for a house, a car, or even a vacation. If you try to borrow capital for your start-up, you're likely to make the disconcerting discovery that your friendly banker not only won't lend you the money, he won't even consider it. You may wonder if you've developed bad breath or leprosy, but the actual explanation is simple: above all, the bank is concerned with how you are going to pay back the loan. If you have a good job, banks will lend you money even if you admit that you intend to spend it on something frivolous. They don't care where the money is going; your salary gives you the means to pay it back, and that's all that matters. But if they invest in your start-up, the money will have to be repaid out of cash flow—a very iffy proposition.

This doesn't mean that you have no chance of getting any financing from a bank. Many banks will make secured loans to small businesses, though they prefer established firms to start-ups. Long-term loans secured by real estate or equipment are feasible, as are short-term loans secured by your receivables. Commonly you as the founder will have to put your name on the loan personally, though.

Again it must be stressed: even with a secured loan, your chances of getting the money depend on making a convincing argument that you can pay it back. The collateral is not a positive argument for giving you the loan, it's merely insurance. The decision will be based on your expected revenues.

You should select a bank carefully. First investigate the banks in your area. Find out which ones have a track record of supporting small business. There's no sense using a bank that sees its market as the *Fortune* 500. Pick the three or four best candidates and make appointments to see one of their officers. Don't be shy; if you've raised, or are in the process of raising, equity, you are going to be a pretty large depositor, and you're entitled to some attention. Your objective is not just to select a bank but to develop a relationship with one of its officers. Note that banks hand out vice-presidencies very liberally, so don't be impressed by a title; find out where the person actually is in the organization chart. It's very desirable to deal with the home office rather than a branch; usually the officers at a branch office have very little authority and everything must be referred back to the home office for decision anyway. With each banker, talk over the bank's attitude. Don't request a loan at this time, but find out: on the average, what size of business does the bank deal with? What industries does it feel most comfortable with? What are its loan policies like? What kind of loans does it prefer to make?

The first banker I talked to when I was getting Reaction Design started was very nervous that his bank might be asked for money. It seemed that every third sentence was, "You understand that we don't make loans to new companies." I didn't need or want a loan, but I quickly decided that this bank was not likely to be helpful or interested in working with a small company.

Select the bank and the banker that you find most congenial. Then make it a point to maintain the relationship. Keep your banker posted. Educate her about your business. Send her financial reports. Call her on the phone when something big happens. Take her to lunch a few times a year. Ask her for advice when you have a financial question. Make sure you have a good record as a depositor. When the time comes to ask for a loan, probably after a year or two, you'll be a familiar face, and you'll have somebody in the bank who knows you and your company.

Leasing Again

Leasing firms can be very useful even to a start-up. The big commercial leasing companies prefer to finance only items that are of general use: IBM computers, standard-brand office machines, the most commonly encountered plant equipment. If you want to lease an unusual piece of equipment, you'll probably have better luck with either its manufacturer or an individual investor.

Hitting Up the Government

Traditionally, entrepreneurs have longed for unsecured, long-term loans to finance their start-ups, and these are usually available only from the SBA (Small Business Administration) or certain other government agencies. Of course, there is a good reason why these loans are almost never made by private-sector investors: they are hellishly risky and do not offer anything approaching a commensurate return. Every now and then the SBA gets a big appropriation, but as fast as it loans it out, it loses most of it and finds itself strapped for funds again. The fact that the SBA, a government organization paying civil-service salaries, is unable to attract first-rate talent doesn't help.

If you wish to go for government money, you should keep in mind that the SBA and other agencies that fund small business are motivated by politics much more than by economics. To get an SBA loan, you must first be turned down by banks (because banks don't like the competition). Your chances are better if you ask for a relatively small loan; the government gets more political benefits by spreading the wealth thin, so agencies try to make many small loans rather a few big ones. Fill out the forms with great care; bureaucrats pay a lot of attention to this, because complete and correct paperwork is the way they cover their rear ends. In your application, emphasize political considerations rather than profit prospects; if you have female or minority founders, are locating in a depressed area, or are helping to clean up the environment, it will be a definite plus. It certainly doesn't hurt if you can get your congressman or some other bigwig to put in a good word for you, though you should avoid heavy-handed pressure tactics. Make it clear that you're a Democrat (even if it is a Republican administration at the time) and a liberal. You have nothing but good to say about affirmative action, regulatory agencies, and unionized labor.

The Invisible Banker: Your Vendor As a Source of Funds

Vendors are a source of capital not sufficiently appreciated by most entrepreneurs. Typically, vendors give trade credit of 30 days as a matter of routine—in other words, they give you a short-term loan of working capital. If you ask nicely, they may do even more for you. If you need a big-ticket item of production equipment, for instance, the vendor may help you find someone to finance it, or even finance it directly. Often, the vendor will routinely lease it to you. For the vendor, remember, the prime objective is sales. If you are making a big purchase, or if you are willing to commit your company to make regular purchases, the vendor may be surprisingly accommodating about credit.

Don't Be Shy—Ask Your Customers

Finally, customers can also be a valuable source of funds. If you've found a viable market niche, it implies that somebody really needs what you're planning to sell. Your customers may be willing to help you out by paying cash on delivery, or even in advance. They may be willing to give you a big purchase order or even an agreement to buy a minimum amount of your product; such an agreement may be very helpful in convincing investors to cough up. A customer—particularly if it's a big company—may even give you a loan or buy equity in your company.

Generally, customer financing is based on the need for a secure source for an essential purchase. The customer wants to be sure that you'll provide its needs—and, if possible, that you *won't* provide its competitors. These are the points you should emphasize in seeking such financing. Of course, you must consider what concessions you are willing to make; you may pay for customer financing with a serious loss in flexibility.

Checklist 13–1: Possible Funding Sources

- [ ] You and your cofounders
- [ ] Friends and family
- [ ] Private investors
- [ ] Venture-capital investment clubs
- [ ] Banks
- [ ] Small Business Administration
- [ ] SBICs
- [ ] MESBICs (SBICs set up to loan to minority businesses)
- [ ] SBIR grants (research grant set-asides by agencies of the Federal government)
- [ ] Factoring companies

☐ R&D limited partnerships
☐ Customers
☐ Suppliers
☐ State and local development funds
☐ Venture-capital firms
☐ Going public
☐ Distributors
☐ Employees

"FINDERS"

Before we discuss the technique of negotiating for investment, we should consider the use of intermediaries. There are many people who make their living by in some way mediating between investors and those seeking money. They may call themselves "brokers," "advisers," "finders," or something else. What they have in common is that they offer to introduce you to investors in return for a percentage of the investment.

To the naive, this may look like a good deal. You receive "expert" help with the daunting task of finding and dealing with investors, and after all, the fee is contingent—no investment, no pay, so what have you got to lose? But turn it around for a moment and look at it from the point of view of the investor. He knows that if he makes a $1-million investment in your company, $50,000 will immediately be paid to the "finder." Will this make the investment more attractive to him? What it amounts to is that the "finder" performs a service for you but is paid by the investor. The investor is likely to ask, "why should *I* give this chap $50,000?"

We do not say that you should never seek this sort of assistance. However, you should realize that the primary responsibility for presenting your company to the investor and convincing him to put up money will inevitably be yours. Nobody else can raise money for you. If you intend to use an intermediary of any sort, you must do three things.

First, check him out. Insist on knowing his track record. Get his résumé. Has he participated in any financings in the past, or are you his first project? Ask him about previous efforts where he failed to get an investor. If he says there are none, drop him; he's lying. If he admits to them, talk to the people he represented. Talk to some well-placed people in the investment community. If they've never heard of him, or if they know him and consider him a flake, drop him.

Second, ask what he wants for compensation. If he wants cash up front, drop him. If he wants cash when you get the investment, beware. If he wants stock in the company, it may be a good sign.

Third, find out exactly what he proposes to do for you; it should be commensurate with his fee. If he is just going to give you the phone number of Mr. Moneybags, that is *not* worth 5 percent—even if it's an unlisted number. On the other hand, if he is a respected character in the industry and is going to help you write the business plan, take you to meet investors, participate in the negotiations, and serve on your board of directors until you're well under way, he may be worth his weight in gold.

> Incidentally, this may be a good place to mention a rule that applies not only to 5-percenters but to investors, brokers, customers, employees, and anyone else you deal with in business. If someone tells you how honest he is, put your hand on your wallet. If he assures you that you can trust him, resolve to sign nothing.

THE PRESENTATION

We're now finally ready to meet the investor. At this point, you're actually making a presentation to the investor—be it an individual, a venture-capital firm, a banker, or some other type. You certainly should not go into this presentation without a prepared pitch, even though you may not use it. It's well to treat it as a sales presentation—which is exactly what it is. Focus on the benefits to the investor, not the benefits to you. Try to anticipate possible objections and have answers ready. Don't rely on your advertising (in this case, your business plan) to make the sale for you.

The probing may get quite personal, especially if you're dealing with venture capitalists. Venture capitalists like to say that they make investment decisions primarily on the basis of the quality of the management team. The standard cliché is:

"I'd rather see first-rate people with a second-rate idea than second-rate people with a first-rate idea." In practice, though they won't admit it, they weigh the idea more heavily than this rule would imply—because they're smart enough to ask themselves, "If they're really first-rate people, why do they have a second-rate idea?" Nonetheless, it's certainly true that the presentation will be regarded primarily as a chance to evaluate you and the rest of your team. So be prepared to field questions about your goals, your attitudes, your past failures and successes, and your character.

After you've made your presentation, you must decide whether the investor is serious or not. If he is, you don't want to be dealing with a lot of other prospects. But if he isn't, you certainly can't afford to sit idly while he ponders the deal for months. How can you determine how serious an investor is?

Obviously, it's a good sign if he is positive and approving. If he tells you your widget is the greatest invention since sliced bread and your management team is a bunch of geniuses, you should feel encouraged, though not confident. On the other hand, *any* expression of a negative evaluation signals poor prospects, even if it's a mild criticism.

Speed is a very good predictor of investment propensity. Prospects who move quickly, who want to see your business plan right away, set up an appointment next week—these are good prospects. The languid sort who don't seem to particularly care how long it takes to go through the process are more likely to be just playing with you. Silence means "no." A good rule of thumb is that three unreturned phone calls is a turndown.

Look for the investor who is specific. If she says, "I like your plan, but you need more market research on the second product, and I think you should have more budgeted for advertising"—and especially if she goes on to say, "Fix those and I'll be ready to talk terms"—she's a very hot prospect. Vague types, on the other hand, seldom come through with a check. If he "would like to think it over" or is "not sure about a couple of things"—if he's unwilling to make a commitment but has no specific objections to cite—don't waste much time on him.

Finally, the good prospect is independent—he clearly makes the decision himself. If the investor wants time to consult a committee, or a partner, or a friend, or an adviser, don't hold your breath while waiting for his check.

THE NEGOTIATION

When the investor says yes, you'll be tempted to relax and heave a sigh of relief. Don't. Your troubles are just beginning. Now you have to negotiate the specifics of the deal, and it may not be easy.

Successful negotiating strategy is a whole subject in itself, and we cannot go into it deeply here. Let's just emphasize three principles that are particularly important in making investment deals.

First, *do not negotiate until you are in a strong position.* It's said of bankers that they are people "who loan you an umbrella when the sun is shining and take it back when it rains." The same policy, unfortunately, is followed by almost any type of investor. That's why it's important to seek funding only when you don't "need" it. Make every effort to avoid seeking funds when you're in trouble or up against a deadline. It's best to have the foresight to borrow the umbrella when the sun is shining. But if you didn't, instead of going out for money when you're under pressure, try to muddle through with what you have. Concentrate on getting through the crisis, even if you have to take a few body blows in the process, and get to the point where the situation is stable. *Then* look for funds. You should not sit down at the table until you feel comfortable with the prospect of getting up and walking away if you don't like the results.

Second, *get your objectives on the table right at the start— and get the investor's objectives on the table also.* Many people think that you should hide your objectives from the "enemy." But this is neither necessary nor desirable if you've accepted the first point. If you know clearly what you want, are determined to get it, and are prepared to walk away if you don't, you have nothing to lose and everything to gain by making your position clear. Insist that the other side do likewise. If your goals and the investors' goals are incompatible, you'd better find it out at once, rather than thrash around interminably speaking at cross-purposes. If your objectives and theirs are compatible, getting everything out in the open will tremendously facilitate clearing up the details and reaching a quick agreement.

Third, *aim for a positive-sum deal.* You're going to be living with these investors for a long time. Don't worry about squeezing out the last drop of advantage in the negotiations. Deliberately leave some goodies on the table for them; chances are you'll be amply repaid over the years by their goodwill. The ideal negotiation has both sides coming out whistling. You should feel that you really cleaned up on this deal, and the investors should feel exactly the same way. If it seems impossible for this to happen, maybe the deal shouldn't be made.

Security Blankets and Seppuku Clauses

You probably are not going to come out of the negotiations with an agreement on your original terms. Chances are you'll make some concessions, perhaps some big concessions. They may include taking less money than you'd asked for; taking it later or more slowly than you wanted; giving up more stock for it. The investors may also demand that you change your plan in certain ways.

It's not uncommon for investors to demand that you acquire some sort of "security blanket" to make them feel more comfortable. If you're dealing with bankers, they will probably want to see some solid collateral—"bricks and mortar" or heavy machinery are preferred. Venture capitalists are more likely to demand extra people. Typically they tell you to hire a Marketing VP; if you've already got one, you'll be told to fire her and hire someone better. Leasing companies insist on big insurance policies so they'll be covered if your factory burns down with their equipment in it. You'll be surprised at some of the far-out demands that may be made, and you may have to decide whether to reject the deal rather than comply with an exceptionally onerous restriction. Often the security blanket is quite reasonable, but look it over carefully before you agree.

The investor may want to impose a requirement that you put your own money into the deal. This is absolutely reasonable, of course. If you don't believe in the investment enough to take some financial risk yourself, why should he? But beware the investor who demands that you commit everything you have to the company. What might be called a "seppuku clause" is popular with some investors; you are required to invest everything you own and everything you can borrow. The idea is that if the company fails, you'll be forced to commit suicide, and that this will motivate you to work hard. It probably will, but it will also motivate you to make some very poor decisions. If the investor believes that nothing will make you work except terror, he must not evaluate your character very highly. Invite him to put his money on someone he believes in more strongly.

INVESTOR RELATIONS

We mentioned that financing your company is a sort of sale. As in any other sale, the most frequently neglected step is follow-up. *It cannot be emphasized too strongly that you must absolutely give top priority to investor relations.* Even if you have firm "control" of the company in terms of stock majority, a disgruntled investor can wreak havoc. She can call for special meetings, harass you unmercifully, sue you, sic the SEC or other regulatory agencies on you for real or imagined crimes—never underestimate the problems she can cause. And it's not enough just to avoid making enemies among your investors. You really want them to be happy. You may want to go back to them for more money. If you plan to go to someone else for further funding, you at least want them to recommend the investment. And, from a very simple moral point of view, these people took a heavy risk because they believed in you, and helped you in accomplishing your goals. You owe it to yourself to be good to them.

The primary principle of investor relations is openness. *Keep investors informed—fully, frankly, and frequently.* Of course you will provide them routinely with a detailed annual report. But it's well to give them something in writing more frequently. A quarterly report is about right. It's not so frequent as to be onerous to produce, but it gives them a good feel for the company's progress and prevents a lot of nasty surprises. Small business tends to move fast, and so much can happen between two annual reports that stockholders can sometimes get an unpleasant shock.

Unless you have a really unwieldy number of investors—unlikely until you go public—it's a good idea to augment your written communications with occasional telephone conversations. Just put it on your calendar, or in your tickler file, to call each investor at regular intervals—it may be once a week or once a year, depending on the persons involved. Beware the temptation to hide when things are going badly. No matter how embarrassed you are, fess up and take your medicine—it will be worse if you put it off. And if things are going well, it's nice to thank your investors for their confidence and give them some of the credit for the company's success.

CAUTIONARY TALE: FACING DOWN THE VENTURE CAPITALISTS

Esteem, like so many new businesses, had its genesis in the failure of a large company to exploit a market opportunity. A friend of mine, Karen Kimbrough, had worked for Estee Lauder's subsidiary Clinique for a number of years. She called on plastic surgeons to promote Clinique's products. The surgeons told her about the market, and Karen listened. Unfortunately, she couldn't get her employers to listen to her.

The message she heard over and over again was this: "It doesn't do me any good to hear about Clinique's products, no matter how wonderful they are, because I do not want to recommend that my patients go to department-store cosmetics counters. The people there have no idea what they've been through. They have no idea of their skin condition and aren't competent to treat them. And my patients don't want to go there after they've had cosmetic surgery. Their faces are numb, there are sutures still in place, there's reddening and bruising—they're embarrassed to take off their bandana and show their wounds. The last thing they want is for the public at large to know that they've had cosmetic surgery. What we'd really like is for Clinique to come into our premises and deal with our patients here, where they feel comfortable and our nurses can supervise what's going on."

Karen's superiors at Clinique, quite justifiably, responded, "There is no way we are going to go to all that trouble to capture this dinky-poo little market segment when we can make money so much more easily selling to conventional markets. Forget it."

So when Karen got bored with working for a large company and quit Clinique, she had this opportunity simmering in the back of her mind. This was where I came in. She and I had been friends for years, and shortly after she left Clinique we had dinner together. I asked her what she was going to do now, and she said, "Well, I've always had this idea . . ." By the time we left the restaurant we were partners, and that was the beginning of Esteem.

I was impressed with the business concept, and I was impressed with Karen. She, of course, has an excellent background in cosmetics marketing and sales. She knows a large number of plastic surgeons around the country. And, of particular importance, she's experienced in the training of cosmetics consultants. This is critical to Esteem, because the key thing in this business is going to be the attitude and the professionalism with which our counselors (as we will call them) deal with their clients. These are people who have just had their faces redone—they need help, not hype.

Finally, Karen is a tall, attractive, mature individual who is gentle and supportive and really cares about people. Her ability to project that attitude and to instill it into our personnel is vital to Esteem's company culture.

After our initial meeting in April 1984 we began to do some market research and to focus on the nature of our products and how we would sell them. We spoke to over a hundred plastic surgeons; the vast majority stated that they would welcome such a product line, especially with the feature that they would be sold in their offices. We also did some focus group-work with a number of women who had undergone cosmetic surgery, and they responded very positively to the idea of having a specially trained cosmetics consultant deal with their problems, starting shortly after surgery.

This has been very encouraging, but the important thing that all this work taught us is that we need to think of Esteem not as a purveyor of products in bottles but as a service business. Specifically, we are selling a therapy—one that is an important adjunct to the physician's therapy. Once we looked at it this way, it opened up a number of opportunities. First off, there are patients who have undergone plastic surgery—not only cosmetic surgery but repair of trauma, burns, and other disfigurements. Then there are cancer patients whose skin has been damaged by the side effects of chemotherapy or radiation. There are also psychiatric patients— women who receive cosmetic services, combined with attention and care, show improved recovery rates. (There is considerable clinical evidence to back this up, from studies conducted by the British Red Cross and others. The effect apparently is due partly to the physical, medicinal effect of properly chosen cosmetics, partly to the comforting attention provided, and partly to the improved morale and self-image that result from having a more attractive appearance.)

Once we focused on the idea of Esteem as a service company offering what in essence is a form of therapy, we could see that the chemical formulation of our products would not be the crucial factor in our success. We put together an excellent, high-quality product line, but we realized the key factor would be selecting and training our cosmetic counselors. They have to be much more like nurses than salespeople, having a high degree of expertise and a deep understanding of and empathy with our clients.

Karen was the sparkplug who conceptualized the company, organized all these ideas, and worked out how to implement them effectively. My job was to help out with some of the business aspects, get the business plan assembled properly, and lead the search for capital.

We had the business plan ready to go to market by the early part of October. When it came to financing, my first thought was doctors. Doctors in this country tend to have large incomes and serious tax problems. Many of them dabble in venture-capital investments. One of my standard rules of thumb is that the best way to finance a company is to find an investor who understands the industry, the technology, or the market already. That greatly reduces the amount of education you have to do, and also reduces the investor's nervousness. So in this case doctors (not necessarily plastic surgeons, though) seemed like good prospects.

Now I don't happen to know a lot of doctors, but I do know quite a few accountants, and boy do they know a lot of doctors. I located several prospects. However, it soon became clear that they were, as one often finds, window-shoppers. They were intrigued with the idea, they wanted to show off how smart they were and how rich they were and how much they knew about venture investing. They wanted to flirt with us, to talk at cocktail parties about how they were being wooed by a new company and thinking of investing. Fortunately, after years of experience, I've learned to spot this type fairly quickly, so we dropped them and examined some more traditional venture-capital avenues.

We went on to a venerable venture-capital firm up in Boston and had a meeting with them. Unfortunately they inflicted on us one of their junior partners, who proceeded to give us a primer in starting new companies. He droned on about how you should do it, the team you should have, and so forth. This was information I didn't really require, and his patronizing attitude made heavy demands on my patience. Since he punctuated this lecture with a series of snide remarks about the frivolity and dispensability of the cosmetics business and plastic surgery, Karen was also feeling a bit aggravated. It was a display of almost comical arrogance of a sort that, I'm sorry to say, seems increasingly common among the younger set in the venture-capital industry.

Naturally, an old gray wolf like me doesn't like to listen to advice from a fuzzy-cheeked MBA, but I can normally stifle my irritation when more than a million dollars is at stake. However, it was clear in this case that the young fellow in question was not a serious investor; what he really wanted was to show off what a shrewd venture capitalist he was. So I thanked him for his advice, reminded him that I'd had actual experience in starting one or two companies myself, and we ended the meeting.

At another prominent Boston venture-capital firm, Karen handled the presentation by herself. One of the firm's associates had done the original work, and she liked the deal—as a woman she could appreciate what was involved. So she arranged for Karen to meet with her and the firm's senior partner. Karen, who is charming and amusing, soon was in comfortable conversation with him. He too began to question the underlying assumptions. He said it was hard to believe that women in this demographic group, or any other for that matter, spent $1,000 per year on cosmetics. The three women in his life—his wife, his daughter, and his aunt—didn't spend anywhere near that much and didn't need to. Karen looked him straight in the eye and said in her Southwestern drawl, "Well, this is Boston, and *most* of the people up here don't look very good."

This firm did not participate in our first-round financing. However, it expressed an interest in joining a second-round financing, should we need one for a national roll-out. The firm told our lead investors that not only did it believe in the idea, but Karen Kimbrough had done a wonderful job of dealing with its senior partner. He said, "I've never been dealt with that way by an entrepreneur, and I loved it."

We finally connected with a French merchant banking company, which ultimately became our lead investor. I met the chairman of this outfit at a party shortly before we had the business plan complete, and told him about the concept. He was somewhat intrigued, so I followed up a couple of weeks later by sending him the business plan. I ran into him again at Thanksgiving at another party and was pleasantly surprised when *he* began to try to sell *me* on the deal. He told me how smart it was and how brilliantly conceived, what he thought it could go to, and how he planned to sell it to his clients. I'd already heard from his number-two man, who'd called me somewhat earlier and said, "We really like this idea, and we like Karen Kimbrough, and we really think this company should be in very strong hands." Of course I had a notion whose hands he had in mind, so I expected this firm to at least participate in the financing, and in fact it came in all the way as lead investor and actually put together the deal. These people put up a big chunk themselves, then went out to their clients and said, "We're in this thing, and we've been successful for you in the past. We suggest you put up X dollars." This is the way venture-capital deals are frequently assembled. We had some private investors whom we brought in ourselves for smaller amounts, who completed the $1.1-million first-round financing.

Of course there were the usual tedious and frustrating delays as the various groups involved did their due diligence and ground out the detailed legal prose, and it wasn't until July of 1985 that we got funded. But that was okay—we still had a lot of work to do ourselves in getting the company set up.

Now we're off and running. As you might guess by now, in accord with my usual principles, we aren't wasting any of that hard-earned $1.1 million on building a manufacturing plant or developing overhead expenses. We are formulating a line of products, with the somewhat special characteristics needed. They will be manufactured by a first-rate European cosmetics firm. It will do the production under our guidance, it will do the packaging that we specify, it will attach the labels that we will provide, and it'll send over a complete line of products ready to sell.

We'll be operating out of Karen's apartment on the fashionable Upper East Side of Manhattan initially, though we may rent a very small office if we really need it. Since we deal with our clients in the doctor's office, we don't need a facility. When we get bigger a larger office will be necessary, and we might bring packaging in-house, but only the very largest cosmetics companies have any business doing manufacturing.

This company illustrates many of the key points in doing a successful funding. We had a clear need in the market, a first-rate founder, and a well-written business plan. We could demonstrate that we'd done our homework. We selected prospective investors carefully; recognized and quickly dropped poor prospects; and developed a lead investor who helped to bring in the rest of the money. Finally, we negotiated on a basis of equality with the investors.

HDS

Appendix
Some Unavoidable
Topics

Nobody but a lawyer can tell legal from illegal, and the lawyers can't tell right from wrong anymore.

Larry Niven, Jerry Pournelle
*Oath of Fealty**

Every year it gets more difficult to run a business. Laws are passed, regulations appear, court rulings are laid down. Today, almost anything you do in business involves legal hassles with the government. Zoning, building permits, fire-department inspections, OSHA, sales-tax collection, payroll deductions, workers' compensation, business permits, licensing—there is an almost endless list even for the most simple and harmless business. If you are involved in a regulated industry, such as chemicals, transportation, pharmaceuticals, or dozens of others, the restrictions and harassment are an order of magnitude worse. It is important to realize that all this is *intentional*. Small companies cause a lot of trouble for their large competitors, and the purpose of government regulation is to restore the advantages of size.

The entrepreneur doesn't want to get involved in this sort of thing—indeed, doesn't even want to think about it. Unfortu-

*(New York: Simon & Schuster, 1981), p. 196.

nately, it can't always be avoided. The purpose of this Appendix is to give you some tips on staying out of trouble and minimizing hassles.

HOW TO STAY OUT OF COURT

The first principle of business law is that invoking the law is to be avoided at almost any cost. Ambrose Bierce defined a lawsuit as a process which you go into as a pig and come out of as a sausage. And the legal system is much worse now than it was at the turn of the century. Anyone who lives in a large city is aware that the criminal-justice system has pretty much broken down. You may not realize, however, that civil law is in just as bad a shape.

> Recently a foundation of which I am a director bought some land near Los Angeles for a new facility. After the deal was closed, the owners decided they could get more money elsewhere and simply reneged. Our attorney tells us that in California there is a standard wait of five years for a civil suit to go to trial.

Lawyers used to tell their clients that justice was slow and uncertain. Now it's even slower, but more certain—more certain to produce an unjust outcome. Juries routinely decide cases on "Poor Fellow Theory" (if a "little guy" gets hurt, *somebody* must pay, regardless of responsibility) and award damages on "Deep Pockets Theory" (whoever has or seems to have a lot of money pays, whether guilty or not). There has always been some of this, but appeals courts no longer reverse such decisions.

The business community has responded to the breakdown of the legal system by gradually developing the alternative of using negotiated settlements and arbitration. The threat of lawsuit is still used, as the threat of nuclear war is used in international relations, but the parties generally realize that there are no winners if the threat is executed.

You can generally stay out of court by following a few simple rules.

1. *Deal with honest people.* As we mentioned in Chapter 3, Providence, which gave the rattlesnake its rattle as a warning of its poisoned fangs, has similarly equipped dishonest people with a danger sign. The crook, no matter how hard he tries to appear honest, will invariably suggest some sort of shady or off-color transaction early in his acquaintance with you. He literally cannot help it.

When I was in graduate school, the chess club went to the Oregon State Penitentiary for a match with the convicts' club. My opponent, when he got into a bad position, tried to move a knight diagonally. It was inconceivable that I would overlook the "error," but he just couldn't help himself. It was an interesting lesson in criminal psychology.

In any case, it really pays to investigate important business associates before you make heavy commitments. Always check the references of job applicants. Look into the backgrounds of your cofounders very carefully before you accept them. Check out the history and credit record of a customer before you ship that big order. If you're a trusting soul and don't like going to all this trouble, remember that just one mistake about the honesty of an associate may *put you out of business.*

2. *Get it in writing in advance.* This applies to contracts, sales agreements, employee relations—anything that may have important consequences. Even if a formal legal document is not needed, get it down on paper; that way, everyone knows exactly what was decided.

Modern case law in the United States is coming up with some pretty incredible decisions requiring employers to predefine offenses that will result in disciplinary action. Fired workers are going to court saying, "Nobody told me I'd be fired for stealing"—and increasingly, the courts are ordering them reinstated.

For the last six years I've been keeping a little business diary. At the end of the day I jot down a few notes about what was done and said. I doubt that it would have much legal weight, but on several occasions I've benefited greatly by my ability to refer to a written record. When one associate attempted to welsh on a prior commitment, I was able to say, "On April 12, here in this office, you told me . . . And on June 3, I called to check and you said . . ." It made a decisive difference in collecting what for me at that time was a large sum of money.

3. *Always use an arbitration clause.* At the end of every contract or agreement you sign, put in: "Any disagreement between the parties shall be settled by arbitration under the auspices of the American Arbitration Association." This is by no means foolproof, and your attorney will tell you that there are a number of complications arising from such questions as appeal from the ruling of an arbitrator to the courts. However, it gives you significant protection—and if the other party resists the insertion of an arbitration clause, you may wish to look over its background for a history of litigiousness.

4. *Don't put temptation in people's way.* Again and again, people who had previously been honest are convicted of embezzlement, Ponzi schemes, pilferage . . . and in court, they say, "I never did anything like that before, but it was so *easy.*" Today the buzzword is "trust" of your employees, and that's great. But when it comes to items that can have large financial consequences, you'd be wise to take the attitude that trust must be earned by a record of integrity—and even so, keep an eye out for danger signals.

5. *Don't let small problems become big ones.* When a conflict comes up, don't hesitate to deal with it immediately—and resolve it permanently. If it's allowed to fester, the various parties are likely to develop increasing hostility, cynicism, and bitterness. A misunderstanding becomes a disagreement, a disagreement an argument, an argument a feud, and a feud a lawsuit—all for want of the courage to sit down and thrash it out before it becomes serious.

6. *Don't rely too much on contracts.* There's ultimately no such thing as an "iron-clad" contract. If the terms become too onerous for the other party, there's generally *some* way for it to wiggle out—legally or not. In such a case, you're almost always better off renegotiating or settling than trying to force compliance.

DEALING WITH THE GOVERNMENT

The government is like a water buffalo: bad-tempered, vicious, and enormously powerful, it can do a lot of damage even on the rare occasions when its intentions are good.

The best way to deal with government at all levels is to stay out of its way. It's a shame to say this, because if business-people were more courageous and regularly stood up to the bureaucrats, this country would be a much healthier and wealthier place. However, what would be good for the country is generally fatal to the individual business!

Small businesses most commonly go wrong by thinking that the government is sincere. Since the stated purpose of an agency is to promote workplace safety or reduce pollution, the naive entrepreneur thinks that by running a safe or nonpolluting operation he will be okay, without the trouble of reading all those complex regulations. Wrong. The only thing that counts is being in compliance with the letter of the law.

Among the major pitfalls that damage or destroy small businesses are the following:

Tax violations. When your business gets desperately short of cash, it can be awfully tempting to delay—just for a few days—your payroll-tax withholding payments. Forget it. The IRS is *mean.* It will wipe out your business without the slightest mercy. If it fails to collect from a corporation, it will come down on its managers, directors, stockholders, or anyone who happens to be standing in the area. Pay the IRS *first.* If you can't pay, run for it. It's said that Paraguay may be safe.

Pollution. One good thing about being a new company is that you can start with a clean slate. Some big companies have crud in their backyards that dates back a century or more, and now they have to try to clean it up. You, on the other hand, can start clean and stay clean if you're willing to take the trouble and accept the expense. In view of the current paranoia about pollution—especially chemicals and radioactivity—it's a good policy. Keep in mind that when you hire someone to come and haul away your waste, that does *not* end your responsibility. If he dumps it in the river and disappears, the EPA will come down on *you.* So be careful about whom you deal with.

Safety. As mentioned, you must comply with the letter of the regulations from OSHA and other agencies, even if it results, as it sometimes does, in reducing rather than increasing safety.

> A hint: OSHA inspectors aren't very well trained. They tend to concentrate on a few standard hazards—looking for uncovered V-belts on pulley-driven equipment is a great favorite. Another hint: keep a Polaroid camera at the plant. If there's an inspection, go around with the inspector and snap a picture of any alleged violation. Ask him to sign the back of the photo. (Of course, you are very courteous and cooperative.) Often this will result in citations being changed into suggestions that "you take care of the problem and we'll forget about it."

Quite aside from the fact that it reduces regulatory hassles, it really pays to run a safe ship. Once your employees get the idea that you don't care about their safety, their attitude will become nasty and they'll be on the phone to OSHA every time the air conditioner is out of adjustment. But don't rely on your employees' stated concern about their safety and health! You must lead.

THE INSURANCE CRISIS

As this is written, the business press is full of stories about the liability-insurance crisis. Perhaps by the time you read this, tort reform will have been accomplished and the problem will have disappeared. Then again, perhaps it won't . . .

Many types of liability coverage are now unavailable or unaffordable. A small company, particularly if it is innovative, may have serious difficulty getting insurance. There's no real cure for the problem, but here are a few suggestions.

1. *Analyze your risks.* Here's where a good independent insurance agent can make a real contribution. All insurance consists of playing the odds. It's much like playing poker or craps—if you don't know the odds and the payoffs, you'll get fleeced.

2. *Have a risk-control program.* Your insurer will usually be happy to help you in reducing your exposure, and thus your premium. Locks, alarms, a sprinkler system and other fire protection—often a small investment of this sort can result in

substantial savings on insurance. There are also steps you can take to reduce your liability exposure. Again, consult your agent. Ask the company to send a risk-control adviser to inspect your company.

3. *Buy only the coverage you need.* Insurance policies are often loaded with special coverage items that sound good but actually represent minimal risk. Don't pay for any coverage unless you see a real need for it from your risk analysis. Beware of impulse buying.

4. *Use high deductibles.* Although insurance companies publicly bitch and moan about multimillion-dollar settlements, most of their payout goes for the large numbers of small claims. You can often save a lot of money by taking the highest possible deductible. Remember, the purpose of insurance is not to pay for every loss but to cover the catastrophic loss.

5. *Go naked until you have something to cover.* A small, new company with a chronic cash shortage is not a very attractive target for ambulance-chasers. You may not need heavy liability coverage at this stage. In fact, if you pay a fortune for a big liability policy, you may just be making yourself into a target.

Bibliography

STARTUPS AND SMALL BUSINESS

Forrest Frantz. *Successful Small Business Management*. Englewood Cliffs, NJ: Prentice-Hall, 1978.

A readable text with a strong focus on the "Mom and Pop" type of small business.

Donald M. Dible. *Up Your OWN Organization*. Santa Clara, CA: Entrepreneur Press, 1974.

A popular and easy-to-read introduction to entrepreneuring. Stronger on pep talk than specifics, but has some useful advice, especially the list of 40 ways to finance your company.

Gordon W. Baty. *Entrepreneurship: Playing to Win*. Reston, VA: Reston Publishing, 1974.

The bible of Route 128. Solid, specific advice on the practical problems of entrepreneurship, and lists of tough questions for you to answer on every topic. The emphasis is on high-tech start-ups with one founder or a small founding group. Includes a valuable chapter on bankruptcy and how to survive it.

Richard M. White, *The Entrepreneur's Manual*. Radnor, PA: Chilton, 1977.

The Silicon Valley equivalent of Baty's book. The emphasis is mostly high-tech, but the discussion includes a variety of other business types. Focus is on start-ups with large founder groups. The book is specific and explicit but discusses issues at a strategic rather than tactical level, concentrating on the development of formal management systems rather than day-to-day problems. Altogether a very good complement to Baty.

Hans Schollhammer and Arthur H. Kuriloff. *Entrepreneurship and Small Business Management.* New York: Wiley, 1979.

A solid and useful textbook, though a bit dry in style.

William D. Putt, Ed. *How to Start Your Own Business.* Cambridge, MA: MIT Press, 1974.

This is a collection of essays by various authors on special topics in start-up management. It covers a number of areas generally neglected and is a useful backup to more general works.

Stanley R. Rich and David Gumpert. *Business Plans That Win $$$.* New York: Harper & Row, 1985.

Rich and Gumpert have produced a first-rate book about business plans, with a great deal of valuable information about other aspects of the start-up process. Particularly useful is the Rich-Gumpert Evaluation System, a simple matrix that gives you a fast—and generally sobering—look at how investors will view your business.

Robert S. Morrison. *Handbook for Manufacturing Entrepreneurs.* Cleveland, OH: Western Reserve Press, 1973.

Aimed at the "owner-operated" manufacturing concern, this book is devoted to the management of established businesses but still has much that is relevant to start-ups. It's loaded with useful hints from a seasoned CEO.

TRUE STORIES OF BUSINESS

Charles N. Aronson. *Free Enterprise.* Arcade, NY: Aronson, 1979.

This is the autobiography, in stupefying detail, of a machine tool entrepreneur. Recommended for prospective entrepreneurs from an academic or big-business background; the immense mass of gritty detail can be very instructive. The account of Aronson's trials and tribulations when he sold his business is especially sobering.

William Rogers. *Think: A Biography of the Watsons and IBM.* New York: Signet, 1969.

An instructive account of the growth of the granddaddy of growth companies.

John H. Dessauer. *My Years with Xerox*. New York: Manor Books, 1971.

Subtitled "The Billions Nobody Wanted," this book refutes much of the conventional wisdom about "market-driven" and "technology-driven" companies.

Don Gussow. *Divorce—Corporate Style*. New York: Ballantine, 1972.

Gussow sold his small publishing company to a major conglomerate—and found he didn't like the results. His account of the sale and the negotiations to buy back his company is both interesting and instructive.

Paul Freiberger and Michael Swaine. *Fire in the Valley*. Berkeley, CA: Osborne-McGraw-Hill, 1984.

An entertaining and instructive account of the birth of the microcomputer industry and many of its most important start-ups. A good introduction to what it's like to be in a real growth market.

GENERAL MANAGEMENT

Peter F. Drucker. *Management: Tasks, Responsibilities, Practices*. New York: Harper & Row, 1974.

It's almost presumptuous to praise this treatise on the theory and practice of management by America's foremost thinker on the subject. This is a gold mine of useful and practical ideas for any manager.

Peter F. Drucker. *Managing for Results*. New York: Harper & Row, 1964.

This book contains a valuable collection of techniques for evaluating and improving your business. Drucker's emphasis is on efficient cost calculation and the determination of product profitability.

Thomas J. Peters and Robert H. Waterman. *In Search of Excellence*. New York: Harper & Row, 1982.

A deserving best-seller, this book is devoted to a study of well-run big companies, which turn out to run themselves using important small-company values.

PERSONAL MANAGEMENT

Richard N. Bolles. *What Color is Your Parachute?* Berkeley, CA: Ten
  Speed Press, 1972.

This perennial best-seller is aimed at job-hunters, but much of it
is relevant to entrepreneurs. Becoming an entrepreneur certainly
should qualify as a "career change," after all. Bolles provides
some very useful exercises to help you identify your strengths
and interests.

Peter F. Drucker. *The Effective Executive*. New York: Harper & Row,
  1967.

An invaluable guide to making yourself a better manager. Must
reading for every entrepreneur.

Alan Lakein. *How to Get Control of Your Time and Your Life*. New York:
  Signet, 1973.

A very useful work on time management.

John T. Molloy. *Dress for Success*. New York: Warner Books, 1975.
  Also: *The Woman's Dress for Success Book*. Milwaukee, WI: Fol-
  lett, 1977.

Californians can probably skip these items, but in the rest of the
country, especially the East, the right clothes can make a big
difference in how you're perceived by customers and financiers.
Some of the details of Molloy's "research" should be taken with a
grain of salt, but you won't go far wrong following his advice.

John T. Molloy. *Molloy's Live for Success*. New York: William Morrow,
  1981.

In this book, Molloy broadens his coverage from clothing to
manners, personal habits, speech, and other factors that influence how you're perceived by other people. Again, some of the
"research" is a bit flaky, but there is much sound advice.

HEALTH AND FITNESS

Durk Pearson and Sandy Shaw. *Life Extension: A Practical Scientific
  Approach*. New York: Warner Books, 1982. Also: *The Life Extension Companion*. New York: Warner Books, 1984.

Controversial though they are, these authors know their stuff scientifically, and they provide an entertaining and instructive account of the various ways in which nutrients can lengthen your life and enhance your health.

Porter Shimer. *Fitness Through Pleasure.* Emmaus, PA: Rodale Press, 1982.

All of have certain things we have to do, and certain other things we want to do. This book tells you how to maintain your health without having to give up either.

Laurence E. Morehouse and Leonard Gross. *Total Fitness in 30 minutes a Week.* New York: Pocket Books, 1975.

You may not achieve "total" fitness, but his book is certainly a useful guide to staying in shape with minimal expenditure of time.

Alice K. Schwartz and Norma S. Aaron. *Somniquest.* New York: Harmony Books, 1979.

Insomnia is an occupational hazard for entrepreneurs. Here is an excellent practical guide to curing it.

SPECIAL TOPICS

Bob Stone. *Successful Direct Marketing Methods*, 2nd Edition. Chicago: Crain Books, 1979.

A superb book, informative, detailed, and readable, which covers every aspect of direct marketing. Indispensable if you are going to use direct marketing, this book is additionally an excellent introduction to general marketing principles and advertising techniques.

Jerome D. Wiest and Ferdinand K. Levy. *A Management Guide to PERT/CPM*, 2nd Edition. Englewood Cliffs, NJ: Prentice-Hall, 1977.

A useful overview of program evaluation and review technique (PERT) and related methods for project organization. We recommend it for research and development managers, but anyone who has to plan and schedule a complicated project can benefit from these techniques.

Daniel D. Roman. *Research and Development Management.* New York: Appleton-Century-Crofts, 1968.

One of the few works available on this subject and perhaps the least inadequate of the lot. Tends to be too general but at least asks some of the important questions.

Delmar W. Karger and Robert G. Murdick. *New Product Venture Management.* New York: Gordon & Breach, 1972.

An excellent book, comprehensive and specific. It is aimed primarily at the analysis of new-product introductions for large companies but contains much of use to small companies and even start-ups.

C. D. Tuska. *An Introduction to Patents for Inventors and Engineers.* New York: Dover, 1964.

An excellent introduction to the basics of patent law.

W. Edwards Deming. *Quality, Productivity, and Competitive Position.* Cambridge, MA: MIT Center for Advanced Engineering Study, 1982.

Wandering, disorganized, and brilliant, this book is a gold mine of useful ideas for quality control. Deming makes the subject of statistical quality control not only interesting but exciting. Not all of these techniques can be readily applied to small businesses, but Deming will stimulate your thinking about QC and productivity in many ways, and the book is worth reading for its entertainment value alone.

Richard Sanzo. *Ratio Analysis for Small Business.* Washington, DC: Small Business Administration, 1977.

A useful though somewhat elementary guide to the use of ratio analysis.

Robert Morris Associates. *Statement Studies.* (annual).

This reference provides the median values of various financial ratios for about 300 different lines of business.

Glossary

bridge financing: Money—usually a short-term loan—intended to keep a company going until an expected permanent financing is arranged. A venture-capital fund will sometimes make such a loan to keep a company from expiring before negotiations for an equity deal can be completed. Of course, the bridge loan gives the venture capitalists a stranglehold on the entrepreneur, thus assisting them in negotiating the kind of deal they want.

CEO (Chief Executive Officer): The head of the business. In the old days, the title was President, but now it's common for the CEO to be Chairman of the Board, while the President is COO, or Chief Operating Officer. The distinction between being "executive" and "operating" is generally unclear, but the latter is clearly second in command.

CFO (Chief Financial Officer): What used to be called the "controller" or "comptroller." Anyway, the person who's in charge of the money. Keep an eye on him.

close: To get a customer to sign on the dotted line or otherwise formally commit to a purchase. The part of selling that separates the amateurs from the professionals.

cold call: A sales call in which the salesperson takes the initiative in contacting a new prospect.

D&B: A report from Dun & Bradstreet on a company's creditworthiness. It includes recent payment record with the company's creditors, plus a lot of other information about the company's sales, officers, financials (if D&B can get them), the appearance of the premises, and so on.

depreciation: Accounting for the gradual wearing out or obsolescence of a fixed asset. This involves "writing off" part of the value in each accounting period. You have some options as to how you do so, but there are a number of weird restrictions imposed by the IRS and the FASB.

entrepreneur: Originally, the owner/operator of a business. Today it is increasingly used to denote the CEO of a small business, regardless of his equity position, if any. From there it seems to be being extended to any manager in any company, large or small, who claims to operate in an "innovative" or freewheeling fashion.

equity: The portion of a business's value that represents the property of the owners. Equivalent to **net worth.**

focus: The act of selling a single product—or at least a very simple and unified product line—into one market. Lack of focus is generally a disaster for a start-up.

inventory: Goods that you are holding for sale. If you are a manufacturer, raw materials and work in progress are also inventory. Though an asset on the balance sheet, the larger your inventory, the larger the cost of carrying it.

leverage: A general approach to business operations in which use of the owner's equity is minimized. This may be accomplished by debt financing of various sorts, including receivables financing and payables financing; leasing; joint venture; and many other variations. Also known as "OPM," or "Other People's Money."

leveraged buyout: This is the purchase of control of a company, using borrowed money; often the buyers are the management. The assumption is that the cash flow of the company will be adequate to handle the debt service and then some. Consequently, leveraged buyouts are usually restricted to mature companies, since growing enterprises drink cash instead of throwing it off.

limited partnership: A partnership in which some of the partners have limited liability—that is, they cannot lose more than their investment. The limited partners are legally forbidden, however, to participate in management in any way. Primarily used for tax shelters.

manager: Someone who organizes work—which, to be done successfully, requires being organized. "If you can't command yourself, you can't command others." (Chinese fortune cookie)

market analysis: Information about a specific market for a specific product, including: who buys it, why they buy it, where they buy it, how they buy it—and how much they're willing to pay for it.

market-driven: Refers to a company that allows its direction, especially the nature of its future products or services, to be determined by its customers' expressed wants. Venture capitalists tell us that this approach is the key to success. Well-known market-driven companies include Osborne Computer, Keuffel & Esser, and Photostat.

market share: The proportion of the market for your goods or services that is held by your company. You can make it as large or as small as you like, by redefining the market under consideration.

market strategy: A specific plan for selling a specific product, including to whom it will be sold, where it will be sold, how it will be sold.

mezzanine financing: An infusion of capital intended to prepare a company for going public.

net worth: The difference between your company's assets and its liabilities. If it reaches zero, it's generally time to quit and start something else.

private placement: A financing in which securities are sold to a limited number of individuals, venture-capital funds, and/or corporations. Federal and local laws impose restrictions, and the securities are in general "unregistered," which makes them less liquid.

public company: When a company has permission from the Federal government to sell securities—stock, in particular—to the general public, it is said to be a public company. Otherwise it is "privately held," and fairly onerous restrictions are placed on its opportunities to solicit potential investors. A public company has access to large capital markets, and because its stock may be listed and "publicly" traded, investments in it are much more liquid. On the other hand, it must meet certain disclosure requirements.

R&D partnership: A **limited partnership** formed to conduct R&D. If the R&D is successful, the limited partners receive a return from the royalty stream produced by the invention. Once a popular tax shelter, but recent and projected changes in the tax laws may result in its extinction.

recession: An opportunity to acquire for peanuts the assets of people who thought a booming economy was a good time to start a business.

rep: Short for sales representative. Basically a free-lance salesperson who works for you on straight commission. The majority are one-person firms with a desk and a telephone. However, some quite large rep organizations exist, which can handle quite complex sales problems (such as exports) in a very useful manner.

sales cycle: The time required to complete a sale, starting with the first contact with the customer and ending when you get paid.

sample: A statistical term used in market research. The limited group of customers or potential customers you interview is a "sample" of the total class of customers. The size of the sample needed can be calculated mathematically and is surprisingly small; a few thousand respondents can be used reliably to poll the entire U.S. population—if they are properly chosen.

segment: Another term from market research. A market segment is a portion of the market that behaves in a distinct manner. Affluent customers, for instance, may constitute a class different from middle-income customers. Beware of thinking in terms of product segmentation rather than market segmentation!

SIC (Standard Industrial Classification) code: A method of classifying a line of business, with a unique number associated with each industry. Unfortunately, the indexing method has not been updated for some time, which reduces its usefulness when you're dealing with new industries.

technology-driven: Refers to a company that is committed to introducing a certain technology and convincing the market to accept it. Current venture-capital thinking is that this is a sure recipe for failure. Well-known technology-driven companies include Bell Telephone, Ford Motors, and Xerox.

terms: Terms of sale are generally set by custom in each industry or market. "Net 30"—that is, customer should pay the invoice amount within 30 days of the invoice date—is common in most industrial markets. Discounts for prompt payment (typically 2 percent for payment within 10 days) are also used.

VAR (Value-Added Reseller): A distributer who buys goods, enhances them in some way, and sells to the ultimate consumer. For instance, in the computer business, a VAR might buy microcomputers, then attach special peripherals and provide software to sell the systems for a specific application.

Index